An Introduction to World Religions

Edited by

Khaleel Mohammed

With Contributions by

Professors: Zoe Close

Sandra Wawyrtko

Wil Hansen

Angela Feres

Arashmidos Monjazeb

A Polymath Learning LLC Product

Acknowledgments

Were it not for students who took the time to indicate what they liked or disliked about texts that we have used, or pedagogical methods that we have utilized, this book would not have been possible. Like true scholars, they have blazed a path for those who now embark upon the introductory study of world religions. We thank them all, and dedicate this book to them.

Contents

Foreword.....and Caveats

In my many years of teaching introductory courses on World Religions, I have never found a text that I consider truly suitable. Students usually have about sixteen weeks in which to learn about many different faiths while also keeping up with the other subjects of the university curriculum. Most authors have packed such excruciatingly detailed information into their various chapters that one has to wonder if their aim is to impress with the encyclopedic information at their command rather than to impart knowledge. The instructor using such a text often does not have a chance to make HER voice heard since she is so busy regurgitating the material. Students are forced to read pages upon pages that contain information more suitable for the advanced specialist than the undergraduate learner. With this in mind, we have tried to produce a work that allows for a grasp of knowledge while not overwhelming with detail.

This book represents the combined work of several specialists. Professors Zoe Close, Sandra Wawyrtko, Will Hansen, Angela Feres, Arashmidos Monjazeb and I have tried to give enough information that allows for a teaching foundation while still allowing each professor enough time to somewhat personalize the information. Chapters have been kept to a length that we consider adequate for professors who may wish to focus on some aspects more than others, or, in some cases, abandon some information altogether in favor of material they may wish to present.

We have also produced a Companion Workbook that will allow students to review with preparation for simple exams that are the norm for courses of this level. Some religions are presented in more detail than others, representing their presence in the North American Religious mosaic. Since this is our first cooperative effort, and we are striving to produce a work that will be used with for maximum pedagogical benefit, we have issued this initial edition as a course-reader. As such, you may find that some chapters may have suggested sources for more information while others may not, or others may provide a bibliography while others may not. We trust that within a short time of observing how the professors work with the text, we will be able to edit and emend as needed.

We trust that both professor and student will be able to use this book as a way to making the introductory foray into the study of religion an enjoyable learning experience.

Khaleel Mohammed
Professor, Dept. of Religious Studies,
San Diego State University

Introduction

MOUNT SOLEDAD CROSS, SAN DIEGO, CALIFORNIA

Learning Goals

- *Understanding the Importance of Religion Today*
- *Defining Religion*
- *Major Features of a Religion*
- *Understanding the problem of grouping religions.*
- *Typologies of Religion*
- *Outlining Approaches to the Study of Religion*
- *Dealing with the question of the Existence of God.*

The Importance of Religion

In 2008, a Pew Foundation poll found that 90% of Americans claimed to believe in God. This survey of Americans seemed to mirror the situation in the rest of the world. Christian missionary movements in almost every country, the rise of activists in the name of religion in many of the Middle Eastern countries, and the ubiquity of religious discourse on the internet are some of the strongest supporting evidence.

In the presidential elections of the United States, some people, in an effort to discredit Barack Hussein Obama, claimed that he was a Muslim. Mitt Romney was identified as a member of the Latter Day Saints Church, and the question about America's readiness for a Mormon president was raised. In the wake of 9/11, many people started questioning the values of religion in general, leading to a tremendous increase in the enrollment in Religion Studies classes at community colleges and universities. One previous pope objected to Turkey's becoming a member of the European Economic Community on the basis that it would change the "Christian" character of Europe.

When a New York Muslim group decided to build what it called a Muslim Community Center near to the site of the World Trade Center that was destroyed on 9/11, some groups protested and the matter made the headlines both at home and abroad. The Constitution of the United States promotes the separation between Church and State, and this has been the reason cited for a long battle over the War Memorial Cross on Mount Soledad in San Diego—since one claim is that religious symbols should not be on public property.

SUPPORTERS AND OPPONENTS OF THE ISLAMIC CENTER NEAR TO GROUND ZERO IN SEPTEMBER 2010.

All of the foregoing would seem to indicate the continued rise of religiosity. Yet, a poll by the Pew Foundation in 2012 showed that most Americans were identifying less with structured religion. Of the 4006 people interviewed, one-fifth said that they were religiously unaffiliated. Many others have chosen to identify less with any particular set of ideas that identify them with any particular religion, since individual concepts of morality in a modern world are often at odds with traditional religious ideas.

What is Religion?

In our discussion thus far, we have referred to "religion" on several occasions. Yet, it is almost certain that if we were to question a large group of people and ask them to define religion, their answers might give the impression that the same term is not being described. There are those who, based on their own spiritual views, might jump to define religion as "a belief in God." This would mean that religions which have a belief in many gods would be excluded, or those which do not have a god-idea as one of central importance would not qualify for inclusion. And this brings us to the purpose of a definition: it has to encompass everything that falls within its ambit, and yet, exclude that which is outside of its scope. Since this book is designed with the concept that "less is more"—meaning that it is concise to allow students maximum benefit from their readings, and to allow professors the room to add their own expertise to discussions, we will provide our chosen definition only. Of course there may be several definitions that are appropriate, and as such, we do not make the claim for any singular correctness of the one for which we have opted.

Many authors attribute the origin of the word to the Latin "religare"—to join, presumably in reference to the bond between humans and the gods. This presumed etymology, however, is not unanimously accepted, and Cicero, for example, is said to have traced it to "relegere"—to read again. Others have pointed out that the word is a western coinage and may perhaps contain some erroneous notions. Jesus, for example, never spoke of "religion," but rather of law.

Professor Leonard Swidler of Temple University defines religion as:

An explanation of the ultimate meaning of life and how to live accordingly based on a notion and experience of the transcendent.[1]

Explanation of Professor Swidler's Definition

An explanation of the ultimate meaning of life and how to live accordingly based on a notion and experience of the transcendent

PROFESSOR SWIDLER

Note that, instead of "God," Professor Swidler uses "transcendent"—to indicate that which lies outside the range of ordinary perception. It could refer to God, or gods, spirits, or even emptiness, among other things. This definition is wide enough to cover several different ideas, and yet restrictive enough to NOT cover those concepts that may not fall within the concept of religion. It excludes, for example, those "ultimate meanings" of life that do not focus on a transcendent such as, for example, secular humanism, or communism. These movements may be defined as "ideologies," thus separating them from "religion." Along with this definition comes the concept of what are considered as the key characteristics

---

[1]http://globalethic.org/Center/intro.htm. Accessed May 22, 2014.

of religion. It may be argued that religions are so different that it is difficult to speak of characteristics that we may seek to find in all of them.

Nonetheless, we can generally assume that religions contain what are known as **the four 'Cs"**:

Creed: That which outlines everything that goes into explaining the ultimate meaning of life.

Code: That which covers ethics and customs of action that somehow follows from one aspect or another of the Creed.

Cult: That which covers ritual activities such as prayer, or definition of sacred space.

Community: That which pertains to relationships among followers.

The Problem of Typology

One of the commonest classifications of religions that we see in older works is "Eastern" and "Western." In an age of globalization, these labels are problematic, since, even though they may accurately present the origin of a particular movement, they may not indicate that religion's place in the contemporary world. Hinduism, for example, has its origins in India, but the religion has followers in what we may loosely define as 'the east' and 'the west.' Mauritius, Guyana, Trinidad, Belize, the United Kingdom, The United States, Germany, South Africa and the Netherlands are just a few of the places with sizeable populations of Hindus. Another problem with the "East" and "West" grouping is that these terms are generally in reference to Europe and the "New World" as opposed to Asia. This means effectively that Africa and Australia are not considered.

Although Judaism, Christianity and Islam all have their roots in a common geographical area—the Middle East—many researchers, until recently, considered Islam an Eastern religion. This was presumably because the majority of the world's Muslims reside in the East. But Muslims also live in the West, not as a foreign people to that part of the world, but as its natives. Their interpretations of Islam are unique to them, and so today, Islam is considered a western religion. Yet, the majority of Muslims still live in Asia, Africa and Eastern Europe. A Guyanese Muslim often has different customs—even in religious expression—than, for example, a Pakistani or Saudi Arabian Muslim. Clearly then, this labeling is inadequate.

One of the typologies suggested is that of **Prophecy** religions as opposed to Wisdom religions. In this concept, Prophetic religions are those that deal with revelations and scriptures from a God. Wisdom religions, by contrast, promote the insight that comes from reflection and meditation, often under the guidance of a sage. Yet, in the same way that there is difficulty defining religion, so too there is difficult in formulating any absolutely accurate typological approach. While, therefore, we may attribute some specific characteristics qualities to certain religions, it has to be understood that religion is always evolving, and that we have to constantly review our conclusions.

There is also the concept of "scriptural" as opposed to "oral" religions—but this type of approach is also problematic because many religions that are now scriptural began as predominantly oral religions. Classifications such as "primitive," "native," or "primal," all denigrate concepts that may actually be extremely advanced. Our approach is to avoid seeking any absolute typology although we do group into what may be considered Indigenous, Prophet, Western, and New Religious Movements. These will be discussed in more detail later in this book.

Today, one sees departments of Religion that have specialists in Chinese Religions, Japanese Religions, African Religions, New Religious Movements—all bearing testimony to the fact that at best, we can group religions that are similar in outlook, but that it is problematic to seek to typologize ALL of the known religions of the world.

In addition to the typology issue, there is also the problem of **essentialization** or **essentialism**. To essentialize is to assume that there are certain characteristics that are intrinsic to the item or subject being studied. While this may be possible in some cases, it fails to recognize, especially in the case of religions, that interpretations differ and that what may be seen as an "essential" in one part of the globe, may not be so in another. Although we recognize that this is a problem, to a certain extent we do so in parts of this book since we are simply presenting a survey of world religions, and not an extremely detailed study. This book is designed as a university text to be covered within a single semester, meaning that in order to summarize, we must sometimes essentialize. When, for example, we speak of the Indigenous Religions of America, how many religions will we cover? There were many tribes when the first European settlers arrived here, with different concepts of the transcendent. Yet, most religion texts examine a few major beliefs and then generalize. For this reason, we will examine a few tribes, and note that our examination is to be considered in light of those tribes only, and not as representative of the beliefs of all the native peoples.

Essentialization/essentialism

Web definitions

> Essentialism is the view that, for any specific entity, there is a set of attributes which are necessary to its identity and function. ..
> http://en.wikipedia.org/wiki/Essentialization.

In today's world, based on the massive immigration/emigration movements, we see the formation of new religious ideas based on multiple distinct sources. Each new religion does have an element of such combination to form its basis, because religions are necessarily developed from older ones. The term for such mixing from multiple sources is **SYNCRETISM**. A modern example is Santeria, mixed upon concepts from Roman Catholicism, Vudun and other African religious ideas. One has to be very careful when using the term however, as some faith followers do not like it, for it denies originality, and may be perceived to devalue the inherent truth of a particular path. If one, for example classifies Sikhism as a syncretism of Islam and Hinduism, a response may be that the truth is what it is, and it is shared by other religions, it does not follow that it was "imported" from that religion.

There is also another category that one often discusses under terms coined in the 1980s: **New Religious Movements** (NRMs), or **Alternative Religions.** These are religions that may be described as young or started within the last few centuries, and are often disparagingly referred to as **cults.** As such, they may not yet have received recognition as a standard denomination or body. Many of these movements base themselves as being rooted in older religions and claim some sort of new revelation, interpretation, or response to circumstance. They may respond to modernity or to problems that the older religions cannot address in a manner that seems compatible with current values. Some such movements are neo-paganism, the Unification Church, the Hare-Krishna Movement.

Why are there religions?
As Karen Armstrong has pointed out in her book, "The History of God," an argument can be *Homo sapiens* also being *Homo religiosus*. The presence of food offerings at the interment of the dead indicated that at quite an early stage, humans felt that there was some form of life after death—for were it not so, then the food would not have been needed. There is no lack of theories on the presence of religions, or why there should or should not be religions. All of these, however, are speculative.

70000 YEAR OLD STONE CARVING OF PYTHON'S HEAD FOUND IN BOTSWANA AND SAID TO BE ONE OF THE EARLIEST EVIDENCES OF A RELIGIOUS ARTIFACT

Karl Marx observed that religion is the opiate of the masses; Emile Durkheim said that religion is simply useful. Other researchers have argued that humans seem to have some sort of God gene, given the seeming predisposition of our human ancestors to religion, and our continuing adherence to what passes as religion in modern times. Rather than speculate further, perhaps it is better to simply revisit Professor Swidler's definition and note that one of the dominant aspects of religion—although this may not hold equally for all, or even be present in all forms of religion, is that it seeks to provide an explanation for the ultimate meaning of life. It offers answers as to what happens after we die, the reason why life is the way it is; it offers explanations of suffering and the general human condition, among other things.

On the Nature of the Divine: which came first?
If we accept the Biblical story of creation as historically reliable, then it would seem that the first concept of the divine was that there was one God. Certainly that concept has evolved throughout the centuries, but some have called it an *urmonotheismus*—a sort of primordial monotheism, the term used to denote the worship of a single god. The evidence, however, even in the Bible itself, does not allow a unanimous agreement on this concept. A survey of the world's cultures will reveal several different ideas, and to argue for the historical primacy of one over the other is not an enterprise that we are concerned with in this introductory approach. To give an

example of how cherished ideas can be misleading: it is held by many that Judaism was the first to introduce the concept of monotheism. Yet, investigation will show that ancient Egyptians also had the idea of a single God. Even in the Bible, Moses' argument with Pharaoh is not about monotheism as such, but rather about the TRUE God—for Pharaoh thought that he himself was God. There are other arguments to show that it is possible ancient India also knew the concept of monotheism. These arguments are, to reiterate, based on speculation rather than absolute knowledge. One of the strongest scholarly arguments, as far as biblical religion goes, is that the idea of monotheism is a retrojection on the history of Israel. Scholars such as Theophile Meek, Morton Smith and Mark Smith, for example, argue that the progression seems to have been from polytheism (worship of many gods) to henotheism (worship of a single god as superior to others that may be worshipped) to monolatry (worship of a single god while acknowledging that others may exist, but are not to be worshipped by a particular people), and finally to monotheism, wherein only a single god is acknowledged.[2]

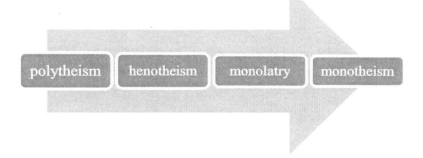

A diagram of the view towards an evolved monotheism

Approaches to the Study of Religion

There are many ways in which one may approach the study of religion. There is of course the faith based model which is common in seminaries. This may also be called the insider-confessional model,

---

[2] See Theophile Meek, "Monotheism and the Religion of Ancient Israel" in *Journal of Biblical Literature* 61, No. 1 (March 1942), 21-43; Morton Smith, "The Common Theology of the Ancient Near East," in *Journal ofBiblical Literature* 71, No. 3 (September 1952): 135-47, and Mark Smith, *The Origins of Biblical Monotheism*(Oxford and New York: Oxford University Press, 2001), 149.

because "confession" indicates that one adheres to that religion being taught, and is necessarily an insider. This makes such a person an "outsider" to a faith other than her own. Along with such an approach comes an occasional lack of objectivity, for such approaches are often underlined by someone assuming her personal faith to be the one, true, religion and all others either false or inferior. Another approach is to study religion from an anthropological perspective, as one examines the history of human culture and thought. One may also analyze religion from a psychological perspective. Some even examine religion purely for its reliance on myth—a myth in this sense being the use of a story in such a way that it may be embellished and evolve through time. There are, then, several approaches to the study of religion.

In a secular university, we prefer the position of what is known as the **phenomenological** approach. This means that we examine religions with emphasis placed on the way a follower of that religion experiences, understands and expressesher path. We avoid criticisms, polemic and many theories that may be advanced. This is only a general approach, and not necessarily absolute. Our concern is that we do not make **value judgments**. When we present Islam for example, our concern is on discussing the faith the way a Muslim sees it, and in like manner, when we study Christianity, it will be from a Christian perspective. The difference from a seminary is that we are not issuing judgments: the focus is not to gain converts, but simply to inform in an honest and respectful manner.

Does God exist? Do Science and Religion oppose each other?
This question is an old one that has resurfaced in recent years. Nietzsche had postulated that with the rise of modern and industrialized society, humans would have no need of God and that the divine would thus die: Gott ist tot (God is dead). This idea brought about a new term: theothanatology: The study of the death of God. In modern society, this idea seems to have revivified itself in the form of militant atheism. This has resulted in debates that focus on the negative aspects of religion and that the world would be better off without such a construct. Religion, some argue, is against science, relying upon that which cannot be proven, that which is irra-

tional, and exists only in the imagination. Others counter that this argument relies on the sensate things, and that most of the stabs at religion are in fact denials of only certain theological ideas that do not represent the entire gamut of world religions.

The fact is that religion and science operate in different areas. Religion is founded upon faith, and not everything that exists can be proven. The American scientist Stephen Jay Gould has coined the acronym **NOMA:non-overlapping magisteria.** This means that science and religion each has a domain of authority, and that they need not overlap: "the magisterium of science covers the empirical realm: what the Universe is made of (fact) and why does it work in this way (theory). The magisterium of religion extends over questions of ultimate meaning and moral value. These two magisteria do not overlap, nor do they encompass all inquiry (consider, for example, the magisterium of art and the meaning of beauty)."

In his wonderful book, *The Great Partnership: Science, Religion, and the Search for Meaning,* Lord Jonathan Sacks has expressed the NOMA idea somewhat differently: he points out that we need both science and religion.[3]He cited Albert Einstein's famous saying, "Science without religion is lame; religion without science is blind."

To argue then about God or no-god seems to be an enterprise that is a waste of time since neither party in this debate is agreeing upon a standard by which accurate truth can be measured. Nonetheless, the study of religion, as pursued in this class, is not about the existence or absence of a God, but rather, as earlier noted, from a phenomenological perspective. We are concerned with what a believer's view of religion is, and how it shapes the world at large.

---

[3] Jonathan Sacks, *The Great Partnership: Science, Religion, and the Search for Meaning*(New York: Schoken Books, 2011), 7.

RABBI JONATHAN SACKS[4]

[4]http://www.ou.org. Accessed February 18, 2014.

Science is about explanation. Religion is about meaning. Science analyses, religion integrates. Science breaks things down in their component parts. Religion binds people together in relationships of trust. Science tells us what is. Religion tells us what ought to be done. Science describes. Religion beckons, summons, calls. Science sees objects. Religion speaks to us as subjects. Science practices detachment. Religion is the art of attachment, self to self, soul to soul. Science sees the underlying order of the physical world. Religion hears the music beneath the noise. Science is the conquest of ignorance. Religion is the redemption of solitude.

We need scientific explanation to understand nature. We need meaning to understand human behavior and culture. Meaning is what humans seek because they are not simply part of nature. We are self-conscious. We have imaginations that allow us to envisage worlds that have never been, and to begin to create them. Like all else that lives, we have desires. Unlike anything else that lives, we can pass judgment on those desires and decide not to pursue them. We are free.

All of this science finds hard to explain. It can track mental activity from the outside. It can tell us which bits of the brain are activated when we do this or that. What it cannot do is track it on the inside. For that we use empathy. Sometimes we use poetry and song, and rituals that bind us together, and stories that gather us into a set of shared meanings. All this is part of religion, the space where self meets other and we relate as persons in a world of persons, free agents in a world of freedom. This is where we meet God, the Personhood of personhood. . .

Jonathan Sacks, *The Great Partnership*, 6.

On February 4, 2014 there was a television debate between Bill Nye, "The Science Guy" and Ken Ham, a proponent of the "New Earth" theory that claims, based on a reading of the Bible, that the earth is only 6000 years old. Many saw this as a debate that should never have occurred. Some scientists claimed that, by accepting such a debate, Bill Nye granted publicity and credibility to something that has long been debunked. Facebook and Twitter pages were inundated with views about the debate.

BILL NYE AND KEN HAM, THE DEBATERS

Here is an excerpt from one blog:

"But Ham is insidiously wrong on one important aspect: He insists evolution is anti-religious. But it's not; it's just anti-*his*-religion. This is, I think, the most critical aspect of this entire problem: The people who are attacking evolution are doing so because they think evolution is attacking their beliefs.

But unless they are the narrowest of fundamentalists, this simply is not true. There is no greater proof of this than Pope John Paul II—who, one must admit, was a deeply religious man—saying that evolution was an established fact. Clearly, not all religion has a problem with evolution. Given that a quarter of U.S. citizens are Catholics, this shows Ham's claim that evolution is anti-religious to be wrong.

So evolution is not anti-religion in general. But is it atheistic? *No.* Evolution takes no stand on the existence or lack thereof of a god or gods. Whether you think life originated out of ever-more complex chemical reactions occurring on an ancient Earth, or was breathed into existence by God, evolution would take over *after* that moment. It's a bit like the Big Bang; we don't know how the Universe came into existence at that moment, but starting a tiny fraction of a second after that event our science does a pretty fair job of explanation.

I can't stress this enough. The conflict over the teaching of evolution is based on the false assumption that evolution is antagonistic to religion. This is why, I think, evolution is so vehemently opposed by so many in the United States. The attacks on the specifics of evolution—the claims about irreducibility of the eye, for example, or other such incorrect statements—are a symptom, not a cause.[5]

---

[5]http://www.slate.com/blogs/bad_astronomy/2014/02/05/creationism_debate_should_we_engage_anti
_science.html. Accessed February 8, 2014.

Glossary

Animism   The belief that everything is filled with spirit.

Alternative
Religions: These are religions that may be described as young or started within the last few centuries, and are often disparagingly referred to as **cults.** As such, they may not yet have received recognition as a standard denomination or body.

Agnosticism: The belief that the presence of God cannot be proven, and one therefore does not know. In lay terms, it is usually defined as the claim that while there is no outright rejection, one says that convincing proof has not been offered for the existence of a God.

Atheism: "no god"—this is the rejection of any form of theism, whether it is in the form of monotheism or polytheism.

Deism: The concept of a supreme being who created the world, but has allowed it to pursue its own course, without giving it any sort of organized religion. In this case, one knows God by reason and observation.

Henotheism: The supreme status and worship of one god while acknowledging that there are other lesser gods that may be worshipped.

Immanent: Present and operating within the material world.

Theism: This is the idea that the one God, before whom there was nothing, created everything and who makes its will known by revelation, and is involved in the governance of this world.

Monolatry: Acknowledgement that there may be other gods, but that only one god is worthy of worship.

Monotheism: The belief in the existence of only one God.

New Religious

Movements: These are religions that may be described as young or started within the last few centuries, and are often disparagingly referred to as **cults.** As such, they may not yet have received recognition as a standard denomination or body.

Nontheism: In this position, the idea of God is basically seen as irrelevant: it is impossible to prove there is a God, and the possibility that there may be a god exists. Nonetheless, given the insolubility of a reliable answer, one neither asserts nor denies the supernatural.

Pantheism: The idea that divinity exists in everything.

Phenomenology:
The study of any religion with emphasis placed on the experience, understanding and expression of its adherents.

Polytheism: The belief in several gods.

Theothanatology:
The study of the death of god.

INDIGENOUS RELIGIONS

By Khaleel Mohammed, Dept. of Religious Studies, San Diego State University

THE CARVING OF CHIEF CRAZY HORSE, A WORK STILL IN PROGRESS

Learning Goals

- *Understanding the appropriate terms used for topic*
- *Explain problems of Studying Indigenous Religions*
- *Outline approach of Western Scholarship*
- *Explain briefly about Iroquois/Dakota/Apache/Inuit Traditions*
- *Provide very brief overview of African Religion*
- *Define Complementary/Conflict Dualism*

Introduction

Today, many scholars use the term "indigenous" or "autochthonous" to describe any religion created by a particular group of people that identify with a particular place, and which has remained specifically associated with that group. These coinages are quite different from the earlier derogatory terms that were used. The process of colonization came with Christian missionary activity, and from this perspective, any religion other than Christianity, or the ones known to the colonizers, were seen in a negative light. Some of the descriptions used were: primitive, primal, basic, non-literate, oral, native, tribal, and aboriginal. Each one of these terms is problematic. The descriptions, **primitive**, **primal**, and **basic**, need little explanation, for they all connote images of an early state in some process of religious evolution. **Oral** and **non-literate** may truly describe most indigenous religions but fail to take into account that there are also peoples, such as the Mayans and Aztecs that had writing systems. The term "native" is one that can be seen as offensive, such as in Africa, where in the past, it gave the impression of lack of development and civilization. Even the words **tribal** and **aboriginal**, that might seem lexically correct, have been used as terms of denigration. It is therefore difficult to find any adequate term, for the same drawbacks that apply to "aboriginal" may be said to apply to "indigenous." The contention however, is that **indigenous** or **autochthonous** is more neutral in tone.

In an introductory course on World Religions, it is difficult to study indigenous religions since most texts dedicate a chapter that seeks to grossly generalize the thousands of such religions into some qualities that allow for **essentialization**. The focus of this text is on the living religions of the world, and as such, we will only cursorily touch on some of the major indigenous traditions of North America and Africa—while acknowledging the existence of many more in Australia, South America etc.

Today, it is extremely difficult to find an indigenous religion that has not undergone transformation due to outside influence. Most have in fact undergone some form of **syncretism**, wherein they have incorporated ideas from foreign traditions. We still, however, describe them as indigenous, since the followers of these religions have woven the imported ideas into their religious worldview, and have not sent out missionaries to seek to convert others to their belief system.

The Problems of Studying Indigenous Religions

It is easy to learn about a religion that has its beliefs and history recorded in written texts. If someone wants to know about Judaism, Christianity, Islam, Hinduism, or Buddhism, all she has to do is visit a local library or bookstore. The information may not always be reliable—especially in cases where authors might adopt a polemic stance against the religions about which they are writing—but the reader has ability to research and compare from a vast array of written works.

Some researchers have also operated under the idea that the major religions of the world are all we need to study, and that indigenous religions somehow represent the ideas of primitive people. Researchers have proven, however, that ideas and concepts, the drawings and symbolisms of indigenous religions are as complex as that of the more popular religions of the world. It is in fact very difficult to study indigenous religions for a variety of reasons. There is the issue of language—which in the vast majority of cases cannot be taught in universities, but must only be learned by living among its speakers. Even when the language has been learned, it has to be done to such a level of fluency that the religious and spiritual ideas of the religion can be understood by the researcher.   The background of the researcher must also be taken into consideration: is the motivation of study the objective need to learn, or to convert the people to some other religion? Will there be a market for such research after it is completed? Today, one can obtain a Ph. D. in some aspect of Jewish, Christian, Islamic or Indic Religion studies and expect to find a professorial position in her specialty. A researcher, however, who goes to the jungles of Guyana to study the religious life of the Akawaio people might find an extremely limited amount of openings, if any at all, that might reward her research. Nonetheless, the research continues, although it is not always under the rubric of religion. Anthropology, Ethnomusicology, Art, and even Pharmacology are some of the disciplines under which one might find studies being done.

Indigenous Religions and Western Scholarship

Until very recently, religion studies in the overwhelming majority of the western world's universities were done under the aegis of churches. Often the idea was to train missionaries to convert the "savages" to the "true" religion. The religious ideas of these targeted peoples were often exaggerated in the most negative forms, and shown as being in some stage of development that would culminate in success only if they were to give up their autochthonous beliefs in favor of Christianity.

We also must note that the reports of indigenous religions, especially those we are told that existed at the time of the Spanish, Portuguese or English exploration of the "new world" did not come from the adherents of those faiths. Rather they were written by outsiders, trained to see only one worldview as correct. Early reports were written by explorers and missionaries who often relied on translators, and then used as authoritative texts.

A Summary of Indigenous American Religions

Regardless of their denominational differences, the early European settlers in America saw Christianity as their common religion. If they spoke of "freedom of religion," they referred to the idea of different paths WITHIN Christianity. This outlook meant that that autochthonous people were seen as a convenient enemy or people to be converted. The indigenous people of North America were like the Canaanites of the Bible: they were to be decimated by a foreign people, bringing arms and diseases that they had never before witnessed.

In time, the tribes were to be largely slaughtered and dispossessed, and had to end up living on reservations. The movie industry generated films that depicted the native peoples as savages in the "oater" or "Cowboy and Indians" genre.

Scholars often take distinct geographic regions and then compare the religious beliefs and rituals of the peoples to show the diversity of religion. Although this approach shows that one cannot generalize, it still obfuscates many of the differences and ideas of groups. In selecting one group from a particular region, it is possible that the many other tribes from that area that might have had different beliefs will be overlooked. This is, sadly, one of the unavoidable consequences of trying to do an overview of the myriad traditions that formed the American religious mosaic before the decimation of the autochthonous people. Our presentation relies heavily on the material supplied by Western Virginia University Project on the study of Indigenous religion, as well as the information from various Canadian or American government establishments. In almost every case, the spread of modernity has brought about a syncretism, and so we often use the past tense to describe the indigenous beliefs. Today, some people are trying to revivify the "older" systems or acknowledge their existence alongside the more dominant Christianity.

The commercial use of sacred symbols or drawings has also been the source of much debate, especially when such usage seems to show lack of respect. The logo of the Cincinnati baseball team, "The Cincinnati Reds" is one such example that has created controversy. Even the San Diego State University's "Monty" has not been without its opponents.

SAN DIEGO STATE UNIVERSITY'S "MONTY"

The Iroquois

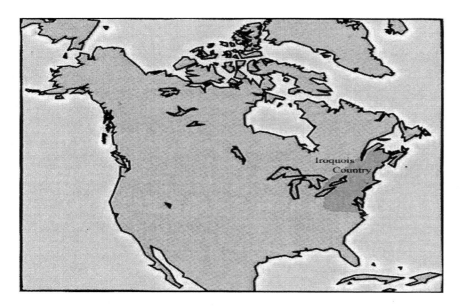

The Iroquois people had an extremely well-developed belief system. Their religion was characterized by a monotheistic belief in an all-powerful creator known as the "Great Spirit", or "Ha-wenne-yu." The Iroquois failed to see the need in developing a detailed conception of their creator. This knowledge was thought to be above and beyond their capabilities to understand. His power was administered to the material world through a class of inferior spiritual existences, by whom he was surrounded. While divine attributes concerning the Great Spirit remained undeveloped, the Iroquois gave detailed descriptions of this lower class of spirits that interacted with the material world. They were known as "Invisible Agents" or "Ho-no-che-no-keh." The power possessed by these spirits was given to them by the Great Spirit and were the manifestations of his unlimited power. Some of these spirits were given names; however, they were often identified with the object or force that they presided over. For example, He-no, one of the more important spirits, was given the thunderbolt and controlled the weather. He had the form of man and wore the costume of a warrior.

The Iroquois belief acknowledged the existence of evil in the world. Evil is represented by the brother of the Great Spirit, "Ha-ne-go-ate-geh", or "the Evil-minded." This evil spirit exists independently and controls its own inferior spiritual beings. These agents of evil also exist in the material world and are here with the specific purpose of causing evil. The believer is left to choose either obedience to the Great Spirit or submission to the Evil-minded. It is important to note that the Iroquois developed the idea of an immortal soul. This soul was judged by the Great Spirit upon the death of the body. The threat of punishment in the afterlife increased morality concerns, which aided in the success of the Iroquois Nation. The Iroquois did not have police and they didn't need them. Their code of honor was seldom broken because citizens feared public disapproval. Only two crimes were named, theft and murder, and both were punishable by death. Violence committed by drunken men was overlooked because rum was believed to have power that extended beyond human will.

CANADIAN COMMEMORATIVE POSTAGE STAMP

The ritual ceremonies practiced by the Iroquois tribes were systematic worship services that occurred in accordance to certain seasonal periods throughout the year. The rituals were handed down through the generation and remained unchanged for centuries. Festivals most commonly occurred during important agricultural periods. Worship and thanks were given to the Great Spirit for protection and survival. One of the "Invisible Agents" was usually honored depending on what time of year the ceremony was taking place. The ceremonies were led by "Keepers of the Faith", or "Ho-nun-den-ont." They were not an organized priesthood like one would imagine, but rather a loosely organized council of qualified individuals who were assigned the task of maintaining the ritual practices of the Iroquois people.

The Iroquois were first encountered by the white man around 1609 during the height of Dutch exploration. The league spent the majority of the seventeenth century at war with neighboring tribes as well as French invaders. Their influence spread through the northeast and reached a culminating point around the turn of the century. Within fifty years of this time, the power and population of the once proud Iroquois Nation was cut in half. White settlers had moved into their territory and forced the Iroquois to give up their homeland.

The belief system of the Iroquois was the closest a Native American civilization had come to the complex theology of Christianity. One major difference between the two religions is evident when looking at how each faith explains humankind's participation in the workings of the universe. While most Christian denominations sought to participate actively in the evolution of their world, the Iroquois saw humankind as too insignificant to take part in the grand scheme of the Great Spirit. For example, many Christian denominations, like the Puritans of New England, believed that they were the chosen people of God and were working toward the creation of a true "Kingdom of God" located in America. The Iroquois, on the other hand, believed that the world was as it should be, and there was nothing that could be done by humankind to change this fact. This idea would eventually change somewhat as the Iroquois were influenced more and more by European Christianity. Furthermore, their ideas concerning punishment in the afterlife were also influenced by Christian concepts. The idea of purgatory seems to have seeped into the Iroquois belief system sometime during the white man's invasion.

While the Iroquois Nation was the strongest Native American civilization east of the Mississippi river, their integration into the dominant white culture went relatively smooth compared to most other instances of integration among the native tribes of North America. This may have been due to the similarities between their belief systems which made it easier for the two races to find common ground. The religion practiced by Iroquois descendants is remarkably similar to the one practiced by their ancestors. The similarities between the two distinct religions seem to have saved the weaker Native American system from extinction.

The Dakota

ROUGH DEPICTION OF LOCATION OF SIOUX TRIBES

The Dakota, or Sioux as they are commonly called, inhabited the Great Plains and prairies surrounding the modern states of North and South Dakota, as well as Minnesota. This was their home until they were forced out in the mid-1800s to make way for mining companies. The Dakotas were less organized and more spread out than their cousins in the east, the Iroquois. Their society was based almost entirely on the hunting of bison, which provided them with virtually all of their survival needs. Their territory consisted of seasonal hunting grounds that forced the tribal units to live a nomadic lifestyle on the plains. There was no need for permanent settlements due to the fact buffalo herds would rarely stay in one place for long. The Dakota's existence centered on the movements of the herds, and as such they relocated during the seasons.

There was no separation of the natural world from the world of the supernatural. This unity in nature was thought to be beyond the comprehension of humankind and could only be shared in through the practice of rituals. The "animating force" that acted as the common denominator of the universe was known as "Wakan Tanka." This Wakan Tanka was beyond definition or comprehension. The physical world was composed of the manifestations of this animating force. In essence, they believed that every object was spirit, or "wakan." This is known as ANIMISM—the idea that everything is imbued with spirit. For this reason, the Dakota held a docetic view of the universe in which nothing was real. Everything in the material world had only the appearance of being real. Like the inferior spirits in the Iroquois belief system, Wakan Tanka employed the use of "Wakan people" to interact with the material world and control the lives of men. These characters were often the objects of worship and praise.

Holy men attempted to explain this Watan Tanka to the Dakota people. They did not concentrate on strict religious doctrine or structure due to the ambiguous nature of Wakan Tanka. Instead, they served as guides to assist Dakota people in coming to their own personal understanding of their place in the universe. It was believed that humankind is required to serve the Wakan people who administered and controlled the forces that surrounded them. White Buffalo Woman was one of the most important Wakan people to the Dakota. Their myth states that she gave the Dakota people the "Calf Pipe" through which they could communicate with the invisible spirit world.

A Lakota peace pipe, advertised for sale on www.peace-pipes.com

The Dakota people see themselves as inseparably related to the bison. A bond existed between the two that was steeped in religious tradition and survival. For this reason, the bison played an equally significant role in the Dakota's religious belief system. A co-existence was achieved between these two life forms within an interconnected universe governed by the collective forces of Wakan Tanka. Most of the Dakota's rituals were centered on this relationship. Dakota rituals were based on mystical experiences instead of systematic worship. The most important aspect of ritual was the individual personal experience. The experience was usually related in the form of an interpretive dance inspired by a personal vision. The Dakota were encouraged to contribute to the understanding of Wakan Tanka through their own individual relationship with the spirit world.

The religious beliefs and rituals of the Dakota people were not as compatible with Christianity as the Iroquois' were. Their religious ties to their land place them at great odds with the invading white settlers. The unity and balance demonstrated in the Dakota's world contrasted sharply with the one-sided, monotheistic characteristics of Christianity. The Dakota people attempted to retain their own religion in the face of cultural extinction; however, few aspects of their culture were left unaffected by their interactions with whites. A significant influence of Christianity on the Dakota belief system involved the personification of Wakan Tanka. Before contact with European settlers, Wakan Tanka was without distinction. The Dakota seem to have given anthropomorphic attributes to their creator fashioned after the incarnation concept of Christianity.

Image of Crazy Horse, one of the greatest Sioux warriors. Some believe he was never photographed.

The Legend of White Buffalo

Long ago, there was a terrible famine among the Lakota's. The chief sent out two scouts to hunt for food. As the young men travelled they saw a figure in the distance. As they approached they saw that it was a beautiful young woman in white clothing. One of the men desired the maiden and approached her, telling his companion he would take her as a wife. His companion warned him that she appeared to be a sacred woman, and to do anything sacrilegious would be folly. The man ignored the other's advice.

The companion watched as the other approached and embraced the woman, during which time a white cloud enveloped the pair. After a while, the cloud disappeared and only the mysterious woman and a pile of bones remained. The remaining man was frightened, and began to draw his bow, but the woman beckoned him forward, telling him that no harm would come to him. As the woman spoke Lakota, the young man decided she was one of his people, and came forward. When he arrived, she pointed to a spot on the ground where the other scout's bare bones lay. The man raised his bow to protect himself, but she explained that she was wakan/holy and his weapons could not harm her. She further explained that if he did as she instructed, no harm would befall him and that his tribe would become more prosperous. The scout promised to do what she instructed, and was told to return to his encampment, call the Council and prepare a feast for her arrival. The woman's name was *PtesanWi* which translated *White Buffalo Woman.* She taught the Lakotas seven sacred rituals and gave them the **chanupa** or sacred pipe which is the holiest of all worship symbols. After teaching the people and giving them her gifts, she changed into a buffalo and left them , promising to return

Under the influence of Catholic missionaries, the story of the Virgin Mary became associated with the legend of White Buffalo Woman. The syncretic blend of the two narratives, wherein Mary is identified as White Buffalo Calf Woman, and wherein the *chanupa* is smoked still continues among many Lakota Christians.

The Apache

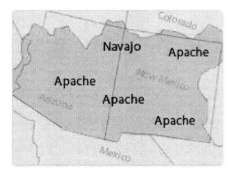

The Apache tribes once flourished in the southwestern desert region of the United States, until they were moved to reservations. Little is known about this nomadic group of autochthonous people that lived a somewhat isolated existence in the harsh environment of the arid southwest. Their territory encompassed the modern states of Texas, New Mexico, Arizona, and extended into parts of Mexico. They were generally nomadic gatherers who relied on scarce resources found in their desert environment for survival. Survival under these conditions was difficult and there was little time for speculating in detail on matters of religion. For this reason, the belief system of the Apache tribes is less developed than the other two tribes mentioned earlier. Rather than concentrate on any large pantheon of gods and goddesses, their belief system concentrated on supernatural cultural figures that interfered little in the daily activities of the people unless called upon to help an individual.

The Apache lifestyle left little room for religious ritual. This non-agricultural society had no reason to celebrate seasonal periods and rarely celebrated any type of annual gathering. All time and energy was spent on survival. Two illustrations of this point lie in the fact that the Apache lacked formal ceremonies for both marriage and death; two events that traditionally involve elaborate ceremonies in most civilizations. Marriage among the Apache focused upon the absorption of the couple into an extended family. Sickness and death were formidable problems for a society that needed every individual's efforts for survival. More importantly, however, was the fact that the Apache lacked an organized belief in an afterlife. This focused all attention towards survival in this world. For this reason, curing rites were the most common form of ceremony demonstrated by the Apache people.

The individual power quest was the foundation of Apache religion. The group, as a whole, was too involved with issues of survival to spend time with religious issues. Therefore, the Apache were encouraged to establish their own relationship with the supernatural forces that surrounded them. Humankind could manipulate these powers—that were eager to be involved in human affairs—for service in both good and evil. Life for the Apache was a struggle for survival governed by one's interactions with these supernatural forces.

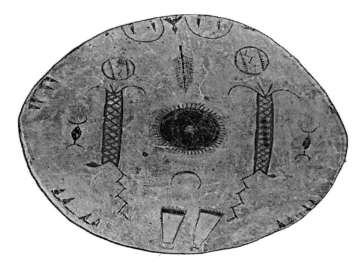

19TH CENTURY APACHE PICTOGRAPH, SOUTHERN PLAINS

The Apache religion was loosely organized and headed by shamans who had the power to communicate with the spirit world. The word for shaman is DIYIN. A diyin's power rested in his ability to heal. This power, if used well, could make the shaman an influential figure among Apache tribes. The shaman was the link that connected the Apache people to the healing powers of the supernatural world.

The Apache tribes were invaded by white culture around 1850. The people and their culture were quickly removed from the land to make way for the expanding American population. There was little time for the Apache to be influenced by Christianity due to the fact that the United States sent military forces to the region before the Christian churches sent missionaries.

GERONIMO, CIRCA 1905

Geronimo (1829-1909), one of the most famous Apache warriors, summed up his indigenous Bedonkohe beliefs thus:

"As to the future state, the teachings of our tribe were not specific, that is, we had no definite idea of our relations and surroundings in after life.

We believed that there is a life after this one, but no one ever told me as to what part of man lived after death ... We held that the discharge of one's duty would make his future life more pleasant, but whether that future life was worse than this life or better, we did not know, and no one was able to tell us. We hoped that in the future life, family and tribal relations would be resumed. In a way we believed this, but we did not know it."[6]

The Inuit

CARVING OF A SEA SPIRIT

Indigenous Inuit belief focused on ANIMISM: the idea that all things, including the forces of nature, had a spirit. These people live in the northernmost part of North America, such as the Yukon, North West Territories, Nunavut, Quebec and Labrador. When someone died, her spirit simply went over to the spirit world, con-

[6] Geronimo, *Geronimo: His Own Story,* ed. S.M. Barrett (New York: Ballantine Books, 1971), 178.

tinuing her existence in that dimension. In hunting, one did not simply kill an animal—but rather something whose spirit could still survive and come back as a demon to seek revenge if certain rituals were not followed. If the proper rituals were followed, the spirit would go into another animal that would again allow for the transfer of its spirit when the animal in which it lived was hunted by the Inuit. The only people who could truly understand and control the spirits were the ANGAKOKS or SHAMANS. These ANGAKOKS used charms, dances, or even went into trances to communicate with the spirit world. In their rituals, they often used masks that they believed had special powers. In the harsh Arctic, survival was ensured by a complex system of taboos and rituals to ensure that no spirits were offended, and that there was harmony with unseen forces. Sometimes the ANGAKOKS would recommend offering gifts to the spirits, moving away from a particular area, or they would even impose some form of penalty on a person who was deemed to have angered the spirits.

Bad weather, sickness, and scarcity of animals for hunting were all blamed upon unhappy spirits. Humans also had souls that could be lost or stolen (causes of illness and madness). The belief was that humans were made of three parts: a body, a name, and a soul. When a person died, it was only the body that died, the spirit and name could continue living in a new body. The names of dead relatives were given to babies, ensuring that the soul and name could continue living.

Some ritual practices for the hunt included the following: sea mammal and land mammal meat were not to be eaten in the same meal; a knife used for killing whales had to be wrapped in sealskin, notcaribou skin. If a seal was killed, melted snow was put in its mouth to ensure that its spirit did not leave when it was thirsty.

One of the seemingly common features of most indigenous religions seems to be in the use of drums, music and dancing to tell stories. In song and dance they told stories of the spirits, and of traditions to be followed. The main instrument of Inuit ceremonies and dances was the shallow, one-sided drum. Most drums were made from caribou skin, or walrus stomach or bladder stretched over a wooden hoop. Drum dances usually occurred inside large snow houses (igloos) with up to 60 people. Throat singing was a popular feature. In the Inuit case, throat singing would be performed by two women, as if they were competing with each other, using sounds from their throats and chests. One would set a short rhythmic pattern, while the other would produce a different pattern altogether. Art and carvings also, to this day, play a large part in Inuit culture. Carvers use parts of animals, stone and driftwood as their media.

Inukshuks were large rock cairns made from balancing rocks that were pushed to the surface by the frozen earth (permafrost). The inukshuk may have been used for navigation, as a point of reference, a marker for travel routes, fishing places, camps, hunting grounds, places of veneration, or any such important function. The simplest and commonest Inukshuk was in the form of a single stone standing upright. It is possible that the later designs of INUKSHUKS may have been influenced by the arrival of Europeans. The more complex designs indicate that the erection of such symbols was traditionally a communal effort.

AN INUKSHUK

The Legend of Sedna

There are many versions of this most popular Inuit story. One of them is as follows:

Once upon a time, before the white men and all others, the Inuit hunted the land and fished the land. In this time, was a great hunter, whose wife had died long ago, leaving a girl child. The hunter would raise the child himself.

The child grew to become a very beautiful woman with many suitors seeking her hand. The hunter was proud for his daughter, she could sew good clothing and in all the land none was so pretty. She was, however, headstrong and would not accept any suitors. One day, a handsome man in a kayak appeared and seeing the beautiful daughter, stopped. "Come with me, daughter, for I am a great hunter and will provide you with food and home" said the handsome man. And so the daughter went.

CARVING OF SEDNA THROWING A BELUGA WHALE

Enroute to her new far off home, they stopped along the way, and the handsome man removed his clothing for the sun was high and kayaking is hard work. The girl burst out into tears, for now standing before her was not a handsome man but a northern fulmar (Bird man) in human form. His eyes black, his muscles bulging. Without the need for human clothing, the fulmar now made good speed and soon he and the daughter were at his nest tent.

Time went by and true to his word, the fulmar provided food and warmth to the daughter and she did not want for anything. Together they had a child.The Father had continued his search for his daughter feeling remorse at how pride had made him treat his only child and after many years of travel he once again found his daughter in the land of the Fulmar. The father arrived when the fulmar was away and seeing his daughter he burst into tears "Forgive me daughter, I have come to take you home". With those words, the father scooped up his daughter and with his kayak began making his way home.

The fulmar returned and seeing his wife gone, set out to rescue her, and in his bird form was able to catch up and try to regain his wife. His wings beat down upon the water as he swooped trying to make the father turn back. The waves grew bigger and almost capsized the kayak, the father in fear of dying, threw his daughter overboard so he could get away, but she held upon the kayak by her fingers.

The father, in abject terror now, took his knife and with one blow chopped off a finger, it fell into the sea and behold, it became a seal and swam away. The hunter chopped another finger, and it too became a walrus. The hunter chopped a third finger, and it became the bearded seal. With each finger being chopped, so the sea mammals were made.

Finally, not being able to grasp the kayak, the daughter sank to the bottom of the seas. As she sank, the Moon Spirit (Tatqeq) and The Air Spirit (Sila) combined together and said "For your hardship, we give you the power of all so that you will become the guardian for the Inuit". With that, Sedna was born and created a kingdom which lies at the bottom of the sea and was once again reunited with her Fulmar husband.

A CARVING OF BIRDMAN BY INUIT SCULPTOR, SAMUEL NAHAWLAITUQ

The father made good his escape, but memories of his daughter gave him great remorse so that one day, he lay down at the edge of the sea and asked his daughter to forgive him. As he slept, the tide came out and reunited him with his daughter. Together all dwell at the bottom of the sea.Now when the Inuit transgress against other Inuit or the land, Sedna will make the sea mammals scarce and cause the seas and the air to storm, displaying her anger to her people. It is then that the shaman must travel down to the kingdom and discover the roots of the problems then solve and rectify them with the people. Only then will Sedna be placated and calm the weather and release the mammals so the Inuit do not suffer starvation.

In some cases, the shaman can enter a trance like state to visit with Sedna or can be given the ability to breathe underwater. Sedna keeps a comb and when shamans visit, it is expected that they comb her hair from algae for she cannot hold the comb herself.

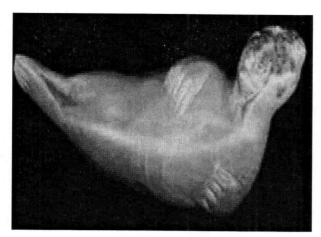

A CARVING OF SEDNA

Reflection on North American Indigenous Religion

The connection between environmental factors and the development of religious systems among Indigenous American cultures should be clear. In general terms, a tribe's ability to develop extensive religious belief systems was directly proportional to its ability to provide for the survival of its people. A large supply of natural resources, as in the case of the Iroquois, provided more time to develop religious ideas. The Apache, on the other hand, had little time to spend on religious thought. They were unable to develop an extensive religious theology due to the amount of time and energy they were forced to put towards survival. Furthermore, the connection between the Dakota's belief system and their environment is glaring. Their dependency on the bison gave rise to a religious system of co-dependent survival within a world characterized by oneness and unity.

A CEREMONIAL DANCE

While each tribe's unique environment impacted its belief system in a different way, all of the four North American indigenous paths we have covered demonstrate similarities in the way in which they view their interaction with the natural world. There is little evidence of a separation between the natural and the supernatural in any of the religions discussed. It can be said that Native American cultures were characterized by an intimate relationship with nature. This relationship was explained in terms of the supernatural and was experienced at the subjective level. Deep religious sentiment permeated most aspects of Native American life in the pre-discovered North American continent even when systematic rituals were absent.

A Very Brief Look at African Indigenous Religion

The very negative early European attitudes towards Africa, along with the Hollywood depictions have been responsible for a very negative view of almost all forms of indigenous African religions. They were largely portrayed as bent upon cannibalism, worship of the devils, and presented in every way possible to make them seem savage and backward.

Based on such imagery, it is sometimes difficult to understand that this large continent has been the traditional home of thousands of different traditions. Their concepts of religion differ greatly, although it is agreed that they focus upon a supreme deity. The role of the Supreme deity is a matter of difference of opinion: in some traditions He created the world himself; in others, the creation was done by lesser deities. Most of these forms are ORAL, maintaining traditions by song, dance, sculpture and other art forms.

A MASK OF THE ORISHA, SHANGO

One of the largest traditions is that of the Yoruba, encompassing parts of Nigeria, Benin and Toga, formerly given the name Yorubaland. These were among the largest groups of people sent to the new world as slaves, and as a result, their influence exists today in many of the forms of religion among the African diaspora. We see, for example, the religions such as Candomble and Santeria, in Brazil and Cuba, or Orisha in Trinidad built upon concepts from Yoruba belief.

Olodumare or **Olorun** is the Supreme Being, over and above everything, beyond description so that even a gender cannot be assigned to IT. This Supreme Being assigns duties to about 400 lesser gods, or those who have some of the manifestations of the Divine in them. These are known as **orishas**. Obatala was sent down to earth by Olorun to create humans, but he did not pay the proper homage to Olorun, and was put to sleep with palm wine. His brother Oduduwa was sent instead, and took the materials from the sleeping Obatala to complete his task.

There are several types of Orishas, and they may exist as rivers, trees, or even in human form. Orishas function almost like **humans**, and can eat, marry, have sex, eat food and do a host of other activities. They may be of either gender. Orishas can often possess people, using these people as the media through which they speak and communicate their wishes. Trickster deities play a special role in Yoruba religion, often serving as messengers among the orishas, and disrupting the normal order of things. This does not mean they are evil. Rather they are part of the worldview known as "**complementary dualism**," wherein the forces that enhance life (good) and those that diminish life (evil) are mixed, even among the deities, working together to create that which is necessary for survival. This, as Robert Baum, explains in his contribution to *A Concise Introduction to World Religions*, is different to **conflict dualism**, where the good and evil are seen as opposed to each other, as in Judaism, Christianity and Islam.

In Yoruba religion there is a special role for ancestors since they are seen to have travelled over to the spirit world and now able to assist their descendants. One of the common trends in many indigenous religions is the role of music and dancing, and in Yoruba religion this is significantly present. So too is the concept of witches (singular **aje**), who exist mostly as women, whose souls can leave their bodies to torment others. Their evil can be countered by medicines prepared by a diviner, a **babalawo**who can read signs to interpret the supernatural influences in a person's life.

YORUBA OFFERING BOWL: These bowls are used to hold kola nuts as offerings of hospitality or as receptacles for the sixteen sacred palm nuts used in divination.

Glossary

Aje	The Yoruba word for "witchcraft."
Angakok	A shaman in the Inuit tradition.
Animism	The idea that all things have a spirit.
Autochthonous	That which belongs, or originates in the place where it is found. Autochthonous religion therefore describes any religion created by a particular group of people that identify with a particular place.
Babalawo	A diviner in the Yoruba tradition.
Chanupa	Sacred pipe, in the Lakota tradition.
Complementary Dualism	Wherein the forces of good and evil are mixed, working together to create that which is necessary for survival.
Conflict Dualism	Wherein good and evil cannot work with each other.
Diyin	A shaman in the Apache tradition.
Fulmar	Birdman in the Inuit legend.
Ha-wen-ne-yu	The Great Spirit, in the Iroquois tradition.
Ho-no-che-no-keh	Invisible agents, the lower class of spirits that interact with the material world, according to the Iroquois tradition.
Inukshuk	A rock cairn made from balancing rocks that have been pushed to the surface by the frozen earth.
Ha-ne-go-ate-geh	The evil brother of the Great Spirit in the Iroquois tradition.
Olorun	See Oludumare.
Oludumare	The Supreme Being in the Yoruba Tradition.

Orisha   A lesser god in the Yoruba tradition, of which there are about 400.

Sedna   The beautiful woman in Inuit legend who drowned at sea, and from whose severed fingers the sea mammals were created.

Syncretism   The incorporation of foreign ideas to a tradition.

Wakan Tanka   The Animating force of the universe in the Dakota tradition.

HINDUISM
MANY BOOKS, MANY GODS, MANY PATHS

By Zoe Close, Chair of Philosophy and Religion, Grossmont College

Nothing of nonbeing comes to be,
nor does being cease to exist;
the boundary between these two
is seen by men who see reality,

Indestructible is the presence
that pervades all this;
no one can destroy
the unchanging reality.

Lord Krishna in the Bhagavad-Gita (2: 15,16)

EXTERIOR DETAIL OF SRI MIRIAMMAN, OLDEST HINDU TEMPLE IN
SINGAPORE

- *Describe Central Features of Hinduism*
- *Explain the term "Hinduism"*
- *Summarize the development/History of Religious Ideas*
- *Describe the Scriptures*
- *Outline Celebrations and Festivals*
- *Explain the Caste System*
- *Explain the Four Stages of Life*
- *Describe Goals of Life*
- *Explain the Ways of Connecting to the Divine/Ways of Salvation*
- *Discuss Hindu Philosophy*
- *Explain Relation to Other Religions*
- *Identify some Modern Movements*

Central Features of Hinduism

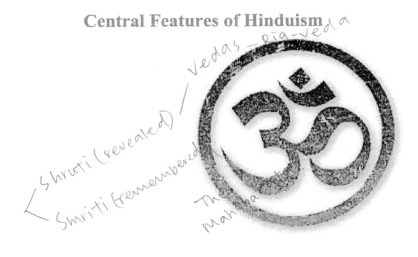

[handwritten margin notes: Vedas—Rig-Veda; Shruti (revealed); Smriti (remembered); The Mahabharata]

OM: A SYMBOL FOUND IN MANY HINDU HOMES.

Although the sacred tradition is the oldest extant world religion, the term "Hinduism" has only been in use since the nineteenth century. "Hinduism" was a term coined by British scholars of "Indology" and used by missionaries who were hoping to westernize the local people. Hindus, themselves, call Hinduism "*Sanatana Dharma.*" Today Hinduism is the religious way of life of the majority of the people of India and of neighboring Nepal. There are many Hindus throughout the world including Britain and the United States. These followers are made up of both Hindus who left India to settle elsewhere as well as new devotees.

Scriptures of the Hindus are categorized as **SHRUTI**, "things revealed (heard)" or as **SMRITI**, "things remembered." The oldest sacred writings, the *Vedas*—belonging to the "things revealed" category—focus on sacrifice, worship, formulas for priestly ritual, and spells and charms. The *Rig-Veda*, the first of the *Vedas*, is, itself, made up of 10 books containing over one thousand hymns. A later work, *The Mahabharata*—belonging to the second category, "things remembered'—is four times as long as the Christian *Bible.*

The number of deities associated with Hinduism is overwhelming indeed. Vedic texts alone, mention thirty-three gods. However, most Hindus believe in a supreme presence whose essence is represented by these deities. These representations emanate from the

[handwritten margin note: 33 gods]

[handwritten: Brahman — universal reality (one soul)]
[handwritten: ↳ Atman]

[handwritten: 波羅門]

sacred qualities of the "supreme one of reality." ***Brahman*** is the concept of Universal Reality, the one soul. ***Atman*** is the soul of each individual which strives to understand that it is part of the one soul, one reality, ***Brahman***.

[handwritten: 生命的本源]

Hindus believe that the human existence is a cycle of birth, death and rebirth (***Samsara***). The same soul remains as it moves through its successive material lives. ***Karma***, meaning "action" in Sanskrit, is the sum of the results of one's deeds over a lifetime. ***Karma*** is the universal principle that determines whether one will be born into a higher or lower status in the next life. Time, itself, is understood by Hindus to be cyclical and eternal in nature rather than linear.

[handwritten: Samsara 輪回]

Brahma, Shiva and Vishnu seated on lotuses with their consorts

Development of Hinduism

The earliest history of Hinduism is difficult to trace with certainty, but the subsequent historical periods coincide with major developments in the religion. The history of Hinduism is inextricably tied to social developments and political change.

Indus Valley Religion (before 2000 BCE)

A sophisticated culture developed alongside the Indus River, an area that is in current-day Pakistan. Although this civilization had begun to dissipate by about 1500 BCE, archaeological remains tell us that it was the dwelling place of about 40,000. Residents lived in houses with water systems that included wells and drainage mechanisms. Harappa and Mohenjo-Daro were the two major cities. In these places raised mounds for temples were discovered. A "great bath" found in Mohenjo-Daro provides evidence that the people practiced ritual bathing. Evidence of fires tells of possible sacrificial practices. A significant number of terracotta figures have been found, female figures that indicate goddess worship. There appears to be a fundamental link between the religious practices of this early civilization and later developments in Hinduism.

SEAL EXCAVATED FROM MOHENJO-DARO

Vedic Religion (~1500—500 BCE)

During this period, the sacred Vedas (what is revealed) were composed. Hindus believe that these revelations are eternal and unchanging and did not have authorship by human beings. The canon begins as an oral tradition that was carefully passed down and not in written form for a thousand years. The priestly class was and continues to be the caretakers of the Vedas. Religious practices of this period focused on ritual sacrifices, many of which were quite elaborate and are still part of present-day rituals. Animals were sacrificed as an offering to various Vedic gods of the earth and sky. Offerings of milk and *ghee* (clarified butter) were also made into the sacrificial fire. The Vedas are exacting about rituals for preparing and consuming *Soma. Soma* involves layers of complexity in Hindu worship. It is a god, a plant and a ritual drink. According to the Rig-Veda, the drink produced hallucinogeniceffects. In the Rig-Veda 8:48 is found, *"We have drunk the Soma; we have become immortal; we have gone to the light; we have found the gods."*

Classical Religion (~ 500 BCE—500 CE)
The composition of more sacred texts occurs at this time. The two great epics of Hinduism, the Mahabharata and the Ramayana, were created in this period. These stories are as popular for Hindus today as they were in the past. The Tantras, works concerned with daily rituals and the building of temples became revered. Some of these texts specified guidelines for offering alcohol in sacrifice and for ritualized sexual practice.

DEPICTION OF KRISHNA AND ARJUNA

Medieval Religion (500 CE—1500 CE)
A significant change in religious practice takes place from around thefifth century. Vedic fire sacrifice as the central ritual gives way to *puja*, the worship of images of deities in temples. The traditions of Vaishnavism, worship centering on the deity Vishnu, and Shaivism, worship focused on the god Shiva, developed into major devotional factions. Regional kingdoms were characterized by devotion to a particular deity. Shaivism, for example, became dominant in South India as it was supported by the Chola dynasty. **Bhakti,** the devotion to a major deity, gave rise to the proliferation of great regional temples during this time.

Temple of Lord Shiva, Chidambaram, Tamil Nadu

Hindu temples are simultaneously to be conceived as places of worship and as the homes of gods. Temple design often evokes natural features—caves, mountains—locales said to be preferred by the gods. During this medieval period, the construction of temples became more complex. The exterior of the temple is elaborately ornamented whereas the inner sanctum is a dark chamber. Guidelines for temple erection were specific as far as the geometry and the decoration; these rules were understood to be in balance with universal order.

Religion of the Moghul Period (1500—1757 CE)
While Hindu practices continued to develop in South India, a new religion, Islam, grew and gained power in the North. As early as the 8th century CE, Islam came to India by way of traders and Muslim armies conquered the Northern provinces. The Turkish Sultanate came to power around 1200 CE and eventually we see the establishment of the Moghul Empire. The practices of Hinduism were tolerated during the rule of Akbar, but persecution of Hindus during the rule of Akbar's great grandson resulted in severe limitations on Hindu worship and in the destruction of many sacred temples.

Taj Mahal: The Jewel of Moghul Architecture

Religion during the British Raj (1757—1947)
The Battle of Plassey in 1757 brought down the Moghul Empire and the British Crown assumed control of India. Initially, Hindus were left alone to practice their religion, but as Christians began to flow into India, they brought with them the zeal to Christianize the Hindus. The Hindu response was to advocate for a return to strict Vedic practices. It was during this time of resistance to the colonial rule by the British that the term "Hindu" began to take on deep political and nationalist meaning in addition to a religious way of life. The most notable reformer is Mahatma Gandhi who believed in the unity of all religions and in a united India. His adherence to the Hindu principle of *ahimsa*(non-violence) was instrumental in achieving independence for India.

Religion in Post-Partition India (1947 CE to present)
In 1947, the birthplace of Hinduism, the basin of the Indus River, became part of Pakistan. The partition of India resulted in the separation of Hindus and Muslims. A new and robust concept in the form of ***hindutva*** (Hinduness) emerged as a galvanizing force for Hindus. Hinduism as a religion became fused with the declaration of India as a Hindu country and Hinduism as an Indian religion.

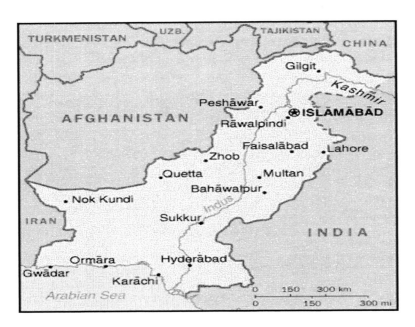

Pakistan Showing Border of India

Many Books

Hindu scriptures are divided into two major categories: *Shruti* and *Smriti. Shruti* is "what is revealed", "what is heard." These texts have no human author but record what is true about the universe as originally revealed to ancient seers called *rishis. Smriti, "*what is remembered" refers to all other scriptures. The purpose of these supplemental scriptures is to elucidate the meaning of Shruti so that the revealed scriptures can be applied to Hindu life. The formal body of Shruti has remained constant for two millennia. All dimensions of Hinduism are grounded in this canon. Following is a complete list of the sacred texts, a brief description of their content and their quantity:

SHRUTI
Vedic

Vedas	Description	Amount
Rig-Veda	Hymns	10 books
Yajur Veda	Formulas for priests	Mostly Prose
Sama Veda	Songs used in Sacrifice	1549 Mantras
Atharva Veda	Spells, Charms, Curses	20 books
Brahmanas	Manuals for sacrifice	Correspond to the four Vedas
Aranyakas	Books of the Forest	Philosophical reflections
Upanishads	"Sitting near a guru"	Philosophical debates on reality. There are 13 primary books, and a total of 123.

SMRITI

PostVedic

Puranas	Traditional Lore	18 Books
Mahabharata	The Great Epic	18 Books
Ramayana	Story of Rama	7 Books
Manu Smriti	Laws of Manu	12 Books
Vishnu Smriti	Vishnu Manuals	100 Chapters
Tantras	Rituals, Yogic	Uncertain Number

The Mahabharata

In section 6 of the *Mahabharata* we find the most-beloved story in Hinduism, "The Bhagavad-Gita," Song of the Lord. In 7000 verses, we have a tale of rivalry between the Pandava brothers and the Kaurava brothers who vie for control of India. As civil war breaks out, Arjuna, a Pandava prince confides in his charioteer that he fears that battle will do harm to his soul; he prefers death to fighting. It is Lord Krishna, himself, who is disguised as Arjuna's charioteer.   Krishna's instructions to Arjuna have two major themes: 1) Arjuna is bound by duty to his warrior caste to fight. Duty to caste and to the divine outweighs his personal feelings; 2) Arjuna's soul, his eternal world-soul, can never be harmed. Killing only affects the body and death is an illusion. Lord Krishna repeats over and over again to Arjuna that the best way to salvation is through devotion to Krishna. Krishna is the both the foundation of Brahman, the world soul, and a loving personal god.

The Ramayana

The Ramayana, a shorter second epic, is the story of Prince Rama. Rama marries the lovely princess Sita, but is forced into exile in the forest by his father who had made a promise to his second wife. Sita and Rama's brother accompany Rama to the forest. While the brothers are hunting, the ten-headed demon, Ravana, kidnaps Sita. With the help of a monkey army Rama wins back Sita. Through many more adventures, Rama is victorious and is deified. The story ends with Rama being understood to be an avatar of Vishnu.

The Most Important Gods of the *Rig-Veda*

Indra——the god of monsoons and storms who wields a thunderbolt

Varuna——the god of the sky

Agni——the god of fire who is evoked during sacrifice

Soma——the deified plant (also a ritual drink)

The primary force of the universe is *Rita*, the principle of order that prevents chaos.

Major Gods of Popular Hinduism

*Brahma*The Creator

*Vishnu*The Preserver

*Shiva*The Destroyer

VISHNU RECLINING ON HIS SERPENT
SCULPTED PANEL OF THE SOUTH FAÇADE OF THE VISHNU TEMPLE IN DE-
OGARH FROM ABOUT 500 CE

In Popular Hinduism, movements have developed around the worship of individual gods. *Shaivism* is the worship of the god *Shiva* and *Vaishnavism* worships the god *Vishnu*. *Vishnu* is usually worshipped in the form of one of his **avatars**, (a manifestation of a god in an earthly form) *Rama* or *Krishna*. *Brahma* is rarely worshipped. One explanation for this is that his job as creator has been accomplished. *Vishnu* is in charge of preserving the universe and *Shiva* must keep the wheel of reincarnation turning. *Brahma* is always represented with four heads. Traditional stories recount this tale: *Brahma* created a woman (**Shatarupa**) to help him. She was so beautiful that Brahma grew heads in all four directions so as to always keep her in his view.

The Four-Headed God Brahma

Devi or Shakti (goddess)

Kali   goddess of destruction and death

Durga   goddess of retribution and justice

Parvati goddess of courtship and erotic love

Ūma   goddess of motherhood and family

All of the above listed are wives of Shiva. Some Hindus focus their worship on one of Shiva's consorts.

Ganesha (Ganesh), God of Good Fortune

Ganesha is the elephant-headed son of Shiva and Parvati. Like a strong elephant he can work hard to remove obstacles and clear the way for success. Ganesha is the most popular god found in Hindu households. His elephant nature never forgets loyalty and devotion. He is usually represented with his mouse and is sometimes depicted riding the mouse as his steed.

Visual Imagery/Symbolismin Hinduism

SHIVA NATARAJA, LORD OF THE DANCE

"Art for art's sake" is not a concept we find in traditional Indian art. The purpose of art in Hinduism is to make the human life easier. The ancient sacred texts promote the use of imagery in the following way: How can the individual meditate upon God if there is nothing for the mind to focus upon? The representations of gods in concrete form give the worshiper a visual image through which to contemplate the divine. One of the most beautiful and culturally/religiously significant representations in Hinduism is that of

Shiva as Lord of the Dance. August Rodin, the famous French sculptor, hailed this work as the perfect embodiment of rhythmic movement. This way of representing Shiva in visual form took hold under the Chola Dynasty during the tenth century CE and is found in many temples in South India. Symbols in Hindu art are fairly standardized. First, we are to understand the dancing of Shiva as the eternal rhythm which is the source of all movement within the universe. He is standing on the dwarf (*Apasmara*) that symbolizes ignorance and sometimes the human ego. The ring of fire around Shiva represents the universe as manifested. The drum symbolizes both Shiva's dance music and the elemental concept of the original sound of the universe. Shiva's lower right hand says "Fear Not", the meaning of the graceful *abhaya* pose. The uplifted left leg signifies the liberation of the soul from *samsara*. This aesthetically stunning and highly symbolic form is often used to represent the whole of Indian Culture.

Traditional Hindu Celebrations and Festivals

In Hindu tradition there are many festivals throughout the year. The following are some of the major celebrations:

Diwali: Festival of lights and the goddess Lakshmi (September-October). The festival symbolizes being lifted out of spiritual darkness and celebrates prosperity. Presents and special sweets are prominent.

Guru Purnima: A festival with a deep spiritual meaning celebrating one's guru through respect and reverence (July-August).

Holi (also known as Phagwah): Celebration of Spring and a festival of colors (February-March). Hindus throw brightly colored powder and water over one another to symbolize the onset of Spring.

Maha Shivaratri (Night sacred to Shiva [February-March]). On Shivaratri, devotees awake at sunrise and bathe in holy water (like the Ganges River) and wear new clothes. On the day of the festival, people fast and spend the day worshipping Shiva. This is the day of Shiva's marriage to Parvati.

Navaratri: Festival of Shakti (in Bengal) or Rama's victory over Ravana (South India) (September-October), the nine sacred nights dedicated to the Mother Goddess.

Dusshera: Celebrated on the tenth day of Navaratri. This signifies the victory of Lord Rama over the demon Ravana, which is often observed with special celebrations and the burning of the effigy of Ravana.

Rama Navami: Commemorates the birth of Lord Rama (April).

Krishna Janmashtami: Birthday celebration for Lord Krishna (July-August).

Ganesha Chaturthi: This celebrates the birth of Lord Ganesha (August-September).

Raksha Bandan: Renewing bonds between brothers and sisters (July-August).

Kumbh Mela: Pilgrimage every 12 years to four cities in India (July-August; (last one 2003).

COLORED POWDERS FOR HOLI FESTIVAL

Many Paths

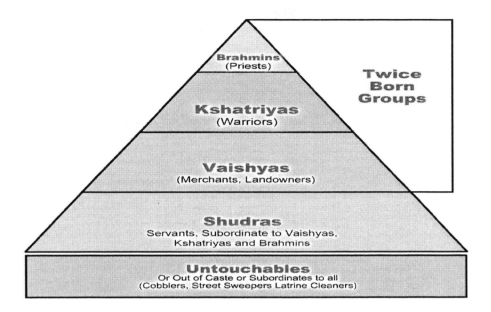

HIERARCHY OF THE VARNA

In contemporary India, the rigid system of social stratification has been weakened; however, the history and content of Hinduism is bound together with *varna*, or the caste system. *Varna* is the Sanskrit word for color and may originate from differences between the light-skinned Aryans and the darker-skinned Dravidians. Vedic society was divided into four classes. Each caste indicates the social division into which one is born and dictates the duties of one's work:

BRAHMIN—the highest of the four **varnas**. This is the priestly caste.

KSHATRIYA—the second class, the caste of warriors, leaders and administrators.

VAISHYA—the merchants, traders, farmers and craftsmen of Hindu society.

SHUDRA—the fourth and lowest class. The Hindu word means "servant." Historically, members of this caste served the higher castes.

All castes are bound by moral duties that include reverence toward the gods, honesty, *ahimsa* (doing no harm), and pilgrimage to sacred places. The three highest castes are understood to be the "*twice-born.*"

Below the four castes, outside of the caste system, are the *Untouchables*, or "outcastes." Westerners would be put into this group. The condition of the outcastes as dictated by tradition is as follows: Their dwellings must be outside the village. Untouchables are dependent on others for food that must be eaten from broken bowls. They perform menial tasks such as digging graves and cleaning sewers. They must wear the clothes of the dead and gather from the dead even basic items such as a bed to sleep on. During the time that Gandhi worked for an independent India he also sought to eradicate the stigma of "untouchability" (too impure for physical contact). Gandhi called them "*Harijans*", Children of God. In post-partition India the concept of "the untouchable" has been outlawed; nevertheless it remains somewhat uncompromising within the social structure. The preferred term today is, "*Dalits*," the Oppressed or Downtrodden.

The Four Stages of Hindu Life

Written in the sacred texts, *The Laws of Manu*, are codes that govern the duties of four stages of the Hindu Life:

STUDENT (Bramchari): This is the first stage of life during which a young man begins the study of the Vedic scriptures. He studies and learns from a guru through adolescence up to as old as twenty four. He must go through a ceremony and wear a sacred thread on his shoulder signifying that he is "reborn."

HOUSEHOLDER (Grihasta): This is the second life stage and the period of adulthood. The individual marries and raises a family. He adheres to the virtues of supporting a household, counseling children and being a good member of the community.

RETIREMENT (Vanaprashta): The third stage of Hindu life offers the individual the opportunity to reflect on life and duty rather to carry out those duties. Once the Householder has a son, he can return to devoting his time to the study of the sacred texts.

THE ASCETIC (Sannyasin):In the final life stage the goal is to prepare for releasing the soul from the body (samadhi). The mind is disciplined to grasp Ultimate Reality.

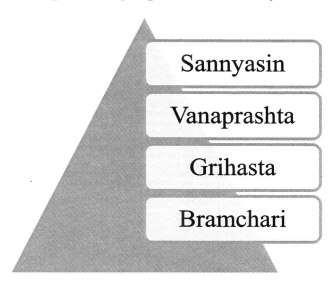

According to these traditional principles, a woman is to be protected by her father in youth, by her husband in marriage and by her sons in old age. She is not understood to be independent. These stages were supposed to have been derived from the Laws of Manu which were designed to ensure the ideal conduct and society. Today, the Laws of Manu do not rigidly control Hindu conduct, but they are still part of the moral code for many contemporary Hindus.

The Four Goals of Life

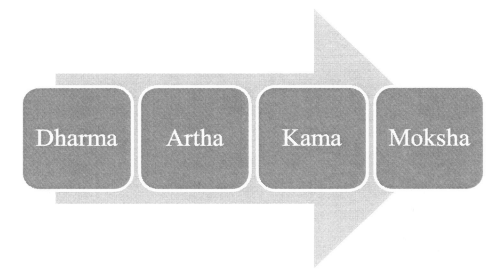

DHARMA(Duty, Righteousness): The universal principle of law, order, harmony and truth that arises from Brahman. Dharma acts as the regulatory moral principle of the Universe. Every individual is bound to carry out their duties specific to their station in life.

ARTHA (Wealth, Success): This is the pursuit of things on the material plane. Wealth is to be acquired, not for its own sake, but to aid in the progression of the spirit. Poverty is not glorified in Hinduism, and it is understood that the way to salvation is difficult if one does not have the basic needs of this life met.

KAMA (pleasure): This is the desire for aesthetic fulfillment. Desiring the beauty of life in the form of music, visual art, literature is a true enjoyment of the earthly life. Sexual passion and the pleasures of the senses are part of this beauty.

MOKSHA (liberation, salvation): This is the final goal of life, freedom from *samsara*, the eternal wheel of birth-death-rebirth. Moksha is also freedom from the suffering that accompanies this cycle.

The primary virtues of Hinduism are *damyata,* the control of self,*datta,* being generous to others and *dayadhvam,* compassion to all.

Yoga

The *Bhagavad-Gita* shows the paths or "Ways to Salvation." These "Ways" are well-established in the forms of Yoga practiced by Hindus.

The Four Yogic Paths to achieve the spiritual goal of salvation

Jnana Yoga: The path of wisdom. The way of knowledge focuses on coming to know that the Atman of each individual is the same essence as Brahman.

Karma: The path of right action. The "Way of Works" involves performing the proper rituals every day. Vedic sacrifice is central to this pathway to release from the eternal cycle. Men and women have different duties regarding family, community, worship and ceremonies.

Raja Yoga: The path of meditation. This way trains the physical body so that the soul can be free.

Bhakti: The path of love and devotion. This way to salvation consists of passionately embracing God in love.

SHIVA MEDITATING

The sound *"Om"* is the standard for focus in meditation. It is the eternal hum of the true and unchanging reality.

Hindu Philosophy

Hindu Philosophy is concerned with both metaphysics (the nature of ultimate reality) and ethics (the moral conduct of human beings). Philosophers construct a systematic understanding of reality and of the human being's place in that reality. There are six orthodox systems of Hindu Philosophy; *Vedanta* and *Sankhya* are two of the most prominent.

Vedanta

Shankara (788-829) is the initiator of the Advaita Vedanta, the most familiar part of this philosophical system. The focus is on distinguishing appearance and reality. *Maya*, Sanskrit for "illusion" is what we experience as reality. We must live in it and deal with it. Human ignorance (*avidya*), keeps us from seeing the true nature of reality. Ascetic living as well as constant ritual and worship will allow us to see that the individual *Atman* is not separate from *Brahman*.

Sankhya

Kapila is credited with originating this system. He interpreted reality during the time of the *Upanishads*. In this philosophical way of understanding reality, there are no gods. There is matter (*Prakriti*) and non-matter or spirit (*Purusha*) and both are real. The ultimate goal of this philosophy is to live in ways that do not involve the material realm so that the individual soul can be set free, set apart from the material aspect of a dualist reality.

Hinduism and Other Religions

Hinduism is connected in various ways to three other Eastern religions. There are major similarities among the four religions, but there are significant differences as well.

The general concept of **dharma** forms a basis for philosophies, beliefs and practices originating in India. The four main ones are Hinduism, Buddhism, Jainism(Jaina Dharma), and Sikhism(Sikha Dharma), all of whom retain the centrality of *dharma* in their teachings. *Dharma* can refer generally to religious duty, and also mean social order and right conduct. In these traditions, beings that live in harmony with *dharma* proceed more quickly toward personal liberation.

BUDDHISM

Karma is a central part of Buddhism. In Buddha's teaching, *karma* is a direct result of a person's word, thought, and action in life. In pre-Buddhist Hinduism, karma has to do with whether the actions performed in rituals are done correctly or not. Therefore, there is little emphasis on moral conduct in its conception. In Buddhism, since a person's word, thought, and action form the basis for good and bad *karma*, moral conduct goes hand in hand with the development of meditation and wisdom. Buddhist teachings carry a different meaning from a pre-Buddhist conception of *karma*.

Gautama Buddha did not deny the existence nor forbid the worship of the popular Hindu gods, but such worship is not Buddhist and the gods are trapped in the same samsaric cycle as other beings. They are not guides to religion, since they need instruction themselves. The focus of Buddha's Noble Eightfold Path is not about worshipping god or achieving heaven in the next life. It is about experiencing Brahma consciousness in this life. The reason is that in all realms, beings are subject to rebirth after some period of time. It is like going around in circles in the round of rebirth despite all the effort and striving. Therefore, the purpose of the holy life in the Buddha's path is about liberation from the cycle of rebirth and experiencing awakening in this very life.

SIKHISM

The Sikh religion emerged during the early 16th century in the state of Punjab in North India. The founder of this faith was Guru Nanak, who from his childhood was attracted to both Hindu and Muslim saints. Born a Hindu, but also inspired by the teachings of Islam, he began to preach the message of unity of both religions. According to him, the basic teachings of both faiths were essentially the same. Nanak attracted many followers and came to be known as a guru or a teacher. His disciples came together to form a new religious tradition called Sikhism. There are currently about 27 million followers of Sikhism in the world, including 500,000 in the United States.

JAINISM

Jainism as a religious tradition was established in India about the same time as Buddhism. Mahavira, one of the *jinas* (conquerors) preached the Jain philosophy around the same time that Buddhism began.

Like Buddhism, Jainism rose against the corruption in the interpretation of Hinduism prevalent at the time. The underlying philosophy of Jainism is that renunciation of worldly desires and self-conquest leads to perfect wisdom. This faith believes in total abstinence and asceticism as practiced by the *Jinas* and the *Tirthankaras* ("crossing-makers").

Western Hindu Movements

THEOSOPHICAL SOCIETY

The term "theosophy" from the Greek means "divine wisdom." During the late 19th century, Theosophical initiate societies emerged. In 1875 Helena Blavatsky (1831—1891) and others founded the Theosophical Society, an organization related to earlier theosophical ideas but departing from them significantly by including concepts from Eastern religion. Blavatsky believed that the ancient spiritual masters had already discovered the unchanging truth about reality. She reached back to the ancient Hindu writings to revive the notion that each individual is god-like and eternal. The popular Krishnamurti (1889—1986) traveled widely and represented Theosophy in his goal to set all human beings free. The movement attracted significant numbers of devotees in the United States as well as Great Britain.

HARE KRISHNAS

The International Society for Krishna Consciousness (ISKCON), known more commonly as the Hare Krishna movement or the *Hare Krishnas*, was founded in 1966 in New York City by A. C. Bhaktivedanta Swami Prabhupada. The society's core beliefs are based on traditional Indian texts such as the Bhagavad-Gita. Their manifesto states that they want to systematically spreadspiritual knowledge to society at large and to educate all people in the techniques of spiritual life in order to check the imbalance of values in life and to achieve real unity and peace in the world. Their hope is to bring human beings closer to Lord Krishna and to encourage awareness that each individual soul is part of the Krishna Godhead.

Swami Prabhupada Wearing the Signature Saffron Robe of the Hare Krishnas

A Hindu Influence on Modern Civil Rights Movements

Mahatma Gandhi's concept of **AHIMSA** became famous during the struggle for Indian Independence. Rather than fighting the British by violent means, he coined the term **SATYAGRAHA** that literally translates as adhering to the truth, but functionally practiced as (non-violent resistance). Martin Luther King and Nelson Mandela were deeply influenced by this concept and espoused it in their own struggle for civil rights.

Local Temples/Centers in the San Diego Area

<u>ISKCON</u>

The temple of ISKCON in the San Diego area is located in Pacific Beach. The first of their principles is that **"An absolute reality exists."** The purpose of worship is to discover that absolute reality and the place of humans in it. Scripture helps us focus on our purpose. The *Bhagavad-Gita* is the primary religious text for understanding God.

The temple houses the deities Krishna and his consort Radha and holds routine devotional meetings, spiritual lectures, music and dance programs, fire ceremonies and vegetarian feasts.

STREET ENTRANCE TO HARE KRISHNA TEMPLE

Vedic Cultural and Spiritual Center of San Diego

This temple is ecumenical and promotes Vedic tradition based on Vedic principles of peace and harmony amongst all people independent of race, religion, national origin, economic status or sexual orientation.

Temple Altar

Shri Mandir

The Hindu Mandir Society of San Diego, an ecumenical Hindu/Jain community temple.

PRIESTS AT SHRI MANDIR TEMPLE

What is it like to be a Hindu in America?

Interview with Kamala Balasubramanian, Professor of English, Grossmount College.

Do you adhere to traditional Hindu beliefs and practices?

I get up each day before sunrise, take a bath to cleanse and do my meditations. One must rise early to avoid being slothful. The bath is symbolic of cleansing the inside as well as outside. I have a closet which I use as an altar. I keep my Hindu pictures and books there; I read a daily devotional and mediate for about 20 minutes. The Bhagavad-Gita *and the gospels of Rama Krishna I favor over earlier Vedic writings.*

What rituals do you perform?

Each Friday I wash my front and back patios and prepare for puja. I make offerings to Ganesha. I especially like this god because the rituals surrounding him are not so structured. Ganesha is sometimes considered to be the "poor man's god." My hibiscus plant yields lovely flowers to offer to Ganesha. He is fond of red flowers. I use a lantern instead of candles so that the wind will not blow out the flame. My non-Hindu neighbors often ask if they can come to my ritual and I like them to join me.

Do you participate in the local Hindu community?

I have attended temple in the past but now prefer mostly to do my private worship. For my children's birthdays, for example, I have taken them to special ceremonies that include the fire ritual associated with the god Agni. The local Hindu community generally tends to remain more culturally isolated. I prefer to be part of the larger American culture.

How do you see the role of women within Hinduism?

I lived with my maternal grandmother when I was growing up in India. I remember her as a strong figure, the anchor of the family, the one who kept the entire household going. She was a very good role model; she was kind and loving, as well as strong. My father arranged a marriage for me when I was nineteen. I did not see my husband until the wedding. I do some Shakti (goddess) worship, but the rituals are very complex. I like to tap into the female power as traditionally understood in Hinduism.

What are the challenges of being a Hindu in the United States?

I much prefer broadening my experience to the whole of American culture than thinking of myself as a Hindu in America. I don't often wear a sari here, but I feel more comfortable in my traditional dress. (A sari is a large strip of cloth, four to nine meters long, that is wrapped to make a skirt and then to cover the shoulders.) I used to wear a ring in my nose piercing as well as my bindi (red dot on forehead indicating Hindu as well as a married status). Here, I don't really like to make myself look different. When I go home to India, the first thing I do at the airport is to change into my sari and replace my bindi. I think that my children and young Hindus in general face more challenges than I do. They have more difficulty sorting out their religious beliefs.

How do you understand the nature of the divine in Hinduism?

A family temple in India has nothing in it but a mirror. You can only see yourself when you enter to worship. The essence of being a Hindu is to reflect and understand yourself. To see the god in oneself and then to see the god in everyone is the foundation of all things.

What aspect of Hinduism is most meaningful to you?

I guide my life by the words of Lord Krishna in the Bhagavad-Gita. He tells Arjuna that he must do his duty. I keep myself centered each day by focusing on doing my duty. Instead of wondering why something undesirable has happened to me or complaining about things, I just keep on doing my part.

LAKSHMAN   SHREE RAM   MATA SEETA   VEER HANUMAN

Murtis at the Shri Mandir Temple

A ***murti*** is an image through which the spirit of the divine presence
of God is expressed. Murtis are made according to strict traditional Hindu guidelines. A special ceremony conducted by a priest is
held to install a ***murti*** in the temple. Priests can then call upon the
divine in the image.

Glossary

Agni   The Hindu god of fire, central to Vedic ritu-
                    al and sacrifice.

Ahimsa   The principle *"Do no harm"* from Sanskrit
                    for "noninjury."

Artha   One of the four goals of Hindu life, the striv-
                    ing to be successful.

Ascetic	The fourth and final stage of the Twice-born life, rejecting the necessities of life in favor of religious contemplation.
Atman	The soul of the individual.
Avatar	The manifestation of a god in an earthly form.
Bhagavad-Gita	Part of the *Mahabharata* containing the story of Lord Krishna disguising himself as the charioteer for Arjuna and teaching him about duty and the eternity of being.
Bhakti	Devotion to and worship of a god or goddess.
Brahma	The god of creation.
Brahman	Ultimate Reality, the power of the universe, the concept of universal soul.
Brahmanas	Vedic manuals containing guidelines for ritual and sacrifice.
Brahmin	The first, highest and priestly caste of Hindu social structure.
Caste	The Hindu system of social hierarchy (*varna*).
Deva	Sanskrit term for god.
Devi	Sanskrit term for goddess.
Dharma	The duty to carry out one's responsibilities virtuously and in accordance with the requirements of one's caste.
Durga	One of Shiva's wives and the goddess of justice and punishment.
Ganesha	Son of Shiva and Parvati, the god of good luck who is represented with an elephant head.

Guru	Title given to a teacher, sometimes a Brahmin
Grihasta	(Householder). The second stage of the Hindu life, the adult phase that includes marriage and family.
Ishvara	Term used to describe a Hindu god or goddess when s/he represents the divine absolutism of Brahman.
Kali	The destructive wife of Shiva who rides a tiger, wears a necklace of skulls and is associated with death.
Kama	One of the four goals of Hindu life, the seeking of aesthetic fulfillment and sexual pleasure.
Karma	Sanskrit word meaning "action" The sum of one's actions over a lifetime that determines the level at which one will be reborn.
Krishna	One of the avatars of Vishnu.
Kshatryia	The second level of the Hindu caste system made up of warriors and leaders.
Lingam	An upright stone representing Shiva and found in temples that are dedicated to the worship of Shiva.
Mahabharata	The long, Post-Vedic epic, composed in the second century that includes the *Bhagavad-Gita*.
Mantra	A meditation technique that focuses on the repetition of a single sound or a series of sounds .
Moksha	Release from *samsara*, salvation.
Om	(Aum) The most famous mantra which represents the sound of the Universe itself.
Parvati	One of Shiva's wives who represents young love and sexuality.

Puja	A ritual offering of food, libation, flowers to a god or goddess.
Puranas	Post-Vedic writings entailing traditional tales of gods and goddesses.
Rama	An avatar of Vishnu and hero of the *Ramayana*.
Ramayana	Tale of Rama and his rescue of Sita from the demon Ravana.
Reincarnation	The cycle of birth-death-rebirth.
Samsara	The ever-turning wheel of the universe that includes birth, death and rebirth.
Sannyasin	The fourth stage of Hindu life, affording the individual the opportunity to become an ascetic.
Sanskrit	The ancient Indo-European language in which the sacred texts of Hinduism are written.
Satyagraha	Non-violent resistance.
Shakti	Term meaning "power" The worship of a goddess who represents some form of power.
Shaivism	System of beliefs and rituals for the worship of Shiva.
Shiva	The Destroyer, one of the major gods of popular Hinduism.
Shudra	Meaning "servant," the lowest Hindu caste.
Transmigration	The process of the soul of an individual being reborn into another body (animal, human) after death.
Twice-born	Term that applies to the three upper Hindu castes that includes a requirement for a "rebirth" ceremony at puberty.

Ūma	One of Shiva's wives who represents motherhood and family.
Untouchables	Individuals outside of the caste system considered too polluting for contact.
Upanishads	The last of the Vedic writings that include stories, contemplations on the relationship of the human to the divine.
Vaishya	The third of the Hindu castes that includes farmers, craftsmen, traders.
Vaishnavism	System of beliefs and rituals for the worship of the god Vishnu.
Varna	Meaning "color," the Hindu word for caste.
Vedas	The ancient sacred texts of Hinduism.
Vishnu	The Preserver, one of the major gods of Hinduism, often represented by one of his avatars, Krishna or Rama.
Yoga	Meaning "yoke" in Sanskrit, a systematic discipline of meditation and control of the body that leads to a desired goal.

LANDMARK IN TORONTO: THE SHRI SWAMINARAYAN MANDIR, BUILT ACCORDING TO TRADITIONAL HINDU SMRITI DIRECTIONS, WITHOUT A SINGLE NAIL

QUESTIONS

1) What factors make it difficult to define Hinduism?

2) What is the relationship of *Atman* and *Brahman*?

3) What are the two classes of scriptures? How are they different?

4) Distinguish among Brahma, Brahman and Brahmin.

5) How does *Dharma* relate to *Varna* ?

6) State the two lessons Lord Krishna gives to Arjuna in the *Bhagavad-Gita*.

FOR DISCUSSION

1) Do you think that the moral principles embodied in Hinduism can be espoused without belief in any of the gods?

2) Do you find Hinduism to be in opposition to contemporary science?

3) Why do you think Hinduism has continued to be a major world religion?

4) Can Hinduism and the history of India be separated?

5) Do you admire Gandhi? Why or why not?

6) Could one practice Hinduism without believing in the soul?

FOR REFLECTION

1) Why do you think Hinduism has so many gods?

2) Would you rather be a devotee of Shaivism or Vaishnavism and why?

3) How do you understand the role of *SOMA* as god, plant and ritual drink?

4) Do you find the principle of *ahimsa* one that all human beings should follow? Why or why not?

5) Why do you think *Agni* is so prominent in the Vedic scriptures?

6) Which form of *Yoga* do you find most appealing and

why?

Recommended Films

The Mahabharata, (1989) directed by Peter Brooks

Gandhi, (1982) directed by Richard Attenborough

Kumare, (2011) documentary by Vikram Gandhi

Samar (1999) directed by Shyam Benegal

Salaam Bombay!, (1988) directed by Mira Nair

Monsoon Wedding, (2001) directed by Mira Nair

The Story of India, (2007) PBS documentary series by historian Michael Wood

Recommended Books

Ganesha Goes to Lunch: Classics from Mystic India, (2007) Kamla K. Kapur

The Avenue of Kings, (2010) Sudeep Chakravarti

The Story of My Assassins, (2009) Tarun Tejpal

India's Unending Journey, (2008) Mark Tully

Let's Kill Gandhi, (2007), Tushar Gandhi

The Elephant, the Tiger and the Cellphone: Reflections on India, (2008) Shashi Tharoor

Bibliography

Dehejia, Vidya, *Indian Art*, New York, Phaidon Press, Inc., 2012

Bryant, Edwin F., *Krishna*, New York, Oxford University Press, Inc., 2007

Eisenberg, Diane U., et al, *Transformations of Myth through Time: An Anthology of Readings*, San Diego, HBJ Publishers Inc., 1990

Flood, Gavin, *An Introduction to Hinduism*, New York, Cambridge University Press, 1996.

Klostermaier, Klaus K., *A Survey of Hinduism*, Albany, State University of New York Press, 1989.

Lopez Jr., D.S., *Religions of India in Practice*, Princeton, Princeton University Press, 1995.

Miller, B.S., *The Bhagavad-Gita: Krishna's Counsel in Time of War*, New York, Columbia University Press, 1986.

O'Flaherty, Wendy Doniger, *The Rig Veda*, London, Penguin Books, 1981.

Local photos by author

Images from Wikipedia sites

BUDDHISM
Buddha, Dharma, Sangha

Sandra A. Wawrytko, Professor of Philosophy, SDSU

THE TRIRATNA DEPICTION OF BUDDHISM (THE THREE JEWELS: BUDDHA, DHARMA, SANGHA)

Learning Goals

- *Introduce The Three Jewels of Buddhism*
- *Relate story of the historical Buddha*
- *Discuss the universal Buddha*
- *Explain the Basic Concepts: the Four Truths, the Eightfold Path.*
- *Explain the Sangha*
- *Discuss the Twofold Truth*
- *Explain the Three Poisons*
- *Explain Nirvana*
- *Describe the Tripitaka: the Scriptural Texts*
- *Evaluate Golden Age of Buddhism*
- *Discuss the different Yanas of Buddhism*
- *Relate about the Dalai Lama*
- *Discuss Rituals in General Buddhism*
- *Analyze Buddhism and Modernity*
- *Discuss Buddhism in America.*

"Better than a thousand useless words
is one single word that gives peace."
Dhammapada, 100

Emptying the Teacup

Buddhism was brought to America by Chinese immigrants from China, early in the nineteenth century. Over time it has expanded from Asian populations to the broader American community. About 40% of our 1.2 million self-designated Buddhists are found in California. However, the increasing popularity of Buddhism in America over the last nearly two hundred years had led to many misconceptions, reinforced stereotypes scattered through various forms of media.

So, before we talk about what Buddhism actually is, we need to empty our teacups of the cold, stale tea representing our presumed knowledge about it, including partial truths and total misunderstandings. Let's begin with one glaring example concerning the identity of the Buddha. Many people imagine the Buddha is a smiling fat guy and it is good luck to rub his belly. In fact, this guy is a late comer to the Buddhist party. Mi-lo Fo (Miroku in Japanese), known as the laughing Buddha, was the contribution of Chinese Buddhists. He incorporates elements that appealed to Chinese audiences—a corpulent figure representing prosperity, often shown holding money (as in the case of this golden boy). Reflecting the generosity of an equally corpulent Santa, Mi-lo Fo also is shown surrounded by happy children. No such figure exists—or would even be conceivable—in Indian or South Asian Buddhism; as a recovering ascetic the historical Buddha was generally portrayed as slim, even bony. The inspiration for China's laughing Buddha is said to be a good-natured tenth century Chinese monk, Pu-tai (Hotei in Japanese), said to be **Maitreya**, the Future Buddha.

Other conceptions about Buddhism have crept into our daily language. A recent story in the business section of the *New York Times* reported: "The Federal Reserve chairman, Ben S. Bernanke, seemed so calm during the worst hours of the 2008 financial crisis that Timothy F. Geithner, then the Treasury secretary, once described him as a central banking Buddha." [7] And then there is the use of Buddhist terms and imagery to sell things.

LAUGHING BUDDHAS

You can buy "Zen" alarm clocks, Zen couches, and even Zen bras! "Buddhist" self-help books, tapes, and other forms of media abound, purporting to teach you how to reveal your true self and how to relieve stress through meditation. There's even a rock band called Nirvana and a perfume named Samsara!

In a perverted way, Buddhism's appeal is demonstrated by the fact that people have co-opted the term for their own purposes, regardless of any connection with the original message. A website for something touted as "Extreme Buddhism" characterizes itself as "a form of Tantric Buddhist Mysticism, although it draws its wisdom

---

[7]Binyamin Appelbaum, "Reflections by America's Buddha of Banking," *New York Times*, January 16, 2014, B1.

and approach from the Truth underlying all mystical pathways and faiths, including Mysticism, Hinduism, Vedanta, Buddhism, Gnosticism and Qabalah." Its list of recommended books includes few books on Buddhist philosophy, and no primary texts (sutras); on the recommended film list you can find, inexplicably, Rambo III.The obvious problem here that Buddhism is characterized as the Middle Way, and hence cannot legitimately be conceived of as extremist.

However, you may have acquired some actual nuggets of knowledge about Buddhism through secondary—things you have read about Buddhism, or perhaps heard from family or friends involved in Buddhist. You may even have had some direct experience, such as meditation practice. It is less likely that you have delved the foundational primary sources of Buddhism the early *suttas* (Pali) that contain the core teachings of the historicalBuddha. As Buddhism evolved over the centuries new texts were addedin which the Buddha generally served as the main character. These *sutras* written in Sanskrit tended to be longer, providing a more complex presentation of the original doctrines.

Basic Buddhism

One of the most captivating chants of Buddhism is that of the **Triratna—The Three Jewels** wherein the adherent seeks refuge in the Buddha, Dharma and the Sangha. This is something upon which all the different sects of Buddhism agree, and in this chapter we discuss the development and beliefs of this path, identified by some academics, as a nontheist movement.

Who—TheBuddha: the One Who Woke Up

The Historical Buddha
The man we know as the Buddha was a role model, teacher, preacher, therapist, philosopher, and social reformer. However, he never claimed to be a god or divine being. Before he became the Buddha he was Prince **Siddhartha** ("he who has achieved his ultimate goal"), a member of the Gautama clan, warriors of the second highest caste, the *kshatriya*. He lived in an area of northwest India that now overlaps with Nepal. In 2013, archeologists found evidence confirming that Buddhism can be dated to the sixth cen-

tury BCE, based on excavations at the Buddha's birthplace, **Lumbini** Temple in Nepal. His birth is celebrated on the full moon of the fourth lunar month.

LUMBINI TEMPLE, NEPAL

His life story has been embellished over the centuries, but the basic account points to an existential crisis that led the young prince to forsake his sheltered, hedonistic lifestyle. The popular version is that when he was born, the wise men predicted to his father, **Suddhodhana** that if the boy did not leave his home, he would become a powerful king, and excel his father in fame. **Suddhodhana**, wanting the best for his son, ensured that the prince lived in the lap of luxury, and did not see or experience any suffering.

Siddhartha was brought up according to the stages of life, passing through the stage of being a **Bramchari**, and then achieving the **Grihasta** status by marrying princess Yashodhara when he was about nineteen years old. The couple allegedly had a son. When his father was away, Prince Siddharta left the palace on different occasions and beheld four things that were later to be called the Four Passing Sights. He saw an old man and understood that all humans must experience the passing of youth and thus grow old. He saw a sick man and learned this aspect of suffering. He saw a corpse and learned the inevitability of death. He was deeply troubled by these three sights, but when he saw a **Sannyasin**, a wandering holy man, he felt that he could learn from him that which would set his mind at ease.

At the age of 29, the prince walked away from his life as a devoted husband, loving father, and future king, intent on solving the perennial problem of suffering in the world. Following the entrenched spiritual models of the time, he immersed himself in extreme asceticism and meditational practices to attain the presumed core identity known as the **atman.**

DEPICTION OF THE FOUR PASSING SIGHTS

Despite Siddhartha's tremendous perseverance and adeptness as an ascetic for six years, the problem of suffering (*dukkha*) remained. He excelled in all the teachings he had learned from numerous masters, but remained unsatisfied. He had been in close association with five fellow ascetics, also seeking solutions to the problems of life. Dissatisfied with what he had learned, he left his companions and settled beneath what became known as the pipal or wisdom tree, determined to succeed in his quest or die in the process. In some traditions, he spent seven weeks in this position.

His practice of meditation has been greatly misunderstood. Although there are many ways to meditate, the form developed by the Buddha is not a trance, dream, daze, spell, stupor, reverie, daydream, abstraction, or wool-gathering. In fact, it is the antithesis of these confused characterizations. It involves awareness, clear insight, attentiveness, wakefulness.

DEPICTION OF PRINCE SIDDHARTHA LEAVING HIS RICHES FOR THE "GREAT GOING FORTH."

Supposedly it was under this bodhi tree that he received his Awakening, and received the insight that was to manifest itself in the path we now know as Buddhism. This awakening came with the realization of a Middle Way that rejected the extremes of asceticism and self-indulgence.

DEPICTION OF THE PRINCE AT THE HEIGHT OF HIS ASCETICISM

The Universal Buddha

The historical Buddha, also known as **Shakyamuni** (Sage of the Shakya tribe) Buddha, never claimed that his awakening was unique. Quite the contrary, he encouraged others to validate his experience on their own. This led to the concept of a Universal Buddha, which was set forth in many Mahayana texts. The universal principle of awakening was associated with the **Tathagata,** literally the one who is both Thus Come and Thus Gone, or ever abiding in the world. Buddha nature is never born and therefore cannot die, but continues to exist as the foundation of all reality. Potentially any and every being can wake up to their inherent reality, referred to as Buddha-mind or Buddha-nature. This potential is not restricted to human beings, for the *Lotus Sutra* repeatedly speaks of Buddha wisdom as "the wisdom embracing all species."

What—The Dhamma/Dharma

The teaching or message of the Buddha is what **he woke up** to or as. In the most basic sense it is the Middle Way between the extremes of hedonism and asceticism recognized in the Buddha's form of meditation that stopped the encumbrance of mental constructs to reveal clear insight into reality. The Buddhist option can best be described as **nondualism** in that it avoids the simplistic either/or dualism that demands we choose between being a libertine or being subject to strict control, between anarchy or the constraints of order.

DEPICTION OF PRINCE SIDDHARTA BECOMING THE BUDDHA "AWAKENED ONE"

FIRST SERMON AT SARNATH

The very first lecture given by the Buddha was at Sarnath. After he had attained awakening, he returned to his five erstwhile companions. They saw the change in him and became his first disciples.

They later became enlightened, and were thus known as **arhats**—those who had freed themselves from attachment and thus, had freed themselves from **samsara**. In his first lecture, he addressed them expounded the famous **Fourfold Noble Truth**. These can be read as a medical prescription. The first three truths lay out the diagnosis:

1. Life is experienced as *dukkha*, suffering or dysfunctionality (literally an ill-fitting axle)
2. *Dukkha* is caused by *tanha* (thirst or craving)
3. To end **dukkha**, end *tanha*
4. The antidote for our dysfunctionality lies in the EIGHT-FOLD PATH.

The fourfold noble truths have been rendered in many different expressions, all providing the same meaning as above.

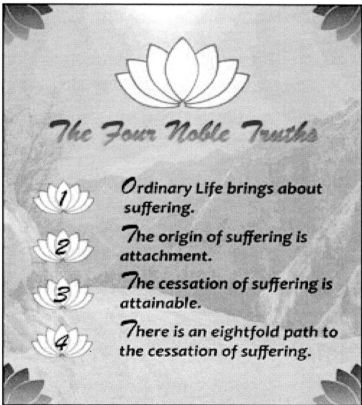

ANOTHER RENDITION OF THE FOURFOLD NOBLE TRUTHS

The Eightfold Path

The antidote for our dysfunctionality, the Eightfold Path, can be categorized into three components, optimally followed by using all of the precepts at the same time:

WISDOM (Deconstructed Thinking).
   1.   Right Understanding/views
   2.   Right Thought/Intention

ETHICAL CONDUCT (Compassion).
   3.   Right Speech.
   4.   Right Action/Intention
   5.   Right Livelihood.

MENTAL DISCIPLINE (Inner Cultivation).
   6.   Right Effort/Will.
   7.   Right Mindfulness/Awareness.
   8.   Right Concentration.

THE EIGHT-SPOKED DHARMA WHEEL

ANOTHER CHART OF THE EIGHTFOLD PATH

How—The Sangha

The historical Buddha realized it would be difficult for others to duplicate his autonomous awakening. So he organized asocial support network, community of those who live in accordance with the **Dharma**. Sometimes the Sangharefers to monks (**bhikshus; in Pali: bhikkus**) and nuns (**bhikshunis; in Pali: bhikkunis**), at other times it inclusive of all Buddhist practitioners, whether monastic or lay.

Legend holds it that at first only men were permitted to join the Sangha, which accepted people from all levels of society. Upon the entreaties of his stepmother, Mahaprajapati, who had raised him after the death of his mother, the Buddha allowed women to become monks. His wife Yashodara also became a **bhikshuni.**

GROUP OF BHIKKUNIS IN LOS ANGELES[8]

Basic rules for life in the Sangha evolved over time, as issues arose, elaborated in the Vinaya texts. They are encapsulated in the 10 Precepts. The first five apply to all Buddhists; the next five are specifically for monastics:

1. Non-injury to other beings (*ahimsa*)
2. No stealing
3. No sexual misconduct
4. No lying
5. No intoxicants

6. No vanity about appearance
7. No frivolous music, dancing, entertainment
8. No luxurious beds
9. No wealth and ostentation (money and jewels)
10. No eating beyond specified times

In addition to universal moral rules, the list reflects an avoidance of distractions that would interfere with one's practice or create differences among people.

[8]http://shambhalasun.com/news/?p=16236. Accessed February 27, 2014.

SOME BASIC CONCEPTS

The Buddha's awakening meant that he viewed some concepts differently to how they had been traditionally perceived. One was on the idea of the idea of reincarnation, or the samsara. In Buddhism, there is no eternal soul. There is, however the law of karma that shapes our lives. When we die, our karmic accumulation, like a flame, continues to burn—the way a flame can be transferred from one candle to another. The karma operates because of our ignorance and delusion.

Why-Ignorance and Delusion

Elaborations of the doctrines contained in the *suttas* and *sutras* are found in the **Abhidharma** texts, a collection of commentaries. What we take to be reality is in fact a virtual reality distorted by misperceptions, misconceptions, and social conditioning. A frequently used metaphor in Buddhism depicts the mind as a mirror encrusted with dust. When we look into such a mirror we will obviously see a distorted image of ourselves, of our Buddha mind. The dust can be removed by the practice of meditation, revealing our true identity, our Buddha nature. Thus we awaken **as** rather than **to** reality. Here are some of the key aspects of that reality.

Anatta/Anatman: Consciousness as Construct

Our sense of identity as a single, separate, independent existence accounts for many of our distortions and delusions. We often think of ourselves as existing because of permanent soul that is going through the samsara. This is an illusion for there is no soul as such, hence the term ANATTA. This comes from the Sanskrit notion of "no self" meaning that all things perceived by the senses are not "I" or "mine" and as such, we should not cling to them. We are, rather than a soul and body, a constitution of **skandhas.**

The second lecture given by the Buddha deconstructs that illusory sense of ego-self, referred to as *atman* in his time, and points to the five *skandhas* (heaps) that account for our deluded identity.

1. FORM—the five sense organs + mind (the sixth sense), our physical body that allow us to interact with the surrounding physical world;

2. SENSATIONS—arising from the data of the sense;

3. COGNITIVE PROCESSING OF SENSATIONS—the concepts that the mind constructs to label and manage our sense data;

4. VOLITIONS—acts of will indicate our response to the sense data; we are attracted, repulsed or neutral; we want more or we want to avoid it or we ignore it;

5. CONSCIOUSNESS—based on the first five *skandhas* we create a controller, the one who possesses a physical body, experiences sensations, conceptualizes, and acts; we imagine an inner self, the ghost in the machine, responsible for all of this.

Skandha, (Sanskrit:"aggregates")

Pāli : Kandha, according to Buddhist thought, the five elements that sum up the whole of an individual's mental and physical existence. The self (or soul) cannot be identified with any one of the parts, nor is it the total of the parts. They are: (1) matter, or body, the manifest form of the four elements—earth, air, fire, and water; (2) sensations, or feelings; (3) perceptions of sense objects; (4) mental formations; and (5) awareness, or consciousness, of the other three mental aggregates. All individuals are subject to constant change, as the elements of consciousness are never the same, and man may be compared to a river, which retains an identity, though the drops of water that make it up are different from one moment to the next.

Abridged definition of skandha[9]

Ongoing research by cognitive science supports the Buddha's conclusion that this presumed core identity is an aftereffect, an epiphenomenon. Nobel Laureate Francis Crick writes: "The Astonishing Hypothesis is the 'You', your joys and sorrows, your memories

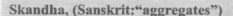

---

[9]http://www.britannica.com/EBchecked/topic/547273/skandhaj. Accessed March 1, 2104.

and ambitions, your sense of personal identity and free will, are in fact no more than the behavior of a vast assembly of nerve cells and their associated molecules."[10] A contemporary Tibetan Buddhist philosopher agrees: "Confused mind is inclined to view itself as a solid, on-going thing, but it is only a collection of tendencies, events. . . . There is no such thing as the ego at all. . . . It is an accumulation of a lot of stuff. It is a 'brilliant work of art.'"[11] A Korean takes a more humorous stance in his poem "The Drunkard":

> I've never been an individual entity. Sixty trillion cells!
> I'm a living collectivity.
> I'm staggering zigzag along,
> Sixty trillion cells, all drunk![12]

Our true identity then is emptiness (*sunya*), which bubbles up once we have emptied out the obstructing illusions and delusions. As Zen Master Hakuin exclaimed—"Forget yourself and become the universe!"

If there is no soul, what is it that is reborn, one might ask. Well, there is nothing to be reborn. When life ceases the kammic energy re-materializes itself in another form. In the paraphrase of one Bhiksu, this unseen energy passes whithersoever the conditions appropriate to its visible manifestation are present. Here showing itself as a tiny gnat or worm, there making its presence known in the dazzling magnificence of a Deva or an Archangel's existence. When one mode of its manifestation ceases it merely passes on, and where suitable circumstances offer, reveals itself afresh in another name or form." This is like the flame of the candle that keeps on burning if it finds a home on the wick of another candle. If not, the flame is extinguished when the candle wax is finished.

Anicca/Anitya: Impermanence
Everything in the world arises, changes and perishes; nothing remains constant for even a single moment.

The fluctuating nature of ego-identity is just one aspect of the on-

---

[10]Francis Crick, *Astonishing Hypothesis: The Scientific Search for the Soul* (Scribner, 1995).
[11] Anam Thubten, *No Self, No Problem: Awakening to Our True Nature* (Shambhala Publications, 2009).
[12] Ko Un, *What? 108 Zen Poems* (Parallax Press, 2008), 39.

going flux of reality overall. The search for universal, eternal truths that riveted the ancient Greeks and subsequent generations of philosophers is itself a delusion. Even the "laws of Nature" once assumed to be inviolable have been found to be subject to change, that is, impermanent. Rather than seeing this as a turn towards pessimism, the Buddhist feels a joyous sense of liberation from our self-imposed delusion of permanency. Letting go of the "eternal" opens the way for a dynamic flow with the flux of reality.

The Twofold Truth

The Buddha's view of reality—grounded in impermanence, non-ego self, and emptiness—certainly challenges what we have been conditioned to accept as common sense. Acknowledging this cognitive dissonance, the Buddha proposes the theory of the Twofold Truth. Not two dualistic truths, but two ways of nondualistically looking at the one truth. Think of it in terms of an iceberg. What is visible on the surface of the water is not the full story of an iceberg; what we see as the tip of the iceberg is real, but only a partial reality, the mundane truth (*smvrti-satya*).

THE ICEBERG IMAGERY

There is so much more to the iceberg of truth that remains unseen because it is below the surface; this is the complete or transcendental truth (*paramartha-satya*).Both views of the iceberg are true, but only one is the whole truth—the Buddha's eye view of an awakened mind.

The doctrine of the Twofold Truth reflects the three step process by which we can broad our viewpoint in order of see the full scope of reality. This process is often used in Chan Buddhism. We begin at the level of GREAT FAITH, belief in some other power as the source of truth. This includes faith in Buddhism—in the **Buddha, the Dharma, and the Sangha (the Three Jewels).** It encapsulates the doctrines of Buddhism, for example "mind is Buddha." However it is suitable only for the unawakened, as a medicine for sick people. Once we begin to recover we must stop taking the medicine, otherwise we will become addicted to it. This is the stage of GREAT DOUBT, which reacts against the previous passivity with "no mind, no Buddha." It is the cure for people who are sick because of the medicine. But one more step is required in this process to arrive at the GREAT DEATH of delusion, the "the mind of no mind." Thinking is no longer stuck on delusions nor does it need to rebel against thought itself. This is the non-discriminating mind capable of self power.

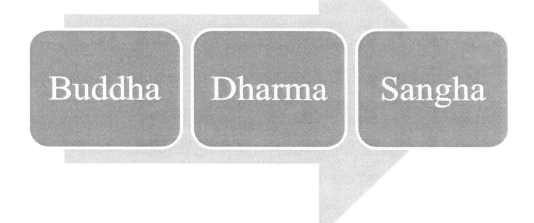

THE THREE JEWELS

Our Experience of Life

This is a common visualization of "reality" as we experience it, held in the grip of Yama or death.

At the core we find the THREE POISONS that are responsible for our suffering.

The Three Poisons

Our errors and misjudgments are assumed to originate in external sources, rather than from an innately evil nature.

These are:

Anger or hatred, represented by the snake, what we seek to avoid, breeding aversion.

Greed or lust, symbolized by the rooster, is what we attracted to, creating attachment.

Ignorance or delusion, the pig, leads us astray.

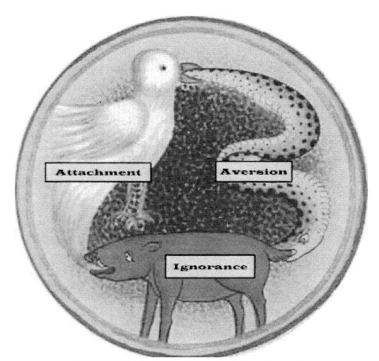

DEPICTION OF THE THREE POISONS

The Ultimate Goal: Nirvana

This is probably the most misunderstood term in Buddhism, often interpreted as being equivalent to the "heaven" of Abrahamic religions.

The Buddha described Nirvana as the ultimate goal, and he reached that state during his enlightenment. One who reaches this stage is also called an **arhat**. At this point, he chose to teach others so that they might also experience this realization, and so when he died, forty-five years later, he then passed through **parinirvana**, meaning completed nirvana.

Nirvana literally means **extinguishing** or unbinding. The implication is that it is freedom from whatever binds you, from the burning passion of the three poisons. Once these are totally overcome, the person is free from egocentrism, a state of bliss is achieved, and there is no longer the need forthe cycle of birth and death. All karmic debts are settled.

The Buddha refused to be drawn on what occurred then, but implied that it was beyond word and without boundaries. Certainly, he saw it in a much different state than our current existence, and not a simple parallel to the process of individual rebirth.

Sacred Texts

Tripitaka or Three Baskets (sutras, vinaya, and abhidharma)

The Buddha did not write down his teachings; there was no need to as his companions learned by association with him. His companions were able, at the first council, to recite the *Sutras* (concepts of doctrine), the *Vinaya* (Monastic rules) and the *Abhidharma*(moral and philosophical treatises of Buddhism, composed after Shakyamuni's death). These teachings were committed to writing by Theravada monks in Sri Lanka in the first century after many monks had died from a severe famine, and there was a fear that the traditions would disappear if they were not preserved in writing. These were written on palm leaves and sorted into three baskets, hence the scriptures are called the **TRIPITAKA** (three baskets).

The Golden Age of Buddhism
Emperor Ashoka 270-230 BCE

Around three hundred years after Siddhartha was born, a man in northern India greatly advanced the cause of Buddhism with a missionary zeal for the Dharma. Ashoka founded the Maurya Dynasty, which occupied much of the subcontinent as well as parts of what is now Afghanistan. Determined to implement the practices taught by the Buddha, he used his executive authority to make Buddhist Wisdom and Compassion the life experience of his subjects. This warrior turned wheel-turning king was responsible for the spread of Buddhism throughout and beyond India.

Ashoka's edicts carved on stone are among the oldest texts associated with Buddhism. He implemented policies to ease the suffering of people and other sentient beings. For example, building road stops for travelers as well as hospitals for both humans and non-human animals. Here is a sample:

"When he had been consecrated eight years the Beloved of the Gods, the king Piyadasi Ashoka conquered Kalinga. A hundred and fifty thousand people were deported, a hundred thousand were killed and many times that number perished. Afterwards, now that Kalinga was annexed, the Beloved of the Gods very earnestly practiced "Dhamma", desired "Dhamma". On conquering Kalinga the Beloved of the Gods felt remorse, for, when an independent country is conquered the slaughter, death, and deportation of people in extremely grievous to the Beloved of the Gods, and weighs heavily on his mind. What is even more deplorable to the Beloved to the Gods is that those who dwell there, whether Brahmans, Sarmanas, or those of other sects, or householders who show obedience to their superiors, obedience to their mother and father, obedience to their teachers and behave well and devotedly to their friends, acquiescence, colleagues, relatives, slaves and servants—all suffer violence, murder and separation from their loved ones. Even those who are fortunate to have escaped, and whose love is undiminished (by the *brutalizing* effect of war), suffer from the misfortunes of their friends, acquaintances colleagues and relatives. This participation of all men in suffering weighs heavily on the mind of Beloved of the Gods. Except among the Greeks, there is no land where religious orders of Brahmans and Sarmanas are not to be found, and there is no land anywhere where men do not support one sect or another. Today, if a hundredth or thousandth part of those people who were killed or died or were deported when Kalinga was annexed were to suffer similarly, it would weighs heavily on the mind of the Beloved of the Gods."[13]

Under Ashoka's rule, Buddhism spread even outside of India, and he was reportedly followed the principles of justice.and good governance, thus becoming an example for Buddhist rulers.

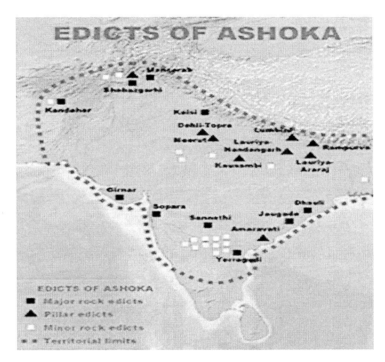

LOCATIONS OF ASHOKA'S EDICTS

The Different Yanas of Buddhism

The Three Vehicles (*yanas*)—**Theravada, Mahayana,** and **Vajrayana**—represent different means or methods of awakening, different forms of transportation if you will.Theravada, the Old Wisdom School or Way of the Elders. They all have the common elements the Three Jewels: **Buddha, Dharma,** and **Sangha.**

---

[13] Romila Thapar, Asóka and the Decline of the Mauryas (Delhi: Oxford University Press, 1997), 255-6.

Theravada(The Way of the Elders)

The first turning of the wheel or first phase of the historical Buddha's teachings based on the earliest written Buddhist textsin Pali. It became the dominant school in Sri Lanka and Southeast Asia, although Buddhism in Vietnam combines Theravada and Mahayana forms due to influences from China. Theravada maintains a strict hierarchy between (male) monastics on the express lane to awakening and the laypeople who support them financially to gain merit for later lives, when they can become monastics.

Mahayanists pejoratively refer to Theravada as **Hinayana** or the **Small Vehicle** due to emphasis on individual practice, a name not used by Theravadans themselves. Theravada, because of its emphasis on the earliest teachings of the Buddha, is often considered as the most conservative form Buddhism. In this school, the way to **nirvana** is seen as best achieved by following the ascetic life of the Buddha, aiming for **NIRODHA**, dispassion, or freedom from suffering caused by attachment. The goal here is to achieve nirvana and thus become an **arhat**, free from rebirth.

Theravadan Characteristics of Reality
      impermanence (*anicca*)
      non-self (*anatta*)
      dysfunctionality (*duhkha*, literally, ill-fitting axle—>
bumpy ride)

Samsara, our experience of reality while asleep, is generally viewed as distinct from the awakened reality of*Nirvana*, like two shores separated by a river.The Dharma is a raft that gets us to the opposite shore.

Main Theravada texts
      Dhammapada
      Commentaries
      *Jataka Tales*stories about the past incarnations of Buddha, often in non-human form, intended for laypersons

Mahayana(The Great Vehicle)

The Great (*maha*) Vehicle is often considered the second turning of the wheel, a reform movement that began in India sometime around the first century BCE to revive the spirit of the original message of the historical Buddha. It features important roles for laypeople, including women, unlike the monk-centered practice of Theravada. It became dominant in East Asia (China, Korea, Japan), especially in the form of Chan/Son/Zen.

The primary focus is on the **Bodhisattva** or Buddha-to-Be who sacrifices personal awakening to help othersawaken, which promotes egalitarian views of the universal potential for Buddhahood. This means that anyone can become a Buddha, and unlike in Theravada Buddhism, **nirvana** is not only achievable after one becomes a monk. This is one of the major differences between Theravada and Mahayana Buddhism, since the former school has no concept of Boddhisatvas. Mahayana, because it incorporates many concepts that the older Theravada school may not accept, is considered the most inclusive of the **yanas**. The focus in Mahayana is not to be an arhat, but to be a Bodhisattava, since in achieving this status, one works for the good of others.

Three Mahayana Characteristics of Reality
Impermanence (*anitya*)
Non-self (*an-atman*)
Emptiness, no-thingness (*sunyata*)

Mahayanarejects a literal interpretation of the river and raft analogy from Theravada. *Samsara*is in fact*Nirvana*, just as the person who is asleep also possesses the Buddha nature. Any perceived differences are due to the deluded or awakened state of the observer.

In the Mahayana school, the Boddhisatvas can be petitioned to for help, almost like the guardian angel in some cultures. There are several different **boddhisatvas**, among them Avalokiteshavara, known for compassion, and venerated in China as Kuan Yin, a female boddhisatva. There is also the Maitreya Boddhisatva (The Friendly One) who will be the next Buddha.

Since the Buddha's teachings allowed for different perceptions, there was no stringent monolith, as shown by the presence of the different schools. And within the Mahayana, there are several different movements as well. There is, for example, the **Madhyami-ka**, "The Middle Way." This Middle Way is because everything in this world is viewed as ultimately unreal, and as such, no position is taken regarding affirmation or denial of perceived realities. In this way, all dharmas are empty of absolute truth, and such emptiness is known as **sunyata**. This means that any dharma is devoid of a permanent and eternal substance.

Within Mahayana, another movement was the **Yogacara,** that focuses upon meditation, holding that we cannot in truth perceive the external world or ourselves: what we think is real is in fact just an idea. Another movement is the **Pure Land Buddhism** wherein the hope of for a rebirth in an ideal setting, achieved by faith in the Buddha and by chanting and concentrating on his name. There is also the **Tendai** sect in Japanese Buddhism that claims to harmonize the truth of all the Buddhist paths.

In China, there was the development of CHAN Buddhism, or as it is more popularly known by its Japanese transliteration, ZEN. This is the idea the self-control is achieved through rigorous meditation. This is to reach the state of *dhyana* reached by the Buddha when he was under the Boddhi tree.

In Japanese concepts of Zen, one learns to think outside the box by the use of **koans,** a seemingly paradoxical statement or question. The effort to "solve" a koan is intended to exhaust the analytic intellect and the egoistic will, readying the mind to entertain an appropriate response on the intuitive level.

Some Famous Koans

1. What is the sound of one hand clapping?
2. If you meet the Buddha, Kill him.
3. If a tree falls in the forest and no one is around to hear, does it make a sound?"

Vajrayana (The Thunderbolt Vehicle)

The Thunderbolt (**Vajra**) Vehicle is regarded as the third turning of the wheel by its adherents, the next phase of development of the Buddha's teachings. It also is known as Tantric Buddhism.The thunderbolt or diamond (the weapon of the Vedic god Indra) symbolizes the use of unorthodox techniques to arouse the sleeper to awaken. These may include breaking formal rules against sexual indulgence, eating meat, and drinking alcohol, with the intent of shocking the practitioner out of deluded complacency, paralleling the shock of being struck by a bolt of lightning. It was the dominant practice in Tibet and Mongolia. Some Buddhists doubt whether it really is Buddhist and call it Lamaism. Esoteric practices involve deep psychological probings, often facilitated through use of the arts (paintings of mandalas, chanting of mantras, ritual gestures of mudras, dance performances).

Vajrayana View of Reality

A thunderbolt is aimed at the heart of *Samsara*, in order to expose the inner *Nirvana*, evoking an unmediated encounter with one's inmost psychological constructs and passions.

The Dalai Lama

One form of Tibetan Vajrayana Buddhism is the **GELUGPA**, founded by Tsongkhapa (d. 1419), and whose followers wore large yellow hats. The term "Dalai Lama" means "ocean of wisdom." In the sixteenth century, a Gelugpa missionary, Sonam Gyatso, went to Mongolia and succeeded in converting its ruler to Buddhism. It was at this time that the ruler coined the term "Dalai Lama," granting it to two predecessors of the missionary and naming Sonam Gyatso the third successor to the title. Soon, this sect became dominant in Tibet and Mongolia. Today, the current Dalai Lama is opposed by the Chinese government because he opposes the Chinese annexation of his land. The Dalai Lama is supposed to be an incarnation of a boddhisatva, the Panchen Lama. The Chinese government views another person as being the rightful incarnation of the Panchen Lama.

Rituals

The historical Buddha opposed ritualism, seeing it as a hindrance in the achievement of nirvana. After his death, however, rituals did develop. People began venerating his birth place (Lumbini), the place where he attained awakening (Bodh Gaya), the place where he delivered his first sermon (Sarnath), and where he attained parinirvana (Kushinagar)—the stage where he was forever free rebirth, and where his *skandhas* were forever extinguished.

In the more conservative Theravada Buddhism, there is the **Buddha Puja**, which means basically paying respect to the Buddha. There is also the concept of the members of the sangha going out each day with their bowls for food.

Mahayana incorporates rituals from other traditions, among them the honoring of the dead, in addition to commemorating his birth, awakening and attainment of **parinirvana**. Vajrayana uses **mandalas**-sacred geometric circular figures that represent the universe. When completed, a mandala becomes a sacred area that serves as a receptacle for deities and a collection point of universal forces. By mentally entering a mandala and proceeding to its center, a person is symbolically guided through the cosmos to the essence of reality. By constructing a **mandala**, a monk ritually participates in the Buddha's teachings.

SAND MANDALA, INDIA 1996[14]

Buddhism in America
In many of the western bloc countries, the teachings of Buddhism with its Nontheism is seen as attractive to many who prefer its focus on life in this world, and its leaving what will happen afterwards in the realm of non-focus. Many famous personalities have

---

[14]http://creativity.denverartmuseum.org/?lesson-plan=the-goal-in-the-mandala, Accessed February 28,2014.

converted to Buddhism, among them, Tina Turner, the singer, and Richard Gere, the actor. Modern politics has brought with it the legacy of violence and fights over land, as in Sri Lanka, Burma and parts of Thailand and the surrounding areas.

In the United States, immigration and conversion have been two of the greatest factors in the rise of the Buddhist population. The practice of zen, as well as the interest in martial arts have created interest in the study of Buddhism. Buddhism does welcome converts and there is a missionary movement. The image of the Dalai Lama as a symbol of peace and his role as a world leader in ethics all provide a positive image for Buddhism.

THE LARGEST BUDDHIST TEMPLE IN THE UNITED STATES, HSI LAI TEMPLE, HACIENDA HEIGHTS, CALIFORNIA.

What is it like to be a Buddhist in America?

Interview with Karma Lekshe Tsomo, Professor of Theology & Religious Studies, University of San Diego.

PROFESSOR LEKSHE TSOMO MEETING HIS HOLINESS, THE DALAI LAMA ON HIS VISIT TO SAN DIEGO IN APRIL, 2012

Do you adhere to traditional Buddhist beliefs and practices?

Buddhism is not so much concerned about beliefs as about cultivating wisdom and compassion. I like to meditate every day to become more calm and peaceful. Meditation on loving kindness and compassion helps me develop patience with people and situations. I like to recite mantras, such as *om mani padme hum*, to wish happiness and enlightenment to all sentient beings. I also like to read the teachings of the Buddha, because they help remind me to pay attention to the quality of my actions, moment to moment. Every action of everyday life is an opportunity to let go of destructive emotions and live a meaningful life.

What school/form of Buddhism do you follow?

My approach to Buddhism is non-sectarian. Most of my teachers are from the Tibetan tradition, but I also have teachers from the Burmese, Chinese, and Korean traditions. From the outside, these traditions appear to be quite different, but they are all founded on the same basic Buddhist teachings and use similar methods to cultivate the mind, such as meditation. There are differences of emphasis and interpretation among the traditions, even different philosophies and goals. For example, Theravada practitioners take *nirvana* (liberation from *samsara*) as their goal whereas Mahayana practitioners aspire to become a fully awakened Buddha. To become a *bodhisattva* and eventually a Buddha takes a very long time, but the ideal of liberating beings from suffering sounds good to me.

What rituals do you perform?

Early in the morning and when I visit the temple, I offer incense, food, and water to the Buddhas and bodhisattvas on the altar. I also circumambulate temples, *stupa*s, and other sacred sites whenever I get a chance. On full moon and new moon days, Buddhist monks and nuns perform a ritual of reciting the monastic precepts. This reminds us to keep the precepts purely and is also a kind of confession ritual. I also make a ritual of practicing mindfulness when making tea in the morning. In a sense, every action of everyday life can be seen as a ritual if it is performed with mindful awareness.

Do you participate in the local Buddhist community?

Wherever I am, I go with my friends and students to participate in as many Buddhist services and community events as possible. I love to visit Buddhist temples of all descriptions: Chinese, Japanese, Korean, Thai, Tibetan, Vietnamese, and so on. Interacting with Buddhists of different traditions is an excellent opportunity to learn about different people's experiences of practicing Buddhism. When I travel to different Buddhist countries, I enjoy participating in services, meditations, and cultural celebrations.

How do you see the role of women within Buddhism?

Buddhist texts present a variety of images of women, some quite positive and some quite negative. The statement of the Buddha that women have the potential to achieve liberation is reassuring and affirms the spiritual equality of women and men. In Buddhist societies, women play many different roles, both domestic and religious, but the powerful, celebrated religious leaders are generally male, not female. In contemporary society, there is now a global movement to encourage greater public participation of women, including the increasing involvement of women as fully ordained nuns and as teachers.

What are the challenges of being a Buddhist in the United States?

The biggest challenge is the lack of systematic Buddhist studies programs. Some Dharma centers hold periodic talks on Buddhism and a few universities provide in-depth Buddhist studies, but there are only a few programs in-between. Another challenge is the lack of support for full-time Buddhist practitioners. In Asia, monks and nuns are supported to live and practice at monasteries, but at present there are very few monasteries in the U.S. There is also a lack of understanding about Buddhism in general and the value of monastic practice in particular. In American society, most people are concerned with money, pleasure, and worldly success, whereas Buddhists understand that these pursuits are only temporarily fulfilling.

Would you consider yourself an atheist or a nontheist? Why?

In the Buddhist worldview, the god realms are possible states of rebirth, so Buddhists are not atheists. But rebirth as a god is temporary, so that is not a permanent solution. For Buddhists, the most important issue is getting free from suffering. The question of whether a supreme being exists is not the pressing issue. Rather than speculate about abstract concepts such as the existence or non-existence of a God or gods, the Buddha suggested that we focus on purifying our minds of greed, hatred, ignorance, and other destructive emotions. That way, we can free ourselves and others from suffering and constant dissatisfaction, and live more peaceful, meaningful lives.

What aspect of Buddhism is most meaningful to you?

The idea that human beings can get rid of destructive emotions and instead develop wisdom, loving kindness, and compassion for all living beings is very compelling to me. It's not necessary to agree to some prepackaged belief system; we can verify the benefits of Buddhist practice for ourselves. The Buddha instructed his followers not to accept any ideas or practices, even his own teachings, until they had verified them through their own experience. For example, we can verify that self-centeredness makes us unhappy, whereas loving kindness and compassion make everyday life more pleasant and trouble-free. Mindful awareness – learning to be attentive to the present moment – helps us avoid problems, make better decisions, and appreciate the precious human opportunity. Putting these teachings into practice, we can live a happy, peaceful, and meaningful life.

Glossary

Abhidharma	Moral and philosophical treatises of Buddhism, composed after Shakyamuni's death
Anatta/Anatman	Literally "no-self." The denial of the concept of an eternal soul.
Anicca/Anitya:	Doctrine of Impermanence.
Arhat	One who has achieved freedom from attachment and rebirth, thus attaining **nirvana**.
Bhikshu/Bhikku	Monk.
Bhikshuni/Bhikkuni	Nun
Bodhisattva	"Buddha-to-be." A stage to perfection wherein one works for the good of sentient beings.
Buddha	Literally, "the one who woke up," or "the awakened one."

Buddha-puja   The ritual of paying respect to the Buddha.

Chan/Zen   Intense meditation.

Dalai Lama   The spiritual leader of the Gelugpa sect of Buddhists.

Dharma   Cosmic Justice, following the Buddhist precepts.

Dukkha   Suffering, Dysfunction.

Gelugpa   A subsect of **Vajrayana** Buddhism

Hinayana   "Small Vehicle"—a derogatory name used to refer to Theravada Buddhism, indicating its limitedness.

Jataka Tales   Stories about the past incarnations of Buddha, often in non-human form, intended for laypersons.

Khandha   Pali for Skandha.

The Eightfold Path The eight precepts that provide a solution to our problems, and which ought to be ideally practiced in conjunction with each other.

Fourfold Noble Truths   The concept that to life is to suffer, suffering is caused by attachment, if attachment is killed, there is no suffering, and that the solution lies in following the Eightfold Path.

Koan   A seemingly paradoxical statement or question to show the limit of the analytic intellect and to rely upon intuition.

Lumbini   Birthplace of Siddhartha Gautama.

Madhyamika   TheMiddle Way where everything in this world is viewed as ultimately unreal, and as such, no position is taken regarding affirmation or denial of perceived realities.

Mahayana Literally "The Great Vehicle," one of the major schools of Buddhism.

Maitreya The future Buddha.

Mandala Asacred geometric circular figure that represents the universe.

Nirodha "Dispassion,"—the attainment of the third of the fourfold truths in Buddhism.

Nirvana Literally, "the extinguishing." That state after which there is no rebirth.

Nondualism Not subject to dualism of any sort.

Parinirvana The state reached by the Buddha when he was freed from rebirth. Some Theravadists use this term specifically for the Buddha and explain the difference between this and **nirvana**thus: Nirvana can be accomplished during one's life. After death however, when there is the state of absolutely no return, that is parinirvana: reached by someone who has already attained **nirvana** on earth.

Pure Land Buddhism A type of Buddhism that preaches rebirth in an ideal setting, attained upon absolute faith in the Buddha and by concentrating and chanting his name.

Sangha The community of monks and nuns; sometimes refers to the entire Buddhist community.

Shakya The tribe into which Prince Siddhartha was born.

Shakayamuni The sage of the Shakyas; another title of the historical Buddha.

Siddhartha	"he who has achieved his ultimate goal." Name of the Buddha at birth.
Skandhas	Literally "aggregates." The five elements that sum up the whole of an individual's mental and physical existence.
Suddhodhana	The father of Prince Siddhartha.
Sunyata	Emptiness. This does not mean non-existence or denial of reality, but indicates rather the undifferentiation through with dualities, entities and distinctions arise.
Tanha	Thirst, craving, attachment, obsession.
Tathagata	The one who is both come and gone. Another title of the Buddha. Often used to indicate one who is beyond transitory phenomena—referring to the Buddha nature rather than the Buddha as a person.
Tendai	A path that claims to harmonize all the different ways in Buddhism.
Theravada	Literally "The way of the Elders," a school in Buddhism.
Three Poisons	Anger, Greed, Ignorance—the cause of our errors and misjudgments.
Tripitaka	The Three Baskets—a reference to the Buddhist scriptures.
Triratna	The three Jewels of Buddhism: Buddha, Dharma, Sangha.
Vajrayana	The Thunderbolt Vehicle: a major Buddhist school.
Yana	Literally "vehicle"—used to refer to the three major schools of Buddhism.

Yogacara   A Buddhist school that focuses on meditation.

Questions

1. Explain the meaning of this koan: "When you find the Buddha, kill him." You may research this online.

2. Explain three major differences between the Theravadin and Mahayanist schools of Buddhism.

3. Describe the Three Poisons

4. Identify and describe each of the four sighs that moved young Prince Siddharta to leave his life of luxury and go forth to seek enlightenment.

5. How would you explain "The Three Jewels" to a group of non-Buddhists.

6. Relate the story of Ashoka with added material that you may have learned about from reading hard copy books or through the internet.

7. Describe the ten Buddhist precepts and explain why you think some are specific to monks and nuns.

JAINISM
The path of Ahimsa

परस्परोपग्रहो जीवानाम्

THIS IS THE SYMBOL OF JAINISM AS AGREED UPON BY A MEETING OF THE DIFFERENT GROUPS IN 1974. IT IS CALLED THE JAIN PRATEEK CHIHNA.

- *Describe the origins of Jainism*
- *Explain the derivation of the term "Jain"*
- *Summarize the general teachings of Jainism*
- *Describe the Scriptures and Sects of Jainism*
- *Outline Celebrations and Festivals*
- *Differentiate between Sallekhana and suicide.*

Introduction

Jainism originated in India as one of the paths within Indian spirituality. It contains themes and beliefs that seem to reflect concepts of Sanatan Dharma, but at the same time, it also has views that clash with what we now know as Hinduism. The ideals of Jainism are strict, with an emphasis on non-violence and self-discipline that is extremely demanding. One of India's most famous personalities, Mahatma Gandhi was said to have based his ideas of non-violence upon the principles of Jainism.

The Origins

According to the Jain tradition, Jainism does not have a single founder. Throughout history, there have been twenty four revealers of truth. Each one is known as a TIRTHANKARA. The word literally means "ford finder. " In this interpretation, life is seen as an ocean. The person who provides the contrivance (**tirtha**) to cross is called a **tirthankara.** Such a person is born as a human, and achieves **moksha** by intense disciplinary practices and meditation. **Tirthankaras** only appear when there is need for renewal or resurrection of the good teachings that have either been forgotten or abandoned. Each **tirthankara** may subtly adapt teachings to suit culture and custom.

The last **TIRTHANKARA** was known as **MAHAVIRA** (great hero). He is said to have lived from approximately 599 -527 BCE. He was a prince and his actual name was **Vardhamana**. He had all the pleasures of life, but at the age of thirty, gave those up to go in search of a solution for pain, sorrow and suffering.

He spent the next twelve and a half years in silence and meditation, trying to conquer all the desires and feelings that attached him to this world. He carefully avoided causing any type of suffering to any creature, going without food for long periods of time. It is said that people would ridicule him, but he would not react. Some would set their dogs on him, but still he stayed calm. When his clothes fell off his body, he did not replace them for he had reached the level of freedom from such things.

He finally reached the stage of perfection, of **nirvana or moksha**. Some say that he meditated for so long that trees grew upon his body. He got the name Mahavira—great hero—when he attained this perfect state. He traveled around until his death in 527 BCE in the village of Pavapuri, about 60 miles from Patna, the capital of present Bihar state. He had attained the state of **ishatpragbhara**: a state beyond life and death, wherein he now exists as a pure soul in another dimension and can neither help nor harm us.

DEPICTION OF MAHAVIRA

TEACHINGS

Mahavira explained that our **KARMA** is what keeps us being re-born. Our desires keep building up karma for us. Our soul is *jiva*, our body is *ajiva*—and our soul is basically held prisoner by our body, based on the accumulation of karma. To be free from this, one must follow a certain ethical path. This path is built upon five great vows known as the **Mahavrata**:

Ahimsa (Nonviolence) : non-violence: not causing harm to any being.

Satya (Truthfulness**):** To speak harmless truth only.

Asteya (non-Stealing): Not to take anything that is not properly given.

Bramachariya (Chastity): not to indulge in sexual pleasure.

Aparigrapha (Non-attachment): detachment from all people, places, or material things.

These vows differ in the terms of rigor in which they are followed. Monks are expected to observe them, along with some additional restrictions, with absolute devotion. Householders follow them with less stringency. One of the daily rituals that Jains follow is called **Kayotsarga**—standing motionless in meditation for long periosd of time. **Kayotsarga** means "the abandonment of the body."

THIS 60 FOOT TALL STATUE IS IN KARNATAKA STATE, INDIA. IT DEPICTS BAHUBA-LI, SON OF THE FIRST TIRTHANKARA, RISHABA, IN THE STATE OF **KAYOTSARGA**, SO STILL THAT TREES AND VINES GROW UP AMONG HIS TOES AND AROUND HIS BODY

Sallekhana

Many outsiders to Jainism have heard the concept of *Sallekhana* explained in rather simplistic terms, and consider it as suicide. This is a misconception. *Sallekhana* is death while in ultra-pure meditation. It is a well-ordered voluntarily chosen death which is not inspired by any passion and is the result of conscientious grad-ual withdrawal from the taking of food in such a manner as would never disrupt one's inner peace and dispassionate mindfulness. There is, therefore, a fundamental difference between suicide and

Sallekhana. Suicide is the result of the outburst of passions, whereas Sallekhana is the result of dispassionateness. It is recommended only when the body is completely disabled by extreme old age or by incurable diseases and the man becomes conscious of the impending unavoidable death and of the necessity of concentrating on the pure qualities of the soul. In the aspirant, there is no dissatisfaction, no sorrow, no fear, no dejection, no sinfulness; the mind is cool, calm and composed; the heart is filled with the feeling of universal love and compassion. It is also called the death with equanimity. Sallekhana is thus a spiritual process of emaciating one's passions and body by internal and external austerities. It involves giving up love, enmity, attachment to possessions etc., and with pure mind; forgiving one's kinsmen and others, and asking for forgiveness. Casting aside grief, fear, anguish, wickedness etc., with all sincerity and zeal, one should allay the innermost passions by scriptural words.[15]

Jainism is most famous for its focus on AHIMSA. The word literally means "to be without harm." As such, in the Jain scriptures it is written, "Do not injure, abuse, oppress, enslave, insult, torment, torture or kill any creature or living being. Mahavira taught that there is no quality of soul more subtle than non-violence and no virtue of spirit greater than reverence for life. In this worldview, both intention and the actual act of violence bring about karma. So too does condoning, or asking anyone to commit violence.

[15] Abridged from http://www.jainbelief.com/intro_jainism.htm. Accessed May 23, 2014.

Sects

There are two major sects in Jainism: the **Digambara** (sky clad), and the **Svetembara** (white clad). The monks of the Digambara go completely naked, often with a peacock-feather broom to clear the path of any insects so that they may not trample upon them. The monks of the Svetembara wear thin white garments. There are several doctrinal differences between the two groups, the main ones perhaps regarding gender and scripture. The Digambara believe that the scriptures were lost very early, and as such do not accept Svetembara collection. They also believe that **Mahavira** was never married, and that only in a male state can one attain **moksha**. The Svetembara, in contrast, do not share the concept of gender specificity for moksha, and believe that the nineteenth **Tirthankara** was female.

Both Digambaras and Svetembaras observe the symbolism of **murtis** or statuary in their prayer rituals. They are therefore called **murtipujakas**: those who use murtis in their prayer. Some reform sects do NOT use such **murtis.** Two such subsects of the Svetembaras are the **Terapanthis** and the **Sthanakvasis.** The Digambaras also have some subsects.

TWO DIFFERENT MONKS: ONE A "SKY CLAD" DIGAMBARA, AND THE OTHER A "WHITE CLAD" SVETEMBARA

Scripture

Mahavira's disciples compiled his words into texts or sutras, and memorized them to pass on to future generations. The texts had to be memorized since Jain monks and nuns were not allowed to possess religious books as part of their vow of non-acquisition, nor were they allowed to write. With the passing of time, some of the texts were forgotten, or others became corrupted. In 350 BCE, many monks and nuns died in a famine taking with them the precious teachings.

The **Svetembaras** believe that most of those texts were saved, and collected in AGAMAS. The **Digambaras** believe that ALL of the **AGAMAS** were lost. Both sects believe that another collection of scriptures, the **PURVAS** were all lost.

FOLIO FROM THE KALPASUTRA (THE BOOK OF SACRED PRECEPTS)

Preservation of the Scriptures

After the famine, monks and nuns of the Svetambara sect held several conferences to preserve the most important Jain texts. Unsurprisingly there were many arguments about which texts were authentic, and different sub-sects still differ over this.

Jain monks and nuns are now permitted to possess religious books, so the Jain scriptures should no longer be in danger.

Concept of God

Jainism does not believe in a CREATOR GOD. The Universe, in this worldview, is eternal—having no beginning or end. The Universe operates by its own cosmic laws, without any need of a manager or creator. This does not mean that Jainism has no concept of a GOD. If a God be a perfect being, possessing infinite knowledge, wisdom, vision, power and the other qualities that denote perfection, then every living being can aspire to that state. One can attain this state upon achieving MOKSHA; as such, in Jainism one may speak of **many gods**.

God is beyond desire, and a being who wants people to pray to him or worship him cannot be a God in actuality. Jain prayers focus on the great qualities of the **tirthankaras** and remind the individual of various teachings.

Glossary

Ahimsa (Nonviolence):
> Non-violence: not causing harm to any being.

Asteya (non-Stealing):
> Not to take anything that is not properly given.

Aparigrapha (Non-attachment):
> Detachment from all people, places, or material things.

Agamas:
> A collection of Jain scripture. The Svetembara believe they were preserved. The Digambara reject this notion and feel that they collections that are referred to as such by the Svetembara are not authentic.

Ajiva:
> The body, flesh. That which is without soul.

Bramachariya (Chastity):
> The state of not indulging in sexual pleasure.

Digambara:
> Literally "sky clad." The monks of this sect wander naked.

Ishatpragbhara:
> A state beyond life and death, wherein one exists as a pure soul in another dimension and can neither help nor harm us.

Jiva:
> The soul.

Katyosarga: Abandonment of the body, an additional vow to the regular Mahavrata five; it means standing motionless for long periods.

Mahavira: Literally "great hero." The last *tirthankara.*

Mahavrata: The five great vows of the Jain ethical path.

Murti: Statuary, depiction of a revered figure used in worship.

Purvas: The name of a set of Jain scriptures. All major sects agree that these have been lost.

Sallekhana: Death from ultra-pure meditation, when the body releases the soul.

Satya (Truthfulness):
To speak harmless truth only.

Sthanakvasis: A subsect of the Svetembara.

Svetembaras: Literally "white clad." One of the major sects in Jainism.

Terapanthis: A subsect of the Svetembara.

Tirthankara: Literally "ford finder." The title applies to each of the twenty four revealers of truth

SIKHISM

Only those who remember the name of God are truly liberated

THE KHANDA: SYMBOL OF SIKHISM. THE SYMBOL RECEIVES ITS NAME FROM THE DOUBLE-EDGED AT THE CENTER, CLEAVING TRUTH FROM FALSEHOOD. THE CIRCLE AROUND THE KHANDA IS CALLED A CHAKAR: A CIRCLE WITHOUT BEGINNING OR END SIGNIFYING THE ETERNAL PERFECTION AND COMPLETENESS OF THE DIVINE, THE TWO SINGLE-BLADED SWORDS AT THE ENDS ARE CALLED KIRPANS, AND THEY DENOTE MIRI AND PIRI, THE TEMPORAL AND SPIRITUAL DIMENSIONS OF A SIKH'S WORLDVIEW: THAT S/HE MUST OBSERVE SPIRITUALITY AS WELL AS SERVICE TO HUMANKIND.

- *Understanding the social setting in which Sikhism was founded*
- *The Birth and Life of Guru Nanak*
- *Summary of the Philosophy and Beliefs of Sikhism*
- *Brief overview of the ten gurus*
- *Understanding the Khalsa and the Five Ks*
- *Rituals*
- *Reform Movements, Modernity, Relationship with other religions*
- *Sikhism outside of India*

Sitz im Leben

The India of the fifteenth century was a land that knew several major religious traditions: Sanatan Dharma, Buddhism, Jainism and Islam. This rich atmosphere engendered several ideas, one among them being a focus on the esoteric and mystical aspects of religion. The Hindus had their caste system, the Muslims had their concept of Islamic law, and the harmony or lack thereof depended on whichever ruler was in power. If he was a fanatic, then there was religious oppression; if he was more irenic, or a believer in syncretic ideas, then different religions were allowed relative freedom of practice.

The Birth and Life of Nanak

Nanak Dev Ji was born on April 15, 1469, in a place called Talwandi, in the Western Punjab, now located about 50 miles south west of Lahore, in present day Pakistan. He was born into a Hindu family, with his father an accountant working for the local Muslim authorities. It is said that the astrologers predicted that he would attain the status of a prophet. He had a unique upbringing, being trained along with Muslim children in Persian language classes, while also observing the learning that was customary for Hindu children. When he was about thirteen, and about to go through the Hindu ceremony of being invested with the sacred thread to denote belonging to a particular caste, Nanak is said to have rejected the thread, asking instead for one that actually symbolized mercy, contentment and truth.

He tended the family cattle and engaged in several discussions of religion with both the Hindus and Muslims, and most probably those who were from the other religious paths. He was known for his keen insight and probing questions. When he was sixteen, he got married, and eventually fathered two children. He took a job as an accountant, and during the day would work at his profession, but at night, along with a Muslim companion, Mardana, would sing hymns and meditate.

When he was thirty years old, Nanak had a spiritual experience that was to change his life forever. He went to the river for his bath, and plunged in. He did not resurface for a long while, and people thought that he might have drowned. After three days, he showed up and revealed that he had had a mystical experience, being taken to the presence of the Divine. God gave him a cup of the nectar of immortality (**AMRIT**), and let him know that he was to be a teacher, calling the people to the way of God. It was then he responded with the words of the **Japji:**

There is but One God, His name is Truth, He is the Creator, He fears none, he is without hate, He never dies, He is beyond the cycle of births and death, He is self-illuminated, He is realized by the kindness of the True Guru. He was True in the beginning, He was True when the ages commenced and has ever been True, He is also True now."

A painting of Guru Nanak

Guru Nanak gave up his job and declared that there is no Hindu nor is there any Muslim. He began to wear a mixture of Hindu and Muslim clothing, and when questioned about his statement, noted that the outward labels were misleading and divisive. Rather people should avoid such labels and replace them with that which was meaningful. When told that the Muslims were staunch adherents to their faith, he said:

"Let God's grace be the mosque, and devotion the prayer mat. Let the Quran be the good conduct. Let modesty be compassion, good manners fasting, you should be a Muslim the like of this. Let good deeds be your Kaaba and truth be your mentor. Your declaration of your faith be your creed and prayer, God would then vindicate your honor."

Guru Nanak took to travelling to spread his message, winning many disciples. They were called **SIKHS** (singular Sikh, meaning disciple). Guru Nanak's teachings were well received by some, and rejected by others. While he accepted certain social norms, he did not accept the idea of statuary depiction of the Divine, although he maintained a belief in karma and samsara. For Nanak, God is beyond our comprehension, beyond need, and we only gain liberation through God's grace.

The great guru died in 1539 at Kartarpur, after having appointed Guru Angad to take his place. He appointed this man over his two sons since he did not feel they were worthy of the leadership position. Muslims and Hindus attended his funeral, and both communities built shrines honoring him.

SHRINE AT KARTARPUR, GURU NANAK'S RESTING PLACE.

Central Features of Guru Nanak's Teachings

God, according to Guru Nanak, was beyond description, known only by experience. God is the only truth, and one can find this by reflection and meditation. God is called by several names: Ek Onkar, Sat Naam, Waheguru. These names simply ascribe to God's uniqueness.

Philosophy and Beliefs

There is only One God. He is the same God for all people of all religions.

The soul goes through cycles of births and deaths before it reaches the human form. The goal of our life is to lead an exemplary existence so that one may merge with God. Sikhs should remember God at all times and practice living a virtuous and truthful life while maintaining a balance between their spiritual obligations and temporal obligations.

The true path to achieving salvation and merging with God does not require renunciation of the world or celibacy, but living the life of a householder, earning an honest living and avoiding worldly temptations and sins.

Sikhism condemns blind rituals such as fasting, visiting places of pilgrimage, superstitions, worship of the dead, idol worship etc.

Sikhism preaches that people of different races, religions, or sex are all equal in the eyes of God. It teaches the full equality of men and women. Women can participate in any religious function or perform any Sikh ceremony or lead the congregation in prayer. [16]

---

[16] Downloaded from www.sikhs.org. Accessed October 8, 2013.

The Ten Gurus

Guru Nanak was the first of 10 gurus, and this period lasted for 239 years, until the assassination of the last Guru, Gobind Singh, in 1708. Each of these masters continued the teaching of Guru Nanak, implementing what was necessary for the formation of the religion we now know as Sikhism.

The second Guru, Angad, developed the script of GURMUKHI, the sacred language of Sikhism, and he also ensured the continuation of the LANGAR: the communal kitchen started by Guru Nanak. The fourth Guru, Ramdas (1534-81), founded AMRITSAR, and breaking from tradition with his predecessors, made the office of the Guru hereditary, and started by appointing his son, ARJAN to succeed him.

Guru Arjan supervised the collection of sayings that were to form the Sikh Scripture, the ADI GRANTH, and he also started the construction of the famous temple at AMRITSAR, known as Harimandir—"The temple of God." In the nineteenth century, the temple was covered with gilded copper and became more famously known as "the Golden Temple."

Unfortunately, the relatively benign atmosphere of religious harmony in the time of Guru Nanak did not last; both the Muslims and Hindus started oppressing the Sikhs and their gurus. The emperor Jahangir (d. 1627) accused the fifth guru of subversion, and had him imprisoned and tortured to death. Guru Arjan was thus the first Sikh martyr.

The sixth Guru, Hargobind Singh, instituted the role of defence for the Sikhs and started the symbolism of the two swords: one to show spiritual authority and the other, temporal authority. The conditions worsened, and under the rule of Aurangzeb (d. 1707), a Moghul emperor, the ninth guru, Tej Bahadur was executed when he refused to convert to Islam.

The tenth guru, Gobind Singh was involved in open war with the Moghul regime, and lost his sons in battle. He was later assassinated by being stabbed. On his death bed, he decreed that, henceforth, there would be no more human gurus. Instead the Adi Granth would be the Guru. It is for this reason that in the Sikh temples, the GURDWARAS, the scripture is treated like a person and addressed as the **Guru Granth Sahib**.

A GRANTHI (RECITER) FANNING THE GURU GRANTH SAHIB

HARIMANDIR SAHIB: THE GOLDEN TEMPLE

The Khalsa

The tenth Guru, Gobind Singh, founded the Khalsa in 1699. Initially he chose five devout followers to the order. The word "Khalsa" means "pure." The Khalsa baptism ceremony is undertaken as part of one's own personal spiritual evolution when the initiate is ready to fully live up to the high expectations of Guru Gobind Singh. All Sikhs are expected to be Khalsa or be working towards that objective.

The Khalsa baptism ceremony involves drinking of Amrit (sugar water stirred with a dagger) in the presence of 5 Khalsa Sikhs as well as the Guru Granth Sahib. The initiate is instructed in the following; (a) You shall never remove any hair from any part of thy body, (b) You shall not use tobacco, alcohol or any other intoxicants, (c) You shall not eat the meat of an animal slaughtered the Muslim way, (d) You shall not commit adultery. The initiate is required to wear the physical symbols of a Khalsa at all times as well as follow the Khalsa Code of Conduct.

Members show their allegiance by observing the five Ks—or what is known as **Panchka Kay**. The five Ks are:

- **Kesh** (uncut hair)
- **Kara** (a steel bracelet)
- **Kanga** (a wooden comb)
- **Kaccha** - also spelt, **Kachh, Kachera** (cotton underwear)
- **Kirpan** (steel sword)

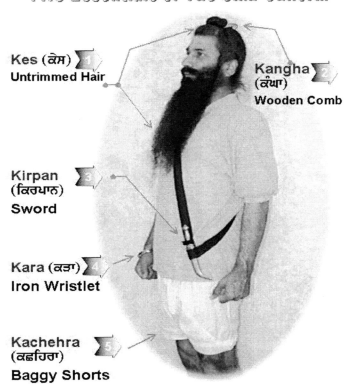

Five Essentials of The Sikh Uniform

Kes (ਕੇਸ)
Untrimmed Hair

Kangha (ਕੰਘਾ)
Wooden Comb

Kirpan (ਕਿਰਪਾਨ)
Sword

Kara (ਕੜਾ)
Iron Wristlet

Kachehra (ਕਛਹਿਰਾ)
Baggy Shorts

A depiction of the 5 Ks.[17]

[17] Downloaded from www.ramgarhiagurdwara.org. Accessed October 8, 2013. The variation in spelling is simply reflective of a different form of transliteration. *Kes* or *Kesh* is correct.

Rituals

There are three main prayers: early in the morning, at sunset, and just before retiring at night. There is regular singing of hymns, known as **kirtan**in the **gurdwaras.**

Reform Movements, Modernity, Relationship with Other Religions

As with any religion, there have been some reform movements in Sikhism. One such movement, the Nirankari rejects several Hindu practices. The Namdharis believe the Gobind Singh did not die, but went into occultation and will return someday. The Sing Sabha rejects the influences of foreign religious influences.

Over the years, the movement for an independent Sikh state, Khalistan, separate from India, has grown. This has caused many problems with the Indian government. The former Prime Minister, Indira Gandhi was assassinated by Sikh bodyguards in revenge for an attack on the Golden Temple. The relationship with Muslims in the area is also rooted in memories of Aurangzeb's attempt to suppress the movement.

Sikhism outside of India

Sikhs are found in large numbers in Great Britain, Canada, and the United States. In Canada and Great Britain in particular, they have large communities and established places of worship. Sikh soldiers have served with honor in both World Wars. Ujjal Dosanjh, a Sikh, was Canada's first non-white premier, serving in British Columbia from 2000-2001. In 2010, Sikh officers were granted the right to wear their turbans in the U.S. Military.

Local Place of Worship

The Sikh community of San Diego is not a huge one. They worship at a gurdwara located at 12269 Oak Knoll Road, Poway.

Sikh Temple in Wisconsin

Glossary

Adi Granth

Adi means first. Adi Granth is the first edition of Sri Guru Granth Sahib Ji, Sikh Holy Scripture, as was compiled by Guru Arjun Dev Ji in the seventeenth century. The Adi Granth is kept in the Golden Temple at Amritsar, an important Sikh Holy Site.

Amrit

Amrit means nectar. Amrit is prepared from ground sugar and water. Receiving or drinking Amrit means getting baptized in Sikh religion.

Amritdhari

A Sikh who has received Amrit and gone through the Khalsa initiation ceremony. Also known as the baptized Sikh.

Gurdwara

Sikh place of worship. Gurdwara is a compound word created by combining Gur, meaning *Guru* and *Dwara*, meaning door or house. Thus the word Gurdwara means the door or house of the Guru. The Guru Granth Sahib is always present at a Gurdwara.

Gurmukhi

The sacred language of Sikhs.

Guru   A spiritual leader sent by God. *Gu* means Darkness and *Ru* means Light. Literally translated, *Guru* means 'The Light that dispels darkness'. A Guru is a highly spiritual teacher who has been sent to Earth by God and is in direct communion with God. There has been a total of 10 living Sikh Gurus, who brought knowledge of God. The eternal Guruship (spiritual and temporal authority) is found in the ***Guru Granth Sahib Ji*** (the Sikh Holy Scripture compiled by Sikh Gurus and other devotees who themselves have attained salvation).

Guru Granth Sahib   The Holy Scripture of Sikhs compiled by Sikh Gurus and devotees of God who themselves have attained salvation. Guru Granth Sahib Ji shows the path to attain salvation and to be One with God.

Kachhehra   Special undergarment, drawers or briefs resembling boxer shorts. Kachhehra is worn by Sikhs as a reminder to practice marital fidelity. It is a symbol of self-control. *Kachhehra* is one of the Five Ks.

Kanga   Wooden comb carried by Amritdhari Sikh as a reminder to practice cleanliness. It is a symbol of hygiene and discipline. *Kanga* is one of the Five Ks.

Kara   A steel bracelet worn by Sikh as a symbol of committment to truthfulness, strength, and unity. It is also considered as a visible deterrent to wrongdoing by attaching a symbol of God to the hand. *Kara* is one of the Five Ks.

Kaur   Princess. All female members of the Sikh community adopted Kaur as their last name to abolish the caste system and establish human equality.

Kesh

Unshorn hair usually covered by a turban. Kesh symbolizes spirituality, living in a way God made us and the prohibition of harm to the body. *Kesh* is one of the Five K.

Khalsa

The pure ones. The term is also used as a collective description of the Sikh community.

Khanda

The Khanda is the emblem of the Sikh faith. It consists of four symbolic weapons. The Khanda represents knowledge of divinity and the creative power of God.

Kirpan

A short sword or knife carried by Amritdhari Sikhs as a reminder to fight for justice and against oppression. *Kirpan* is one of the Five K.

Langar

Free food service provided in every Gurdwara Sahib. People sit together on ground and enjoy the food served in the Langar. This act of sitting together on the floor symbolizes humble behavior and human equality. Langar also servers the purpose of feeding the hungry so that no one is left without a meal.

Sikh

A follower of Sikhism. Sikh is a word derived from Sanskrit. Literally translated, the word means disciple or student. In the Sikh faith, the word Sikh means someone who strives to learn about God, is a seeker of God and truth, and someone who follows Guru Granth Sahib Ji to achieve such goals.

Singh

Lion. All male members of the Sikh community adopted Singh as their last name to abolish the caste system and establish human equality.

Waheguru   A name for God. It means 'Wonderful Lord'.

CHINESE RELIGIONS

The Sanjiao (The Three Teachings): Confucianism, Daoism, Buddhism

**LAO TZU, BUDDHA AND CONFUCIUS. FROM A MING DYNASTY PAINTING
IN THE FREER GALLERY AT THE SMITHSONIAN INSTITUTION.**[18]

[18]http://www.asia.si.edu/collections/zoomObject.cfm?ObjectId=7919. Accessed
March 19, 2014.

- *Understanding the term "Sinjiao"*
- *Explain of the Yin and Yang concept*
- *Overview of Daoism, its founder, and main ideas*
- *Outline meaning of Wu Wei*
- *Present short history of Zhuangzi*
- *Summarize concept of Taiji*
- *Assess Daoism and Modernity/Politics*
- *Explain Confucianism*
- *Describe the Five Great Relationships*
- *Illustrate the Five Virtues of Confucianism*
- *Discuss Chinese Buddhism*

When speaking of Chinese Religions, scholars usually refer to what is known as the **Sinjiao: The Three teachings**. This coinage is attributed to **Li Shiqian**, a sixth century sage, who wrote that "Buddhism is the sun, Daoism the moon, and Confucianism the five planets." The expression refers to what was a common practice in China: one could follow all three religions at once, as well as pray to other gods and spirits. Buddhism made its way to China from India in the second century, but Confucianism and Taoism were native Chinese traditions, and they influenced Chinese Buddhism.

These three teachings have certain common factors. They focus more on the value and agency of humans more than upon gods, and are hence said to foster **humanism**. They were also focused on ethics: how to build a better society by right action. They were not too concerned about stories of origin of the world or of people, but rather how to live in harmony with nature.

Before these three religions, there were other beliefs in place. Among these was the concept of good and bad **spirits** that were active in every aspect of the natural world. People prospered in health and wealth, or suffered in sickness and poverty based on the whims of these spirits. Natural disturbances, whether they were earthquakes or floods were all punishments for humans doing that which disrupted cosmic harmony. Such harmony could be restored through **expiation** rituals.

There was also the idea of **Yang** and **Yin.** Heaven was Yang, and earth was Yin, but there is no separation between them as thought—rather they work in harmony, much like light and dark, hot and cold, male and female—denoting the complementary forces of earth. When these forces act in harmony, we have the ideal Dao, the way of the universe.

YANG AND YIN, SHOWING THE COMPLEMENTARY RELATIONSHIP NECES-SARY FOR HARMONY, THE IDEA OF GIVE AND TAKE. IF BOTH FORCES WERE TO ATTEMPT TO TAKE, THEN THEY WOULD NOT WORK IN HARMO-NY AND CHAOS OR DYSFUNCTION WOULD BE THE RESULT.

In addition to the idea of spirits and Yang and Yin, there was also Ancestor Veneration. When ancestors died, they were seen as becoming spirits whose veneration could ensure harmony and good relations. There was also the concept of **I-Ching,** that arose out of the practice of **divination,** the idea of using bones, tortoise shells and other objects to foretell the future. This developed into a highly complex use of sixty-four hexagrams around the Yang-Yin symbol that, when properly interpreted, offered guidance for the individual in the choices of action.

All of the foregoing beliefs blended with the later paths of Daoism, Confucianism and Buddhism to make Chinese interpretations of the Three Teachings very unique.

THE YANG-YIN SURROUNDED BY THE HEXAGRAMS

Daoism

The origins of Daoism are said to go back to the sixth century BCE, from the teachings of Laozi (Lao Tzu) or Lao Tan, whose name means "old master." Traditional reports state that he was from virginal conception and was born old, which explains the name "Lao Tzu." He became a librarian in the city of Loyang where he served for many years. He finally tired of society, and traveled on a water buffalo to the west of China. When he tried to cross the border, the guard recognized him for the sage he was and insisted that he write down his teachings. He then wrote the **Dao De Jing.** There are many varying stories as to how this book was compiled and what Lao Tzu did after supposedly writing it. He was said to have traveled to India, reincarnated into a deity, as is still worshipped as such by some Daoists.

The Dao De Jing
This short book of eighty-one chapters has had an enormous impact on Chinese thought. Its focus is upon attaining harmony between opposites in nature. Dao, according to this scripture, is beyond description, and has no form. Yet, it can be experienced and followed, since it is the origin of everything. Dao is not God, for it has no personality; instead it may be said to represent the principle of the natural order of the universe, encompassing the principles of the Yang and Yin, and promoting the conduct that fosters harmony with the natural order of things. Dao thus seems to be that mysterious, cosmic powerthat we may simply refer to as "the Way." This Way teaches us that things are sometimes best left the way they are, for this is the natural way that leads to harmony. When we seek to move things out of their natural place, we cause discord. There is no ritual worship that is mandatory; instead meditation and contemplation are encouraged.

Wu Wei

Trees grow without trying to grow, and the planets move in their orbit without contriving to do so. It just happens as a law of nature. *Wu Wei* is this principle of "non-action" or "non-doing." It refers to the principle of uncontrived action, living by or going along with the true nature of the world, allowing things to take their natural course. The sages do not seek to act a certain way to impress people with their knowledge or spirituality: they are simply who they are, acting naturally without imposition or attempt to impress. The observance of how a river works explains the power of the natural way. A rock is obviously harder than water. Yet, if a river flows on or over a rock, in the course of time, it will either split the rock or carve an indentation in it. And this will occur without the river "doing" it—rather it will be accomplished by non-action. Since water is an element that adapts itself to reality instead of attempting to fight oppose it, it is the natural element most often associated with Wu Wei.

This principle of Wu Wei may be applied to governance even: a government that seeks to force its edicts upon the people will create disharmony and resentment. The ideal situation is where there is no government—but where there is one, it will be best when it interferes as little as possible in people's lives. When people understand the function of government, and the government understands the nature of people, there will be a case of give and take, and harmony will be achieved.

Zhuangzi (Chuang Tzu)

CHINESE POSTAGE STAMP DEPICTING ZHUANGZI

Zhuangzi was a fourth century BCE Daoistteacher who is credited with expanding on the Dao De Jing by writing his own work that is known as the Zhuangzi. He used a variety of methods to teach that the individual should be able to exist, be who he is, without being forced to conform to certain perceived norms of perception by the society. He noted the different modes of understanding between creatures, and of the inability of expecting everything to function according to "norms."

We are creatures of conditioning, and were our conditioning different, we would perceive the same thing differently. This is because our knowledge is limited and when we use it to understand the unlimited, we make errors and foment disharmony. An example is in the following story, known as **The Happiness of the Fish.**

The Happiness of the Fish:

Zhuangzi and Huizi were strolling along the dam of the Hao Waterfall when Zhuangzi said, "See how the minnows come out and dart around where they please! That's what fish really enjoy!"

Huizi said, "You're not a fish — how do you know what fish enjoy?"

Zhuangzi said, "You're not me, so how do you know I don't know what fish enjoy?"

Huizi said, "I'm not you, so I certainly don't know what you know. On the other hand, you're certainly not a fish — so that still proves you don't know what fish enjoy!"

Zhuangzi said, "Let's go back to your original question, please. You asked me *how* I know what fish enjoy — so you already knew I knew it when you asked the question. I know it by standing here beside the Hao."

From a philosophical form, Daoism morphed into a religious system, wherein a pantheon of deities and immortals were created.

The general teachings of Daoism may be summarized thus:

Wu Wei: non-action, effortlessness, no strain, following the laws of nature to do what is necessary but go beyond this, for such goes against nature itself.

Simplicity: This ties into Wu Wei, for it avoids complexities.

Gentleness: Ways of aggression, violence and war are among the worst disrupters of harmony.

Relativity: As noted in the fish story above, we observe things based on our conditioning, sometimes with our personal interests in mind, attributing to them categories based on preconceptions. Hence for one person, another might seem hideously ugly; to another that same person may be the epitome of beauty.

Taiji (Tai-chi)

A common sight in the morning in China is that of people doing a set of exercises, with slow graceful movements of the arms and legs. These exercises, said to promote better health, and even aid in prolonging the life, are associated with another concept, **Qigong**, promoting **Chi**—loosely translated as "life energy" through proper breathing techniques. The mastery of **tai-chi**, and of **Qigong** (sometimes known as **Chi Kung**) is amazing to behold, as by proper breath control, one can do things that seem beyond belief, such as, for example, allowing bricks to be broken over the head without injury to himself. There are three dimensions to **Taiji** practice: health, meditation and martial arts.

TAIJI PRACTICE IN CHINA

Daoism and Modernity/Politics

Whereas early Daoism seemed more of an individual non-conformist pursuit, several Daoist communities emerged throughout the centuries. The seeming anti-government philosophy made the early Communist government in the 20th century oppress Daoism somewhat. Today, by incorporating beliefs from other religions, such as Buddhism and Confucianism, as well as ideas of gods, Daoism is widespread in Taiwan, Hong Kong, Malaysia, Singapore, and is enjoying government support in China.

The philosophical ideas of Daoism along with its meditative practices make it attractive to many who are looking for a set of beliefs and practices to ease the stress of living in a modern world, without becoming totally secularist. The Mayo Clinic has incorporated Tai Chi as part of its exercise program for stress reduction and for gentle physical exercise.

Confucianism

Is Confucianism a religion? Is it a philosophy or a scholarly tradition? One may say that while Confucianism may be considered as being covered by the definition of religion, it is much more than that. It combines a holistic way of thinking, elements of ancestor reverence, and humanist values to promote an ethical and philosophical system. This Chinese movement has an ancient past, and has extended its influence over other places, among the Koreas, Japan, and Vietnam. Confucianism has been called a "civil religion"—wherein the leaders are lay people instead of priests, and wherein the institutions are those of the school, society at large, and the state, instead of churches. Confucianism encompasses every aspect of daily life, and in this way may be said, to be closer to the idea of the "way" or "law" of ancient Judaism.

LIKENESS OF CONFUCIUS[19]

The founder of this movement is said to be Kong Qiu (551-479 BCE), later known as Kong Fuzi (Master Kong). His name was later rendered as Confucius by Jesuit missionaries. He was from a noble family that had fled from its ancestral home during a time of political turmoil. His father died while he was still a child, but despite living in straitened circumstances, Confucius' mother raised him in a manner that manifested the ideal parent-child relationship. He played the lute, and was a good archer.

Confucius worked as a tax collector for a while, and when he lost his mother, he observed his proper filial duty, venerating her memory. He eventually became a teacher, and then a government adviser. He is supposed to have married, and fathered a son and daughter.

---

[19]http://www.biography.com/people/confucius-9254926. Accessed March 28,2014

At a time when there was great emphasis on State control and law, Confucius thought that the ancestral values from the Zhou dynasty ought to be applied. He believed that every human was basically civilized and cultured, having learned to be so from centuries of wisdom, transmitted from generation to generation. Such achievement, however, was not possible on an individual basis, but only as a society. In human society, people function at the optimum only by working together: each individual dependent upon the contributions of others, as she herself also contributes to the societal well-being. These relationships include parents, children, aunts, uncles, grandparents, ancestors, teachers, government ministers, and all other relatives. Confucius envisaged the perfect society as functions under what he termed **THE FIVE GREAT RELATIONSHIPS.** Several factors influence relationships, among them age, social status or family connection, and thus create a sort of hierarchy of importance. They may be represented by the following schema:

Five Key Relationships	**Appropriate Virtues**
Father-son	Filial piety
Ruler-subject	Loyalty
Elder Brother-Younger brother	Brotherliness
Husband-wife	Love and obedience
Older Friend-Younger friend	Faithfulness

Father-Son (Loving-reverential): This is the most important of the family relations, and is an expression of the Parent-Child relationship. As parents are supposed to teach their children moral values and look after their education, even finding good marriage partners when they become of age, so too children must reciprocate by being dutiful offspring, caring for parents in their old-age. When parents die, they ought to be venerated, through the upkeep of their graves, or having their photographs honored at a home-altar. This forms the paradigm for many relationships, among them the teacher and student, employer and employee, etc.

Elder brother-Younger brother (gentle/respectful): The eldest brother has an authority that may be considered almost like a father over his siblings, and the relationship of mutual duties not unlike that of the first relationship.

Husband-Wife (Good/listening): In this relationship, the husband is protector and breadwinner, with the wife looking after the welfare of her husband.

Older Friend-Younger Friend (considerate/deferential): This is essentially a mentoring relationship, along the lines of a teacher-student connection.

Ruler-subject (benevolent/loyal): Since the primary unit for Confucian values begins in the family, the father-son relationship is placed at the top of the hierarchy. Sometimes, however, the ruler-subject replaces it. The relationship is essentially based on the father-son paradigm, for after all, a good ruler is like a father to his subjects who are like his children.

The above hierarchy reflects itself in society in how people treat and show respect to each other, with good manners being extremely important. The goal is to promote harmonious interaction between the members of a society, i.e. the extended family, and this is achieved by a strict protocol of respect and good manners.

The Five Virtues

REN (JEN): Often translated as "humaneness," this teaches that we function successfully as a society when we are considerate of others. Politeness is a necessary result of this virtue.

LI: This may be seen as the observance of rituals in a proper manner, i.e., doing what is appropriate. This means that for every occasion, there is an appropriate word, and appropriate protocol of action—in short, showing good manners in society.

SHU: This is the idea that you do not do to others what you would not like done to you, and because of its negative wording, is often called "the silver rule."

XIAO: This is the virtue of loyalty, obedience and care that must be shown to family members, based upon the hierarchy of the FIVE RELATIONSHIPS.

WEN: Everyone in society should be involved in a creative pursuit, and this is something that one does at leisure.

Major Texts
Confucius himself left no written texts, but there are collections of pithy sayings and anecdotes that are said to have been compiled by his students after his death. Among these are the **LUNYU** ("Analects"), and the **WUJING**(Five Classics). This literature was to become central to the Chinese educational system, and form the basis for the civil service examination.

Quotations from the Analects of Confucius
[1:6] The Master said: "A young man should serve his parents at home and be respectful to elders outside his home. He should be earnest and truthful, loving all, but become intimate with his innate good-heartedness. After doing this, if he has energy to spare, he can study literature and the arts."

[1:10] Zi Qin asked Zi Gong: "When our teacher (Confucius) arrives in any country, he invariably finds out everything about its government. Does he seek this information? Or is it given to him? Zi Gong said, "Our teacher gets it by being cordial, upright, courteous, frugal, and humble. His way of getting information is quite different from that of other men."

[5:12] Zi Gong said: "What I don't want done to me, I don't want to do to others."

[7:25] The Master taught four things: Culture, correct action, loyalty and trust.

Key Interpreters of Confucius

Perhaps the two most famous interpreters of Confucian thought are Mengzi (Meng-tzu, 372-289 BCE) and Xunzi (Hsun-tzu, 310-220 BCE). Neither met Confucius, nor did they know each other, but Xunzi was aware of the writings of Mengzi (often referred to by the anglicized form of his name, Mencius).

These two transmitted Confucian material, and added their own interpretations and philosophies. Their writings were used by later scholars in Confucian thought to found several schisms within the movement. A very concise analysis of the teachings may be said to be that humans are innately good, but can develop into better citizens of the world with attention to learning and philosophy from the ancient masters. These writings also betray influences of Buddhism and Daoism, two paths that contain elements that are not always in concordance with Confucian ideology.

Confucianism and Modernity

The Communist system of modern China, with its professed egalitarianism, seems to oppose many aspects of Confucianismthat promote a hierarchy of relationships. The modern system of education too leaves little room for what some see as archaic values in a world of technology and human rights. As such, at the onset ofcommunism, many temples were destroyed, and a western based system of education replaced Confucian curriculum. In the twenty-first century, however, there seems to be a softening of the opposition towards the movement, and there is seemingly some sort of harmonious mix. Today, in the hometown of Confucius, his birthday is celebrated with great pomp and glory. Singapore and Taiwan are some of the countries that have Confucian teachings as part of the school curriculum.

Chinese Buddhism

Buddhism is not native to China; it was brought there during the first and second centuries of the Common Era. Initially, many Buddhist concepts seemed in conflict with the native traditions. In Buddhism, the idea of reconstitution of the *skandhas* for a type of reincarnation was in contrast to the Chinese idea of a linear, single lifespan. The Buddhist idea of the *sangha* seemed to oppose the Chinese values on family life, and ancestor veneration. The idea of *anatta*(no-soul) was also in contrast to the Chinese idea of the permanent soul, and the independence of the *Sangha* was quite different to the Chinese idea of the control of the state over all institutions.

Yet, Buddhism proved itself to be open to accommodation, and in the same way that it evolved into different *yanas* (vehicles), so too in China, Buddhist institutions came under state control. The government allowed the monastic community to function, but regulated who could become a monk. The Mahayana form of Buddhism, with its more liberal approach to the incorporation of alien ideas, became popular in China.

An esoteric tantric form, often referred to as *Mizong* or *Tang-mi*, was the result of the morphing of Buddhism to incorporate ideas from Chinese indigenous religious ideas. Among such ideas are there are some scriptures known as *Tantras*, containing great secrets, that on their own, can lead to enlightenment, as long as they are studied under a capable teacher. Among the ideas is that a teaching monk, a LAMA, can chose his future incarnation. The Dalai Lama is the head of the Tibetan school. The Chinese government has opposed his appointment, stating that is has its own incarnation and therefore another Dalai Lama. This tension has spread to the international political scene where the reception of the Dalai Lama by heads of state is often protested by the Chinese government.

GUANGHUA BUDDHIST TEMPLE, BEIJING, CHINA

In addition to the esoteric forms of Buddhism, CHAN (Zen) and *Pure Land Buddhism* are also popular. *Chan Buddhism* focuses on meditation under the guidance of a master. *Pure Land Buddhism* teaches that one does not have to struggle for enlightenment in this life, but should rather try to reach a stage of rebirth in a type of Paradise. This is possible by faith in the Compassionate Buddha. Life in this paradise eventually leads to enlightenment.

Under the SANJIAO concept noted at the beginning of this chapter, many Chinese incorporate ideas from Daoism, Confucianism and Buddhism to carve a path for themselves. Modern China also knows Islam and Christianity as religions. Islam reached China quite early, and some legends even state that the religion was brought there by one of Muhammad's companions, Sa'd bin Abi Waqqas. Christianity is a much later introduction, being brought by missionaries in the sixteenth century. There is a new movement, Falun Gong, or Falun Dafa, introduced to China in 1992, based on principles of Buddhism. Founded by Li Hongzhi, who currently lives in the United States, this movement claims that "It is a discipline in which "assimilation to the highest qualities of the universe—Zhen, Shan, Ren (Truthfulness, Compassion, Forbearance)—is the foundation of practice. Practice is guided by these supreme qualities, and based on the very laws which underlie the development of the cosmos."[20]Since 1999, the Chinese government has labelled the organization as a threat to social stability. Human rights organizations claim that members of *Falun Dafa* are routinely subjected to harassment.

Glossary

Analects	One of the writings based on the teachings of Confucius.
Chi-Kung	See Qigong
Civil Religion	A system wherein the leaders are lay people and the institutions are state governed rather than independent churches.
Confucianism	A holistic way of thinking that combines religion, ancestor reverence, and humanist values.
Confucius	Anglicized name of Kong Qiu, who lived from 551-479 BCE.
Chuang Tzu	See Zhuangzi
Daoism	A movement attributed to Laozi.
Dao De Jing	A short book of eighty-one chapters, allegedly written by Laozi.
Expiation	The act of making amends through ritual, reparation or any other form.

---

[20]http://en.falundafa.org/introduction.html. Accessed March 28, 2014.

Falun Dafa   A philosophical/religious movement in Modern China.

The Five Great Relationships: A Confucian construct that works on a hiearchical relationship structured thus: Father-son, Elder Brother-Younger brother, Husband-wife, Older friend-younger friend, Ruler-subject.

Hexagram   A figure of six stacked horizontal lines used in the I-Ching.

Humanism   A concept wherein the focus is more on the value and agency of humans than on gods.

I-Ching   A Chinese concept based on the Yang-Yinphilosophy, using hexagrams that, when properly interpreted, offer guidance for the individual in the choices of action.

Jen   See Ren.

Kong Qiu   See Confucius.

Li   One of the five virtues. Translated as observance of ritual in a proper manner.

Li Shiqian   A sixth century sage who coined the term "Sanjiao."

Mengzi/Mencius (372-289 BCE)   One of the famous interpreters of Confucian thought.

Mizong   An esoteric form of Buddhism, based on the Tantras. Also known as Tang-mi.

Qigong   "Life Energy." This can be obtained by following Taiji exercises.

Ren   One of the five virtues, translated often as humaneness.

Sanjiao   The three teachings, referring to Confucianism, Daoism and Buddhism.

Shu   One of the five virtues, also known as the Silver rule. It is the concept of not doing unto others what you would not like done unto you.

Tai Chi/Taiji   A set of exercises said to promote better health, often done in slow motion.

Tang-mi   Also known as *Mizong*, an esoteric form of Tantric Buddhism.

Tantra   Scriptures from Chinese Buddhism.

Wen   One of the five virtues, meaning that everyone in society should be involved in a creative pursuit.

Wu Wei   The principle of "non-action"— uncontrived action, living by or going along with the true nature of the world, allowing things to take their natural course.

Xiao   One of the five virtues, denoting loyalty and obedience.

Xunzi/Shun-tzu (310-220 BCE)   One of the famous interpreters of Confucian thought.

Yang   Heaven, one of the polarities in Chinese religion/philosophy, often associated with the male.

Yin   Earth, or one of the polarities in Chinese religion/philosophy, often associated with the female.

Zen, Shan, Ren: Truthfulness, Compassion, and Forbearance—foundational values of *Falun Dafa*.

Zhuangzi   A fourth-century Daoist Teacher.

JAPANESE RELIGIONS

Professor Wilburn Hansen, San Diego State University

The Way of Syncretism

SHINTO GATE[21]

---

[21]http://www.onmarkproductions.com/html/buddhism.shtml. Accessed March 7, 2013.

Learning Goals

- *Discuss the concept of kami and kami-belief*
- *Present summary of Japanese folk beliefs*
- *Utilize and explain terminology relative to such beliefs*
- *Explain early history of Kami Cults*
- *Discuss early reception of Buddhism*
- *Outline concepts of sacred space and worship*
- *Present overview of Japanese Mountain Worship*
- *Discuss Rituals*
- *Analyze the concept of modernity, challenge of Science*
- *Discuss relation between Religion and Politics*
- *Describe relation between community and individual in terms of ethical perspective*
- *Summarize some New Religious Movements in Japan*

Introduction

In the past, most Japanese historical accounts had been preoccupied with a 'single unbroken line of sovereigns' stressing Japanese cultural uniqueness and ignoring or undervaluing the culture Japan had received from China and India. Along with this came a tendency to focus on the economics and politics of the ruling classes while attending to religion as a mere cultural adornment. However, a closer look at even this version of Japanese history shows that the supposed 'single unbroken line of sovereigns' is in fact a lineage of *priestly* rulers extending as far back as perhaps the third century CE when the Japanese kingdom of Yamatai, according to Chinese dynastic history, was reported to be governed by hereditary rulers.

Late in that century, a kingdom based in the Yamato region of central Japan emerged under a succession of kings and queens. This was the historical impetus for the single line of descent theory. The preoccupation with cultural uniqueness gained more intensity in the Tokugawa period (1603-1868), owing to a nativist movement intent upon establishing difference and distance from continental cultures older and more advanced than Japan's. Twentieth-century developments only added to this preoccupation by defining Japan by its unique national polity, that is, the emperor system. This emphasis on nationalistic identity politics is currently being challenged by scholars offering theories that shift the focus of Japanese religious studies to the native Japanese belief in *kami*, indigenous deities, rather than on the Shinto mythology connecting *kami* with the imperial court. This new focus offers a broader foundation for imagining a national personality that could effectively influence subsequent historical development. In other words, religion, particularly folk and popular religion, is being seen more and more as an essential aspect of Japanese culture.

Worldview
The worship of **kami** and kami belief lies at the foundation of Japanese culture. **Kami** are mystical, superhuman forces that have the mysterious power to create, enrich, prolong, or renew any form of life existing in the here and now. The earliest signs of this *kami* worship can be seen in female clay figurines or phallic rods excavated in pre-agricultural stone-age sites. Later, as well as at present, worship of *kami* can be seen in community festivals and individual devotional activities.

Life affirming agricultural *kami* worship started in prehistoric times and continues to this day. Natural vitality and the creative powers responsible for sustaining it are treasured and worshiped by people in farming communities. Accordingly, those things dead and dying are considered bad luck, dangerous, and sources of impurity that must be kept away or permanently disposed of. Abhorrence of death and the impurity that accompanies it and threatens to spread decay is the opposite side of the life-affirming Japanese proclivity. These all-important matters of maintaining the purity of life and staving off death and the impurities that come with it have from ancient times been entrusted to experts in the field, that is, shamans, spirit mediums, or ritual specialists of various sorts.

AMATERASU, KAMI OF THE SUN, EMERGING FROM THE CAVE

Family or clan tutelary deities as well as deities of nature, *kami*, were routinely invoked and worshiped for their divine assistance; however, this usually required some medium or ritual specialist to connect the worshiper with the worshiped. The ancestors of the first emperors were originally the most powerful and effective mediums between humans and *kami* and eventually came to be considered as *kami* themselves and thus inherently divine. Buddhism, when it was imported from the continent, added to this native emphasis on the need for ritual mediums and priests. Confucianism, another continental import, also contributed to this native Japanese tendency, owing to Confucian ethical teachings that advocated hierarchy and awareness of one's place within that hierarchy; that is, unqualified humans were required to go through proper channels to importune the more important *kami*, a task thatrequired trained and approved go-betweens.

Finally, in general the Japanese religious worldview leans toward particularism as opposed to universalism. There are a vast number of *kami* that have small, defined roles of spiritual governance. *Amaterasu Omikami*, the most well-known of Japanese *kami* as the mythical progenitor of the imperial family, is not omnipotent. This particularist tendency made room for the import and inclusion of various foreign religions, allowing Buddhism, Confucianism, Daoism, and much later Christianity to be practiced alongside native religious practices.

Japanese Folk Beliefs

Scholars have for some time attempted to reconstruct historically, as well as by other means, a presumed ancient Japanese animistic belief in superhuman spirits, in essence, traditional folk beliefs supposedly rooted in time immemorial. Usually this reconstruction causes the de-emphasis of written traditions dependent upon previously literate foreign cultures, and directs the scholar toward stories found in native oral traditions. Most of the stories surviving and focused on for such efforts were collected one hundred years ago when an ambitious Japanese folklore movement was headed by the scholar and ethnologist Yanagida Kunio, who feared that the rapid modernization of Japan would mean the loss of traditional beliefs and values. Yanagida focused on storytelling bound up within the daily life activities in rural Japanese villages assuming that these stories would contain themes that reflected timeless native Japanese values, principles, and aspirations. Those folktales he collected did not focus on grandiose political mythology nor did they explain the creation of the world or the sacred purpose of the human being, rather they spoke of beneficent and relatively humble *kami* who guarded such things as the home, the hearth, and even the family outhouse.

A sampling of such stories should render some of the flavor of Japanese folk beliefs. There are quaint stories of unique Japanese creatures such as the *kappa*, an amphibious boy who lives hiding in rivers. His coloring is green and he has a bowl-shaped indentation on the top of his head, which he must keep moist. Stories of this creature are often used to explain unforeseen misfortune or are used to find a scapegoat for those who would rather not admit to certain social transgressions. For example, this *kappa* could be blamed for unwanted pregnancies and also for deformed children, becoming the basis of a rationale for abandoning and killing those children who would prove to be burdens or social embarrassments.

Another such creature that the Japanese folk stories usually scape-goat is the part-bird but mostly human creature called the *tengu*. Any misfortune that occurred in the uncharted wilderness of Japan could be attributed to this creature. From the Japanese medieval period onward accusing social enemies of being *tengu* in disguise also became a standard way of vilifying suspicious strangers, especially shady Buddhist monks who seemed beyond the power of society to control.

Some non-mythical creatures also came to take on supernatural identities in Japan. Foxes gained a reputation for being mischievous tricksters made all the more dangerous by stories of their shape-shifting ability and their assumed delight in fooling humans. There are many stories of women who appeared as foxes in human form determined on ruining honest but simple men. Cats are also seen as tricksters, and the animal called *tanuki*, which looks like a large raccoon, the Japanese word often translated as raccoon-dog or sometimes badger, is even more famous for taking joy in deceiving, killing, or otherwise harming humans on a whim. Also in this country village Japanese imaginary demons lurked everywhere. Folklore attests to traditional forms for a variety of Japanese demons. Some are depicted as having horns or tusks and others are typically red or blue.

There are also famous she-demons, shriveled old women called *yamamba*, or mountain hags,that have their own brand of malevolence prepared for the unfortunates who should cross their paths. However, there are exceptions such as the kindly *yamamba* who raised the legendary super boy *Kintarô* renowned for his strength.

DEPICTION OF A TENGU, ON THE FRONT COVER OF THE AUTHOR'S ETHNOGRAPHIC WORK, PUBLISHED BY UNIVERSITY OF HAWAII PRESS IN 2008.

A MODERN CERAMIC TANUKI DOG[22]

Early Historical Developments: The Rise of the Imperial Kami Cults and the Early Reception of Buddhism

About the time of writing of the oldest extant Japanese histories, *Kojiki* (712) and *Nihon Shoki* (720), two imperially commissioned documents supporting the heavenly lineage mythology of the imperial family, imperial *kami* cults enjoyed official state support while Buddhism was both supported but also restricted by that same state government. Any type of Buddhism that served the interests of the imperial court and was compatible with the established Japanese worldview sanctioned by that court was encouraged. Buddhist teachings that were incompatible were restricted or discarded. This litmus test for survival served to adapt Bud-

---

[22]http://www.onmarkproductions.com/html/buddhism.shtml. Accessed March 7, 2014.

dhismand prepare the way for a distinctively Japanese Buddhist thought and culture.

The imperial family's ancestral *kami*, Amaterasu Omikami, was originally simply referred to as the sun deity. Over time this deity was personalized and during the reign of Emperor Temmu (631-686) she came to be known as *Amaterasu Omikami*, "Great Heaven-Illuminating Deity." She had been worshiped simply as the heavenly ancestor of the imperial clan, which was of course by blood or by service related to the other clans, but was still simply one clan deity among many. However, as Emperor Temmu and his successors proceeded to build a nation-state headed by the emperor, *Amaterasu Omikami* and her shrine at Ise came to occupy a place above all other clan *kami* and shrines.

It was at this time that the hierarchy of *kami* solidified with *Amaterasu Omikami* taking precedence over all other clan *kami* as well as nature *kami* and the regional tutelary and folk *kami*. A schedule of *kami* rites and festivals was established and regulated in the government instituted *Taihô* code (701), which included an article concerning *kami* worship. This code demonstrates the rise of Japanese religious group consciousness and is an early expression of Japanese thought taking form in the beliefs and practices of a developing system of *kami* worship.

In this same time period Buddhism, officially recognized as entering the country in the year 552, was receiving both official patronage and strict government regulation. The Code for Clerics of 624 is an example of strict regulation of this foreign born tradition. The code strictly regulated the activities of the members of the Buddhist order in Japan. Its dictates were strongly punitive with each of its twenty-seven articles containing a range of penalties for violating that particular article. At this time the propagation of Buddhist teachings among the populace was also prohibited. The government hoped to prevent popular dissatisfaction with present standards from developing into mass resistance based on the promises of the Buddhist teachings. Still, propagation to the masses was occurring; for example, the Buddhist monk *Gyôki* (668-749) became famous among the people for his charitable works and was censured in 717 for 'inciting the masses' in violation of the Code for Clerics.

IMAGE OF GYOKI

The patronage that was extended to Buddhism at this time can be best recognized in the increase in temple construction activity. In 624 there were forty-six temples in Japan but by 692 the number reached five hundred forty-five, increasing by more than ten-fold in less than seventy years. Temple building became popular for a variety of reasons. The emperors and their courts built temples because they were thought to ensure the protection of the nation by *buddhas* and *bodhisattvas*. The building of private clan temples also became popular as these were thought to guarantee the peace and prosperity of the clan by serving as monuments venerating clan ancestors. Temple building came to replace the older practice of tomb building using massive mounds of earth, which the government had started to restrict. The introduction of the Buddhist custom of cremation around that time also helped contribute to the decline of ostentatious tombs. Buddhist images were also included in these temples to enhance their ability to protect the clan. This trend in clan temple building is an example of how Buddhism in Japan became associated with ancestor veneration, demonstrating once again how the Japanese adapted Buddhism to suit native purposes.

The imperial capital was moved to Nara in 710 ushering in the *Nara* period (710-794). The Buddhism of the Nara period is defined by the so-called **Six Schools of Nara Buddhism**. The Six Schools together constituted a curriculum of Buddhist scholarship. The texts and teachings of the six Nara schools as well as other texts and teachings imported during this time period would later develop into the sects called **Tendai**, **Shingon**, **Pure Land**, **True Pure Land**, **Nichiren**, and **Zen**, those that still best represent the diversity of Japanese Buddhism to this day. While Japanese priests in *Nara* gained an intellectual understanding of the religion, they had not yet made the teachings a unified comprehensible philosophy truly their own. That is to say, at this point Buddhism was a huge collection of foreign knowledge on which the Japanese had yet to put their particular stamp.

Later Historical Development: Kami and Buddha
In the late Heian period of Japan, which includes the tenth and eleventh centuries, the imperial system of autocratic rule went into decline and power spread out to aristocratic clans then further branched out to warrior families in the provinces. The centralized system of *kami* worship collapsed and the *kami* cults of different political and social groups: the court, local elites, warrior groups, and occupational groups began to develop independently. *Kami* worship was becoming decentralized and no longer just a tool of the imperial government. This trend continued into the medieval period (12th – 16th centuries) when the imperial family lost most of their political power to the warrior shogunal houses. In this same period Buddhism flourished and spread throughout all sectors of Japanese society in many new and diverse forms. Although this period is known as the greatest period of religious innovation for Buddhism, *kami* cults in this same period also developed into independent religious institutions to which current Shinto lineages can reliably and historically trace their origins.

This is also the time period when *kami*and Buddhist deities were amalgamating and combinatory cults became prevalent. As a result, many objects of popular worship were perceived as having a dual identity, both as *kami* and as buddhas. Accompanying this merger of *kami* and buddha, theological Shinto doctrines of increasing sophistication were formulated and written down. These two trends and the interplay between them shaped medieval *kami* cults into institutions that would create the Shinto establishment we think of today.

During the prehistoric period, *kami* ritual was a local or clan-based practice that followed the cyclical patterns of nature and society. Its aim was to ensure the prosperity and peaceful existence of the community, be it clan or state. *Kami* worship was predominantly a communal affair that did not address the concerns of individuals. However, once *kami* became widely identified as manifestations of Buddhist deities, their function came to resemble that of buddhas and bodhisattvas. Individual believers began addressing their hopes and wishes for this life and the next to *kami*, just as they had previously been doing to Buddhist deities.

The distinction between private and public *kami* ritual had become vague in the Heian period just preceding this; for example, the clan (private) rituals of the Fujiwara family at **Kasuga** shrine had become part of the official (public) ritual calendar. However, the blurring also started to move in the other direction as individuals start performing their private devotional practices at public communal shrines. The collapse of the imperial system of funding official shrines by assigning households to be taxed by certain shrines fell into disuse and shrines became more autonomous as they found they had to find their own sources of revenue. This situation forced the shrines into attempting to attract believers from beyond their original communities, and new private rituals were fashioned and propagated for this purpose.

These ritual and social changes required theological explanation and medieval schools of *kami* thought such as *Ryōbu Shinto* and *Ise Shinto* arose. The theory-building techniques of these schools were based on Buddhological precedents. It was in this context that the term 'Shinto,' which previously had been little more than a synonym of *kami*, first began to take on sectarian meanings. Only then did the notion arise that the *kami* were the most appropriate deities to bring salvation to Japan and the Japanese. In this process we can see the seeds of the anti-Buddhism of the early-modern period being sown already in the medieval period. By the end of the medieval period *kami* worship as Shinto had been transformed almost beyond recognition from the private or public *kami* cult worship of the classical period.

KASUGA SHRINE

In modern Japanese society, Shinto and Buddhism appear as two clearly distinct entities. However, this distinction was imposed on the Japanese religious landscape only by the 'shrine temple separation edicts' of 1868 and the ensuing wave of anti-Buddhist destruction that followed. During the pre-modern period, Buddhist and *kami*beliefs intermingled to give rise to a distinctive religious universe. It is important to remember that this state of amalgamation has been the norm throughout most of the history of Japanese religion; the present state of the separation of Shinto and Buddhism has lasted little more than a century. Thus the amalgamation of *kami* cults and Buddhism is the central topic in the history of the *kami* in Japan.

It is not accurate to regard these amalgamated cults and beliefs simply as an overlay of Buddhist thought and practice put on top in some loose manner of ancient indigenous cults and beliefs. In spite of what many Shinto theologians have claimed, Shinto has not existed throughout Japanese history as the original essentially immutable native religious tradition. Likewise, Buddhism in Japan is quite different from early Indian Buddhism. This foreign import has undergone such radical changes during its long presence in Japan that it is understandable that scholars express doubts whether its Japanese forms can still properly be called Buddhism at all.

Sacred Space and Nature Worship

Agriculture was the foundation of life in ancient Japan. Many shrines were dedicated to the *kami* of mountains who are said to bring the rains and maintain the flow of rivers and streams. In the Heian period there were fifty-three such shrines around the capital and before that the ancient capital of Nara alone had twenty-nine. To the ancient Japanese, mountains were linked to agriculture, the *kami* of the mountain and the *kami* of the rice field were the same. Many contemporary farmers still say that the mountain *kami* comes down in early spring to guard the rice field and returns to the mountain in the fall after the harvest. Villagers echo this belief and strengthen it with seasonal rituals of welcoming and sending off the *kami*.

Mountains in Japan also have an ancient connection to the souls of the dead, and beliefs of that sort have played an important role in the development of ancestor worship. There are two basic—if contradictory beliefs—supporting this connection. One ancient belief has the mountains as the abode of the dead, and reflects the ancient custom of burial on the mountain. The other belief is that the mountains are merely the meeting ground between this world and the next. This is predicated on stories that heaven or the other world exists some place beyond the mountains. In the latter belief complex, the mountain serves as the nexus between this world and the other world, the present life and the life yet-to-come. This tradition makes it reasonable that native shaman and Buddhist ritualists alike would choose to practice in the mountains in order to be near that sacred energy and to facilitate communication with beings from the other world. Although mountains are seen as life-generating forces that provide the water and the divine *kami* protection for rice, they are more commonly known as the world of the dead or the meeting place of the living and the dead—a gateway between this world and the next. In all cases, mountains in Japan are sacred spaces charged with superhuman energies.

Japanese Mountain Worship: Shugendô

Shugendô refers to a religious tradition, still practiced today, that developed its present religious structure after ancient Japanese beliefs concerning the sacrality of mountains were influenced by foreign religious traditions such as Buddhism and Taoism. The core of this religious tradition consists of magico-religious ritual activities performed in response to the religious needs or demands of people in local communities. Those qualified to perform these ritual activities are called *yamabushi*, shugendô practitioners who have acquired superhuman spiritual powers by repeated ascetic cultivation practiced in the mountains.

Yamabushi traveled widely throughout the mountains of Japan during the medieval period, but in the early modern period, in part because of the restrictive policies of the Tokugawa period (1603-1868) government, they were forced to settle down and become a regular part of the local community. However, when this occurred rural communities in Japan already had Shinto shrines dedicated to the local guardian *kami* and Buddhist priests took care of all funerary rites. The role undertaken by the *yamabushi* who settled in these communities consisted of responding to the various mundane needs of the common people. In other words, their religious time and effort was spent dealing with problems of disease and daily life, offering religious services such as fortunetelling and divination, receiving oracles through mediums, offering prayers, and performing exorcisms. In effect, in the Tokugawa period *yamabushi* were responsible for offering practical worldly benefits within the context of the religious activities of the country populace, and should be seen as important figures in that context.

HENRY STEWART, THE FIRST NON-JAPANESE TO BECOME, IN
2004, A YAMABUSHI[23]

Ritual

There are a large variety of rituals practiced in Japanese religion,
as should be expected of a rubric that consists of centuries of multiple traditions with origins in cultures separated by vast distances
both temporally and spatially. However, it might be helpful and
informative to describe seven different types of rituals, or ritual
structures, that for the most part, cross boundaries and are representative of multiple religious traditions practiced in Japan. To
begin there are: rituals for achieving intimacy with the object of
worship, that is, a buddha, bodhisattva, or a *kami*; rituals for communication with the object of worship; rituals performed to
achieve identification with the object of worship; rituals seeking to
achieve the power to manipulate these deities; rituals to receive
oracles from deities; rituals of prayer; and lastly, rituals of exor-
cism.

---

[23]http://www.mfa-gunma.com/en/index.php?go=About-Instructor. Accessed March 7, 2014

WOOD CORE IMAGE OF A BODDHISATVA, C. 775

Modernity: Religion and the Challenge of Science

Western scientific thinking representing the advances of modernity
trickled into Japan throughout the Tokugawa period and the power
and effectiveness of the new ideas and methods had a clear impact
on Japanese religion. However, those modern ideas challenged
some of the very foundations of Japanese identity. Many Japanese
intellectuals were not eager to jettison thousands of years of indigenous wisdom, nor the religious paradigms which for centuries had
helped the Japanese to make sense of the workings of the physical
and spiritual cosmos, and which they had used to explain and emphasize the unique importance of the land, nation, and people of
Japan. Instead, what occurred was a flurry of creative activity evi-

denced in the writings of early modern and modern Japanese intellectuals working in the fields of religion and the various sciences.

What is of particular interest is the role that identity politics played in modern Japanese attempts to redefine space in reaction to the new conditions and situations brought on by modernity. This politically inspired redefinition ranged from new theories concerning the physical nature of the islands of Japan themselves, new theories concerning the meaning and definition of East Asia, and also new theories explaining the importance of the Japanese role in the greater cosmos. The inevitable universal acceptance of certain advances in scientific understanding caused Japanese intellectuals to recontour that science to accommodate and reinforce various homegrown ideas based on religious definitions of Japanese identity.

The widespread acceptance of superstitions in Japan in the nineteenth century was deemed a problem by the Japanese government intent on modernizing society upon Western models and fostering scientific development and technology. The government started an anti-superstition campaign with warnings against, and penalties enforced upon shamans, faith healers, exorcists, fortune-tellers as well as the people who sought out their services. As part of this campaign what had previously been called *tengu* or fox possession was classified as mental illness. Government officials scientifically relabeled these practices to accommodate Western medical diagnoses; for example, a shaman who believed herself to be possessed by a fox was to be diagnosed with a delusional condition with an impressive Greek name. Shamanism was to be replaced by psychiatry, and one sociological result was that the predominantly male profession of psychiatry began replacing the predominantly female profession of shaman.

In actuality, the Japanese government at this time was not trying to eliminate all beliefs in non-scientific supernatural spirits. It was merely trying to control the belief in spirits. The government would still require that all Japanese people believe in some spirits, for instance, the *kami* of the imperial family and their ancestors. In short, government intervention was intended to clarify the authorized 'superstitions' from unauthorized ones. In this vein perhaps,present-day authorized 'superstition' can still be recognized in the enshrined spirits of the patriotic Japanese war dead in **Yasukuni** shrine in Tokyo. In other words, even in the twentieth and twenty-first centuries in Japan spirits can be manipulated for political purposes.

YASUKUNI SHRINE

Religion and Politics

As some scholars have asserted, the pursuit of religious symbols and practices that actually provide benefit in this lifetime can be seen as the 'common religion' of the Japanese people. This is not a feature that is subject to embarrassment; that is, it is not wrong to practice religion for personal gain, on the contrary, in Japan one might be considered foolish to practice a religion that offers no worldly reward. The Japanese men and women who have been responsible for governing the islands of Japan for the last two millennia are representative of that sentiment.

The first imperial histories that contain the mythology in support of the imperial family and support their divine right to govern are evidence of this practical tendency in Japanese religiosity. The fact

that Buddhism was imported from the continent by powerful aristocratic families with political interests who saw the religion as
advanced continental philosophy and technology also attest to this
opinion regarding the practical and political value of religion. Perhaps the clearest example of the connection between religion and
politics in Japan can be seen in the postwar American occupation
government's insistence that the Emperor himself deny his divinity
to the Japanese people. Certainly the continuing problems surrounding visits by the Japanese Prime Minister to the *Yasukuni*
shrine also highlight the deep association between religion and politics in Japan.

Religion and Ethics: The Community and The Individual
Japanese ethics are fundamentally rooted in family and group relationships. As such, it is important that all members of families and
groups; for example, company staff or members of schools, are
aware of their position in the hierarchy, and along with that the duties, responsibilities, and courtesies that accompany that station.
This emphasis on relationships and the debts and other obligations
that cement them is most likely based on ancient clan organization
and the rules that accompanied it, but it is also surely reinforced by
Confucian dictates imported from China well over a thousand
years ago.

Ethical decisions for the individual can be decided based on traditional or family values, but there are also a vast array of specific
Buddhist teachings which can be consulted if one is deeply invested in any such tradition. Choices might also be determined by fortunetelling techniques influenced by Daoist teachings and astrolog-
ical charts originally from China but which flourished in Japan in a
native incarnation known as **Onmyôdô**, or Yin-Yang divination.
These teachings survived in the form of communal folk religion or
small lineage cults. Prayer to native *kami* or other forms of divine
advice or assistance in decision-making might also be sought after
and received according to the beliefs of the individual Japanese.

Modernity and Western idealization of individualism have affected
Japanese social relationships. Disaffected members of groups or

those who for whatever reason feel alienated from society have gained more freedom to form different identities or associations previously unavailable to them. One avenue of escape or freedom from traditional societal ties, which gained popularity in the twentieth century, was to join a New Religion; however, we should be clear that this is by no means the sole reason for the popularity of these New Religions. Still in many cases, the decision to break with the traditional group merely resulted in leaving one group identity for a new, nontraditional group identity.

New Religious Movements
Japanese society started modernizing rapidly in the mid-nineteenth century. Religious communities were also forced to undergo drastic changes. While traditional religions and religious institutions rooted in village communities were sent into decline, religions in urban areas gained in strength. In the twentieth century a number of new religious movements attracted followers and created many new active religious communities.

There are as many as three thousand organizational units in Japan which can classified as an NRM or *New Religious Movement*, and anywhere between ten to twenty percent of the present Japanese populace is said to be involved in them. The founders of these groups are not usually people of high social standing but rather those who have overcome some type of personal hardship that gave them special insight, and also have had some unsatisfying involvement in some other religious group. Therefore this New Religion is usually syncretic and eclectic making it difficult to identify too closely with any one particular religious tradition. As a result, any one New Religion can come with an eclectic collection of religious teachings.

In general Japanese New Religions are optimistic and world affirming. Success and happiness in this life is valued and promised. Emphasis is usually placed on quick relief from personal suffering and active caring for the suffering of the rest of the world. Being Japanese, the deities who deliver this happiness and relief from suffering are often described as buddhas or *kami*. Many of these groups tout the explicit goals of physical health and wealth, while

others seek to perfect Japanese society or else seek to create a uto-
pian society within Japan. Some of these groups emphasize traditional objects of worship such as the spirits of the dead or specific
ancestors. Sometimes the causes of problems are seen as internal
feelings and emotions and problems are overcome using psychological methods instead of traditional apotropaic techniques directed at evil spirits. Sometimes these groups require the formation
of new social units while still relying on typical Japanese group-
oriented psychology as well as the traditional desire to promote
harmonious community action.

The new religions that formed after the 1970s address different
concerns than the older "New Religions." Many of the previous
New Religions in Japan had often seemed directed toward older
women and elderly couples. The New Religions typically attract
young people looking for more idealistic and fulfilling life goals
than what they see as the standard goals set by consumer-oriented,
materialist society. This idealism tends to separate the members of
New Religions from their traditional social groups, causing them to
drop out of 'normal' society. Sometimes magic and miracles can
also play an important part of the religious appeal of these New
Religions.

The new groups also claim to offer an opportunity for the individual to fulfill his or her potential. This attracts young people who
are seeking to discover their inner being and develop their own
spirituality, hoping to bring about a spiritual transformation within
themselves. Often meditation, ascetic training, and psychotherapy
are essential practices in these religious groups. These New Religions can end up combining modern psychological theory and
practice with ancient religious teachings coupled with ascetic and
mystical practices from a variety of ancient religious cultures not
limited to Japan.

The most well-known example of this type of religion is **Aum
shinrikyô**which started in the mid-eighties as a Hindu, Buddhist,
Tantric mix of meditative and ascetic practices borrowing from
various theories about enlightenment and spiritual energy. Aum
had a blind enlightened guru, **Shoko Asahara**, and built up a following with creative marketing. Their recruitment techniques in-

cluded *manga* and *anime* with religious and science fiction topics that attracted young people. Asahara mingled with famous religious leaders such as the Dalai Lama, and in the late eighties his group seemed to be flourishing, although behind the scenes there were charges that members were coerced into staying and pressured into contributing large sums of money to Asahara.

SHOKO ASAHARA

Some leaders of the group started to react to mounting societal opposition by forcibly silencing those who would speak out against them. Asahara and other members of the leadership ran unsuccessfully for seats in the Japanese Diet in the 1990s. In response to society's rejection, they started producing and stockpiling chemicals. In March 1995, members of Aum released lethal sarin gas into the Tokyo subway system, killing twelve and injuring fifty-four. If the attack had succeeded as planned tens of thousands could have been killed or injured.

As one of the most developed countries in the world, Japan has practitioners of many religions residing there. There are outsiders who have converted to Shintoism and Buddhism, and there are Japanese, given the long history of Christianity and later, Islam, who practice, or have converted to these religions.

Glossary

Amaterasu Omikami:
> The Great Heaven-Illuminating Deity, that later became the major kami in Japan.

Aum Shinrikyô:
> A religious movement started by Shoko Asahara in Japan in the mid-eighties as a Hindu, Buddhist, Tantric mix of meditative and ascetic practices.

Kami
> Mystical, superhuman forces that have the mysterious power to create, enrich, prolong or re-new any form of life existing here and now.

Kappa
> An amphibious boy who lives hiding in rivers, and usually seen as a trickster figure.

Kintarô
> A superboy, raised by ***yamambas.*** He was noted for his strength.

Nechiren
> Form of Japanese Buddhism.

Onmyôdô
> A type of fortunetelling technique.

Pure Land Buddhism:
> Sect of Japanese Buddhism.

Shingon
> Sect of Japanese Buddhism.

Shugendô
> Religious tradition that involves concepts of the sacrality of mountains.

Tanuki
> A sort of large raccoon-dog, or badger, that can harm humans.

Tendai
> Sect of Japanese Buddhism.

Tengu   A part-bird but mostly human creature in Japanese folklore.

Yamabushi   *Shugendô* practitioners who have acquired super-human spiritual powers by repeated ascetic cultivation practiced in the mountains.

Yamamba   Shriveled old women, or mountain hags that are generally malevolent. There are exceptions to this norm, and some may be kindly.

Zen   Form of Japanese Buddhism.

JUDAISM

Khaleel Mohammed

"That which is hateful to you, do not unto another: This is the whole Torah. The rest is commentary — [and now] go study." (Saying attributed to Hillel, from Shabbos 31a)

A MENORAH AND A TORAH SCROLL

Learning Goals

- Provide very brief introduction to study of Judaism
- Explain TaNaKh, the acronym for the Hebrew Bible
- Discuss Biblical perspective of history
- Discuss Abraham and his impact on monotheistic traditions
- Provide a summary of the Exodus from Egypt
- Summarize history of Israel after Moses until the Exiles
- Outline concept of Messiah
- Explain Differences between Biblical and Rabbinic Judaism
- Provide overview of Medieval Jewish thought.
- Analyze Judaism in the modern period
- Discuss different denominations in Judaism
- Summarize the modern, academic approach to the Hebrew Scripture
- Discuss Zionism, modern Israel, Judaism in the United States
- Provide overview of Rituals, symbols, commemorations in Judaism
- Discuss Judaism's relationship to other religions

Introduction

Judaism is one of the oldest monotheist religions in the world. Its traditions are unique in the family of faiths that are known as the "Abrahamic paths" because its narratives are shared by Christianity, Islam and other faiths. Judaism is also unique in that Jews do not necessarily have to observe a form of religion, for the term "Jew" identifies a people rather than a set of religious constructs. The history of Judaism is more than four thousand years old, and as such, it is difficult to speak of any one Judaism. The Jewish people had adapted to different conditions in their existence, and as such, one has to be keenly aware of the living tradition, instead of seeking to learn Judaism from scriptures only. The material found in the Hebrew Bible, for example, is referred to as Biblical Judaism. This is quite different from Rabbinic Judaism as we will study in this chapter.

Historical Development

The stories of the beginning of the world, as found in the Hebrew Bible, have fascinated people for millennia. And in modern scholarship, a new question has arisen among academics: were the stories ever meant as literal truth? The parallel of those stories with the Babylonian myths, the theories of Zoroastrian influence on Judaism, the idea that early Judaism was more about henotheism, or monolatry rather than monotheism, all present a vast area of study for researchers. Since our presentation is based on a **phenomenological** approach, we are spared some of the more academic questions that challenge the confessional adherent.

Study of Judaism is not only restricted to the religious aspect, but also deals with the history of a people, much of which is recounted in the document known as the Hebrew Bible.

The Hebrew Bible

The Hebrew Bible is often referred to by an acronym: TaNaKh. This is a term used to refer to a collection of what were individual books, that reached their final form sometime around 200 BCE. Some traditions hold that Moses wrote the first five books—referred to as the **Torah** or the **Chumash**, or the **Pentateuch**. The acronym is thus: **T for Torah**, **Na for Nevi'im** (the Prophets) and **Kh for Ketuvim** (The Writings). One of the most oft-repeated commands in this collection is *zakhor*—to remember. For the Hebrew Bible is not just a book of ethics, but it is also history, explaining why things are the way they are, why Jews are considered to have a special covenant with God, why they are thus a chosen people.

The Composition of the TaNaKh

Torah	Nevi'im	Ketuvim
Genesis	Joshua	Psalms
Exodus	Judges	Proverbs
Leviticus	Samuel	Job
Numbers	Kings	Song of Songs
Deuteronomy	Isaiah	Ruth
	Jeremiah	Lamentations
	Ezekiel	Ecclesiastes
	Books of the Twelve:	Esther
	(Hosea, Joel, Amos,Obadiah,	Daniel
	Jonah, Micah, Nahum,	Ezra-Nehemiah
	Habakkuk, Zephaniah, Haggai,	Chronicles
	Zechariah, Malachi	

The first five books—i.e. the Torah/Chumash/Pentateuch—give us the story of creation, of the primordial human couple (Adam and Eve), of their fall from grace, Noah, and the early history of the Hebrews. It tells of the story of Abraham, the first preacher of monotheism, and his relocation to Canaan, of his descendants who relocated to Egypt, and then of Moses who had to rescue them from that land.

The next set of books, the PROPHETS are given this appellation because they are named after the Nevi'im—those who spoke to the Jewish people in God's name. Finally, there is the section known as THE WRITINGS, consisting of short stories and history that modern researchers often classify as not necessarily true.

The correct reference for the Jewish scriptures is either the *Hebrew Bible* or the *Tanakh*. The term "Old Testament" is a Christian coinage that indicates that the requirements of a previous testament have been replaced by a newer one. While this may be appropriate for Christian belief, it does not adhere to the objective outlook of the academic approach, and as such, we ought not use that term in the classroom. In medieval times, another word for the Tanakh was **Ha Miqra.** This is because the reading of scripture in liturgy was aloud—i.e., it was recited (the word *Miqra* means "that which is recited.")

Biblical History

The basic story, summarized here so as to launch into Judaism at the earliest opportunity, is that God creates the world in six cosmic days. And then God creates a primordial couple to live on earth in a state of bliss, on condition that they do not eat from one particular tree. A serpent tempts the female of the couple (Eve), whose partner (Adam) then follows suit, and they all get exiled from the state of Bliss. This is followed by the story of the children of Adam and Eve, of Cain killing Abel, which some have taken to represent the rivalry that existed between farmers and pastoral folk. There are then genealogical narratives that lead to the story of Noah and the Ark. Noah complies with God's directive to stow on the ark a pair of every living thing because of an impending flood. The purpose of the story is to explain the different races in the area to which the Hebrew Bible became meaningful. One of Noah's sons, Shem, was supposedly the progenitor of the SEMITES, from whom come the Hebrews.

Abraham

One of those in the line of Shem, born in Ur, and called Abraham, was the first to be called to preach monotheism. He had to leave his landand move to Canaan since the idolaters treated him harshly. This narrative is of central importance because it makes a connection between the modern Hebrews/Jews and a particular land.

Abraham is married to Sarah who, because she cannot bear him a son, allows him to cohabit with her maid, Hagar. Hagar does bear a son, Ishmael, but according to the story in Genesis, is a bit arrogant and this causes some ill-feeling between the two women. God's messengers visit Abraham and tell him that Sarah will bear a child. She overhears this, and laughs to herself since by this time, she is an old woman. But God's promise is true, and she does bear a child who is called **Yitzhak (Isaac)**—the Hebrew word referring to laughter, significant because of Sarah's laughter when she was told she would bear a child.

THE SERPENT TEMPTING EVE. FROM A PAINTING BY TITIAN (1490-1576)

Abraham, we are told, loved both sons. But birthright could only lay with one, and this is where Sarah's role as a mother is significant. She asks God that Abraham's inheritance be through her son, and her prayer is granted. The Hebrews are the descendants of Isaac. Sarah notes the play of Ishmael fourteen years older than her own child, and demands the Hagar and her son be sent away. Abraham sends them into the desert and their story will become meaningful many years later in the history of Islam.

God then tests Abraham by asking him to sacrifice his son Isaac on Mount Moriah. The patriarch is willing to comply and it is only when he is on the brink of carrying out the terrible command that an angel calls out from Heaven to him to use a lamb instead. Thus having passed the test, Abraham is promised numerous descendants etc. He lives out his lifespan, and when he dies, the two brothers, Isaac and Ishmael reunite to bury him.

Isaac marries and one of his sons, Jacob, has a vision and even wrestles with God (or a representative of the Divine). At dawn, when the wrestling comes to an end, Jacob receives a new name **ISRAEL** (wrestles with

God). This was the new name for Canaan, the land inhabited by his children. The twelve sons of Jacob from his two wives, Leah and Rachel, become the fathers of the twelve tribes of Israel.

A 1657 PAINTING BY GUERCINO SHOWING ABRAHAM SENDING OFF HAGAR AND ISHMAEL INTO THE DESERT

Jacob dotes on his eleventh son, Joseph, much to the chagrin of the older children who sell him off as a slave. He is taken to Egypt where he is brought up and later rises in status to become a royal adviser and minister in charge of the king's granaries. A famine arises in the surrounding areas, and his brothers are forced to come to Egypt to seek aid. He recognizes and reunites with them, and the entire clan moves to Egypt.

They are initially treated with honor and achieve much success, but in the course of generations, their descendants are envied by the Egyptians for their great numbers. They are enslaved and the Pharaoh passes a law that all the Hebrew baby boys are to be killed at birth. This is the set of circumstances into which, according to the book of Exodus, Moses is born. His mom, fearing for his safety, puts the baby in a raft and places it in the river. The Pharaoh's daughter sees the baby and adopts it. As luck—or Divine plan—would have it, the baby refuses to be suckled by anyone except his own mother. Pharaoh's family does not know that the wet-nurse is indeed the child's mother, nor that the wet-nurse's assistant is Moses' sister.

SACRIFICE OF ISAAC, BY TITIAN (1544)

Moses grows up in the royal household, but when he sees an Egyptian maltreating a Hebrew, he ends up killing the Egyptian and has to flee. He ends up in Midian where he gets married, and one day encounters what is popularly referred to as the Burning Bush. This is where he sees a bush that is on fire, but is not consumed by the flames. Instead he hears the voice of God, and is ordered to go to Pharaoh and obtain the release of the Israelites to return to their land.

Moses does as he is told, but encounters a Pharaoh who is reluctant to heed his words. After being struck with ten plagues, Pharaoh finally relents and allows the Israelites to leave. They have to do this in a hurry, not having time enough to make leavened bread for their journey. Instead they prepare unleavened bread (matzah) and seek to make their exit. Pharaoh pursues them, but God allows them to cross the sea by parting the waves for them. When they complete their crossing, God lets the waters flow over the pursuing Egyptians and drown them.

Thus saved, the Israelites try to return to the land of the forefathers—the land of Israel. It is during this time that Moses receives the Ten Commandments, or the DECALOGUE from God on tablets written by the divine finger. The covenant is renewed, and the terms are rather straightforward: If the Israelites served God alone, He would give them a specific land, and would make them a great nation. These ten commandments were carried in a wooden chest known as the *Ark of the Covenant*. They were to live by the law of God: establishing in effect, a theocracy. The Israelites spend forty years in the desert wandering. Many of them die, and when they near the promised land which is by this time inhabited by others, they are unwilling to take the steps to reclaim it. For this, many of them die without entering the land, and among them is the great Moses. And so the Israelites who enter are led by Joshua, one of the faithful who knew what to do to get the land.

ENGRAVING OF MOSES WITH THE TEN COMMANDMENTS. BY GUSTAVE DORE (1832-1883)

Exodus Chapter 20

And God spoke all these words saying: I am the LORD thy God, who brought thee out of the land of Egypt, out of the house of bondage.

1. Thou shalt have no other gods before Me.
2. Thou shalt not make untothee a graven image, nor any manner of likeness, of anything that is in heaven above, or that is in the earth beneath, or that is in the water under the earth. Thou shalt not bow down unto them, nor serve them; for I the LORD thy God am a jealous God, visiting the iniquity of the fathers upon the children unto the third and fourth generation of them that hate Me; 6 and showing mercy unto the thousandth p. 89 generation of them that love Me and keep My commandments.
3. Thou shalt not take the name of the LORD thy God in vain; for the LORD will not hold him guiltless that taketh His name in vain.
4. Remember the Sabbath day, to keep it holy. 9 Six days shalt thou labor, and do all thy work; 10 but the seventh day is a Sabbath unto the LORD thy God, in it thou shalt not do any manner of work, thou, nor thy son, nor thy daughter, nor thy man-servant, nor thy maid-servant, nor thy cattle, nor thy stranger that is within thy gates; 11 for in six days the LORD made heaven and earth, the sea, and all that in them is, and rested on the seventh day; wherefore the LORD blessed the Sabbath day, and hallowed it.
5. Honor thy father and thy mother, that thy days may be long upon the land which the LORD thy God giveth thee.
6. Thou shalt not murder.
7. Thou shalt not commit adultery
8. Thou shalt not steal.
9. Thou shalt not bear false witness against thy neighbor.
10. Thou shalt not covet thy neighbor's house; thou shalt not covet thy neighbor's wife, nor his manservant, nor his maid-servant, nor his ox, nor his ass, nor any thing that is thy neighbor's.

THE TEN COMMANDMENTS, FROM EXODUS 20

The Israelites after Moses

The land of Israel was divided among eleven of the twelve tribes of Israel. The members of the tribe of LEVI did not receive any land because they are supposed to serve as priests, and are to be supported by the community. Initially, Israel was ruled by JUDGES, endowed by God with special authority. According to the scriptural history, as reported in 1 Samuel, they were not content and insisted upon a king. God granted them their request with the chilling warning as reported in 1 Samuel 8:

[10] Samuel told all the words of the Lord to the people who were asking him for a king. [11] He said, "This is what the king who will reign over you will claim as his rights: He will take your sons and make them serve with his chariots and horses, and they will run in front of his chariots. [12] Some he will assign to be commanders of thousands and commanders of fifties, and others to plow his ground and reap his harvest, and still others to make weapons of war and equipment for his chariots. [13] He will take your daughters to be perfumers and cooks and bakers. [14] He will take the best of your fields and vineyards and olive groves and give them to his attendants. [15] He will take a tenth of your grain and of your vintage and give it to his officials and attendants. [16] Your male and female servants and the best of your cattle and donkeys he will take for his own use. [17] He will take a tenth of your flocks, and you yourselves will become his slaves. [18] When that day comes, you will cry out for relief from the king you have chosen, but the Lord will not answer you in that day."

The first king of Israel was **Saul**, a man who fulfilled all the negative views of what a king would bring to a theocracy. **David** was the second king of Israel and who established his capital in Jerusalem. For this reason, Jerusalem is often called the city of David. He wanted to build a temple to the Lord; this honor, however, went to his son **Solomon.** By all reports, the first Temple in Jerusalem was a magnificent edifice, having a sanctuary and extensive enough to allow for burnt offerings to God.

Kingdoms, however, in order to survive, must exact taxes from the populace. Such taxes can become exorbitant, and after the death of Solomon, this occurred. The ten northern tribes broke away from the authority of Jerusalem to form Israel, or what is known as the Northern Kingdom or Samaria. This event supposedly occurred circa 930 BCE. Thus separated, both kingdoms were weakened. In 721 BCE, the Northern Kingdom (i.e. Israel) was overrun by Assyria, its people chased out of their land, and replaced by immigrants who came there under Assyrian protection.

The Southern Kingdom (Judea) was besieged in 701 by King Sennacherib of Assyria, but despite his huge numbers of troops, he was unable to gain victory. The kingdom of Judah ended up paying tribute to a new power, the Babylonians, but later refused. In retaliation, Nebuchadnezzar 11, invaded Judah, destroyed the Temple and exiled most of the Jewish people to Babylonia in 586 BCE. This is known as the FIRST EXILE.

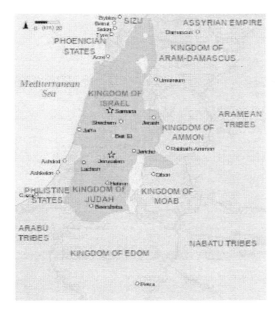

THE NORTHERN AND SOUTHERN KINGDOMS

The First Exile
The Temple was the place where God symbolically resided, and its destruction was supposed to totally demoralize the Israelites. But the reaction to this catastrophic event revealed the ability to adapt to circumstances. An alternative to temple worship had to be developed, and assemblies were formed, each meeting in what was called a **Beth Knesset** (house of assembly). In later centuries the **Beth Knesset** would be known as a **synagogue**. A required minimum quorum for daily worship or the forming of a congregation was decided upon. This amount was set at ten men and is known as a **minyan.** Without the Temple, animal sacrifices were not done, and scholars, known as **rabbis** could study and interpret the Torah. The focus was on how to survive as Jews, and keep the laws of God while in exile away from the Holy land. The focus was on study and understanding the Torah.

There was always the pressing question of suffering: How could God allow this to happen? And should God still be worshipped? Several explanations were offered, in what is known as a **theodicy**. This is an attempt to explain the justification of evil in the presence of an omnipotent God. One explanation was that God had used the Babylonians to discipline an errant King Hezekiah who had shown the riches of Judah to them.

During this time too, several trends developed in Judaism, imported from the surrounding cultures. The idea of Satan as an agent of evil is cultivated, and the Sabbath is seen as a time for Torah study. Aramaic gains prominence over Hebrew and is even used as part of sacred literature.

Cyrus the Great and the Return of the Jews to Jerusalem
Cyrus the Great, ruler of Persia, defeated the Babylonians shortly after coming to power, and in 538 BCE, issued an edict that the Jews be allowed to return to Judea. He was hailed by Isaiah, the prophet, as a Messiah (Isaiah 45:1). The returning Jews found that several changes had occurred among population that had been allowed to remain, and there were some disagreements between the two parties. The ensuing disputes slowed the reconstruction of the Temple, but by 516 BCE, the work was completed enough to allow for a dedication the following year. This marks the beginning of the **SECOND TEMPLE** period.

Ezra, a Torah scribe from Babylonia, and **Nehemiah,** a governor, were aided by the Persian emperor Artaxerxes, recorded the story of the exiles, and saw to the rewriting and revival of Jewish religious practice. In 444 BCE, Ezra read the Torah to Jews assembled at the Temple, and once again, the people agreed to follow the commandments of God, starting a new era for Judaism. It was during this time that the Prophetic books and Writings of the Tanakh were completed. Tradition holds that the books that were to complete the Hebrew canon were completed by about 200 BCE.

Herod the Great, between the years 20-18 BCE completely rebuilt the temple, even replacing the foundation stones. The project was one that he used to seek to establish his name in posterity, and as such, it was known as **Herod's Temple**. It is said that he used 10000 men who took approximately ten years to build the retaining walls around the temple. This gives an idea of the size of the structure. It was designed to serve the approximately seven million Jews that were in the Holy Land. It also became a pilgrimage site for Jews who were from Babylonia, Egypt and the surrounding areas. The temple's magnificence is described by Josephus (circa 100 CE) thus:

Viewed from without, the Sanctuary had everything that could amaze either mind or eyes. Overlaid all round with stout plates of gold, the first rays of the sun it reflected so fierce a blaze of fire that those who endeavored to look at it were forced to turn away as if they had looked straight at the sun. To strangers as they approached it seemed in the distance like a mountain covered with snow; for any part not covered with gold was dazzling white... (The Jewish War, p. 304).

The Second Temple Era and the Significance of Hanukkah

The armies of Alexander the Great of Macedon defeated the forces of Darius in 333 BCE, and in this way, Israel became part of the Greek empire. In 323 BCE, Alexander died, and in the ensuing war for control among his generals, control of Israel fell in the hands of the Seleucids, descendants of Alexander's general, Seleucus. One Seleucid ruler, Antiochus IV (176-153 BCE), was extremely harsh to the Jews, forbidding the possession of Torah and the observance of the Sabbath, as well as circumcision. He dedicated the Temple to Zeus, and placed a dish of pork on the altar. Some of his acts are mentioned in the Books of the Maccabees. His rule was so tyrannical that the Jews rose in armed rebellion. Judah Maccabee and his sons won a great victory over him, and they restored the Temple to Jewish worship. This is what is commemorated in the festival of **Hanukkah**. As some scholars note, the commemoration is not so much the defeat of Antiochus, but the fact that the oil of the Temple lamps that was supposedly enough for only one day, lasted for eight days. This explains the symbolism of the MENORAH, the candelabrum designed after the eight-branched light-holder that was used in the ancient temple.

Why the name Hanukkah?

There are several different explanations. One of them is that is related to the dedication ("hanukkah") of the Altar, [a centerpiece of the Holy Temple in Jerusalem]. According to Avodah Zarah 52b in the Talmud, the Hasmoneans (Maccabees) removed and stored away the Altar-stones which the Greeks had polluted with idolatry, and had to build a new Altar. That is why the festival is called 'Hanukkah' which means 'dedication.'

A RECONSTRUCTION OF THE MENORAH OF THE TEMPLE

The liberation by the Maccabees did not mean the end of all threats. The Jews were still not powerful enough to hold their own against the powerful nations that were vying for domination in the region. By 63 BCE, the Roman general Pompey was in charge of Israel. Apart from this foreign rule, Judaic norms were in conflict with Hellenism, the influence of Greek culture on society. As noted earlier, circumcision of Jewish males made them easily identifiable. Their dietary laws (**kashrut**) and their stringent observance of the Sabbath also conflicted with Greek norms.

Some Jews saw Hellenism as a threat to their way of life, others viewed it benignly, while others even welcomed it. This led to several different groups among the Jews. Under Roman administration, the confrontation with Hellenism continued, but the Jews were allowed most of their ritual observances as long as they paid taxes and did not revolt. Yet, the Romans were foreign occupiers and the Jews were divided in the way they treated this dominance by outsiders, breaking into different groups.

The **Sadducees** belonged to the priestly families, and claimed descent from Zadok, a priest from the time of King David (hence their name in Hebrew, **zadokim**). They accepted only the first five books of the Bible as sacred (i.e. the Torah, or Chumash). They were in charge of the temple and rituals.

The **Pharisees,** another group spoke of two **Torot**: the Written Torah and the Oral Torah, both as sources for Jewish religion and practice. Later Rabbinical Judaism was to develop from Pharisaical interpretations of Judaism. This wider base of foundations was rejected by the Sadducees.

A third group was the Zealots (Hebrew: kana'im), coming from the Greek word *zelotes*, meaning to adhere to with conviction and zeal. They sought to get rid of foreign rule by armed means. The fourth group, the **Essenes** sought to remove themselves from urban society in objection to the way the temple was administered, and to live in celibate communes in the desert. The Dead Sea scroll writings reflect their beliefs.

It was in this situation that the concept of the **Messiah**—an anointed king, deliverer, was born. Many claimants to the messiahship arose, and among them was Jesus. It would seem that he had some ideas that clashed with the major Jewish groups, although he himself was a Jew. When he was eventually arrested he was brought before the SANHEDRIN, the group of Jewish scholars who, in the Roman period, constituted the Supreme Court and the legislative body. They found him guilty of blasphemy, supposedly for claiming to be the son of God.

After Jesus' death, the Roman violations of Jewish ritual and the temple itself grew worse, with temple being plundered, and Roman soldiers engaging in acts of desecration. The Zealots revolted in 66 CE and defeated some armies before being brutally defeated in 70 CE. The temple was burned as was much of Jerusalem. Once again, the Jews found themselves without a central place of worship, and they had to adapt to worship forms not involving temple rituals. It was in this *sitz im leben* that Rabbinic Judaism developed.

THE WESTERN WALL, PART OF THE RETAINING WALL BUILT BY HEROD IN 20 BCETHATES-
CAPED DESTRUCTION BY THE ROMANS IN 70 CE

Rabbinic Judaism

Tradition holds that when Jerusalem was under siege by the Romans, one
rabbi, Yohanan ben Zakkai, a student of the famous Hillel, was opposed to
the activities of the zealots. He counselled against war, but they did not
listen to him. He faked his own death, and his companions prepared his
body for burial, taking him in a coffin out of Jerusalem. He was then taken
to the tent of the Roman general, Vespasian, where he emerged from the
coffin. He prophesied that the general would soon be emperor, based upon
a vision he claimed to have had. His request to the general was simply to
allow him to set aside a place in Yavneh to which he could move his
school and where he and his students would study Torah in peace. The
general supposedly agreed, conditional upon the prophecy being fulfilled.
When he did become emperor, he kept his promise, and this school survived for centuries, being the root from which Rabbinic Judaism developed. It was here that commentaries were prepared and developed the
guidelines that were to ensure the survival of the Jewish people. It was
here that the Mishnah and other famous Jewish works were compiled.

By the year 90, the rabbis had a canon of the Hebrew Bible, the Tanakh, to
which we have earlier referred. Some famous works of this time are:

Mishnah: the Oral Law, compiled in 63 tractates by Rabbi Judah Ha-Nasi.

Gemarah: commentary on the Mishnah, consisting of its Legal material
(*halakah*) and its *Aggadah* (rabbinic narrative traditions that are generally
seen as the non-legal component of *Gemarah*).

Talmud: the compilation of the Mishnah and Gemarah together. There are two Talmuds: the Palestinian (circa 450) and the Babylonian (circa 600).

Midrash: generally a rabbinic explanatory homiletic on any of the five books of the Torah.

The Babylonian Talmud became the central document of Rabbinic Judaism. This document, shaped in a setting where Jews had to come to grips with the pragmatism needed to survive, no longer in their own state or land, is what came to represent Judaism.

With the rise of Christianity and Islam, and the division of the lands of the Middle East and Europe into what we may term "Christendom" and "Islam," the followers of Judaism had to live as a minority subject to the authority of either Christians or Muslims, for the most part.

Medieval Jewish Thought
The rise of Christianity, especially after the time of Constantine came at a great cost to Jews. They were regarded as Christ-killers and persecuted. With the emergence of Islam, they were treated as "People of the Scripture" and granted recognition. It was under Muslim controlled polities that Medieval Jewish thought prospered.

Saadia Gaon (d. 942) lived in Egypt and argued for harmony between reason and revelation, granting precedence to the latter.

Maimonides (d. 1204) is probably the most famous of medieval Jewish thinkers. More popularly known as Rambam (an acronym from his name: Rabbi Moses ben Maimon), he was a medical doctor, philosopher, exegete, and rabbi. He wrote a Jewish law book, *Mishneh Torah*, and the famous, *Guide of the Perplexed*. He showed that Judaism and rational thought were perfectly compatible, and while his writings were esteemed in the Muslim lands, they caused controversy in Europe.

In the twelfth century, a mystic type of teaching, known as **Kabbalah**, flourished within Judaism. This focuses on the divine presence **(shekhinah)** and how it is perceived by humans. Its main text was the **Zohar,** attributed to Moses de Leon (d. 1305). According to Kabbalah, the true essence of God is so transcendent that it cannot be described, except with reference to what it is not. This true essence of God is known as *Ein Sof*, which literally means "without end," which encompasses the idea of His lack of boundaries in both time and space. In this truest form, the *Ein*

Sof is so transcendent that It cannot have any direct interaction with the universe. The *Ein Sof* interacts with the universe through ten emanations from this essence, known as the **Ten Sefirot.**

After the defeat of the Muslims in Spain in 1492, any security that the Jews had known in that land ended. They were faced with forced conversions to Christianity or exiled. They suffered terribly under the Spanish Inquisition, a practice instituted by King Ferdinand and Queen Isabella to ensure that those Jews and Muslims who converted to Christianity were honest in their declaration of faith. The tests for such honesty were often conducted by torture.

Judaism in the Modern Period
Persecution for Jews in late medieval Europe, which was largely Christian was a norm. Forbidden from owning property or holding citizenship in many countries, the image of the Jew as a rejecter of Jesus and therefore as someone to be humiliated took root. Shakespeare in his "Merchant of Venice," and Sir Walter Scott in his "Ivanhoe" depicted them in negative terms, in an era when it would seem there was no limit to the dehumanizing drawings and imageries used to depict Jews.

The Enlightenment brought about **MODERNISM,** with its focus on reason over revelation. Modernity did bring about some changes in the lot of Jews, who realized that they too would have to reexamine their adherence to tradition. This gave rise to several movements for Jewish reform. Some of those movements are Reform, Conservative, Reconstructionist, Orthodox, and Humanistic.

Reform Judaism
In the nineteenth century, in France and Germany in particular, Jewish thinkers had to face the worsening threat to their very existence. Among these thinkers were Leopold Zunz (d. 1886) and Abraham Geiger (d. 1874). Geiger questioned many aspects of traditional Judaic practice, such as circumcision and the liturgy in Hebrew.

In the United States, Rabbis David Einhorn (d. 1879) and Isaac Meyer Wise (d. 1900) focused more on the ethics of the Torah rather than its ritual directives. Today, in most reform synagogues, the males are not required to wear **kippot** (skullcaps), and most of the service is conducted in English or the language of the land. Women can be rabbis or cantors and there is no gender separation in the synagogue. Individuals differ in their views on dietary restrictions.

Conservative Judaism

Solomon Schecter (d. 1915) felt that while Judaism did indeed need reform, radical changes ought to be avoided in order to prevent too much of a rift in the bond between the present and the past. The Torah and Talmud ought to be followed as much as possible, and that attachment to Israel for Jews can never be overlooked. This attachment manifests itself in the modern concept of **Zionism**, the idea of a specific homeland for the Jewish people, established in the land of their forefathers. While there is no gender separation in synagogues, and the language of the land can be used, there is more emphasis on Hebrew, the men wear Kippot, and the traditional dietary restrictions are generally observed.

Reconstructionist Judaism

This may be said to be truly American, founded by an American Rabbi, Mordecai Kaplan (d. 1983). This interpretation rejects the concept of miracles, and focuses on the ethical teachings of Judaism. It rejects the idea of a chosen people, and feels that rituals are of lesser importance.

Orthodox Judaism

This interpretation tries to apply the traditional practice as much as possible in a modern setting. There is gender segregation, and kippot and prayer shawls are worn. It is the denomination that is recognized as the Judaism of the modern state of Israel.

Humanistic Judaism

This is a form on non-theistic Judaism, wherein one observes certain rituals that establish a historical identity, but go beyond the purely religious. In this interpretation, ethics and values should be in consideration of human values and less because they are seen as a divine edict that separates between a chosen people and gentiles.

Hasidism

Hasidism is based upon following a Zaddik, a holy man, who is the channel through which one can connect with God. Hasidic Jews often dress in a manner that observes the ancient edicts, and views that only when one has a good relationship with the Divine can one be a good human being.

Developments in Approaches to Jewish Scripture

The Documentary Hypothesis

Among old traditions regarding the Torah (or the Chumash, or Pentateuch) is that Moses actually wrote them. But detailed analysis by researchers brought to light much evidence to show that the books were written at different times, and by different authors. Academic researchers have suggested the DOCUMENTARY HYPOTHESIS (sometimes also known as the Wellhausen hypothesis). This was put forth by the German theologian Julius Wellhausen (d. 1918). This theory holds that the first five books of were originally independent, parallel and complete narratives, which were subsequently combined into the current form by a series of redactors (editors). The number of these narratives is usually set at four, but this is not an essential part of the hypothesis.

By the end of the 19th century it was generally agreed that there were four main sources, combined into their final form by a series of redactors, R. The formulations were:

The Yahwist source (J): hypothetically written c. 950 BCE in the southern Kingdom of Judah.

The Elohist source (E): hypothetically written c. 850 BCE in the northern Kingdom of Israel.

The Deuteronomist (D) : hypothetically written c. 600 BCE in Jerusalem during a period of religious reform.

The Priestly source (P) : hypothetically written c. 500 BCE by Kohanim (Jewish priests) in exile in Babylon.

This hypothesis has been continually refined, but the basic formulation still remains the same.

Zionism and Modern Israel

From their exile in 135 CE to the modern times, Jews had not known a land they could call their own. Landless and often stateless, they longed for a return to the land of their ancestors. Pogroms in Europe, and then the

Holocaust in which approximately six million Jews were killed underlined the need for a Jewish state. In the late nineteenth century, Theodore Herzl and others founded the Zionist movement, a call for the establishment of a modern Israel. This was done in 1948. The reality is that the establishment of the modern state has not come without difficulty. The land claimed as Israel was not empty: it was inhabited in many areas by Palestinians. While the Arabs initially were welcoming, the duplicity of the British in withholding Arab independence caused them to withdraw their support. To this day, the overwhelming majority of Arab states oppose the state of Israel as it exists, and ask for a return to the pre-1967 borders, a time when the city of Jerusalem was still divided. This continues to be an ongoing dispute between Israel and its Arab neighbors and its Palestinian citizenry.

Rituals

There are traditionally 613 **mitzvot** (singular, **mitzvah**, meaning religious duty), 248 imperatives, and 365 prohibitions. There are several such rituals that may be observed on an individual or a community level. About a week after birth, a boy is circumcised according to the biblical command in Genesis 17 "every male among you shall be circumcised." This was done by a trained *mohel*, but today is often done in a hospital by a trained surgeon.

There is the bar or bat mitvah for the coming of age, when one is supposed to be responsible for observing the rituals. In the case of boys this is a 13 years plus one day, and in the case of girls twelve plus one day. The **Sabbath** is now observed as the day of consecration to God. Given that the Sabbath in Judaism is on Saturday, this was initially a great problem for many Jews in early America where Christian practice observed Sunday as the day of rest.

Rosh Hashanah (the beginning of the year) is another major holiday. This begins with 10 days of reflection, and prayer, followed by **Yom Kippur**, the holiest day in the Jewish tradition. This is known as the Day of Atonement, and many Jews spend it in fasting and prayer, often passing most of the day in synagogue services.

Hanukkah celebrates the victory of the Maccabees over the Antiochus as already mentioned.There is also Passover, celebrating the Hebrews' escape from Egypt, and then there is also **Shavuot**, that commemorates the giving of the Ten Commandments to Moses, also signifying an early harvest. **Purim** is one of the more joyous holidays of the Jewish calendar and is based on events reported in the book of Esther. It is celebrated on the 14th day of the Hebrew month of Adar, and represents the deliverance of the Jewish people in the Persian empire from those who plotted to have them destroyed.

As noted earlier, there are dietary laws, among them prohibitions against pork, or the mixing of meat and milk. Slaughter must be done according to a prescribed format that removes most of the blood from the animal. Such dietary laws are known as **Kashrut**. Marriage is another reason for celebration, usually done under a Huppah, a canopy based on reports from the Bible. Under the huppah, rings are exchanged with the words, "Behold, you are sanctified to me by this ring in accord with the tradition of Moses and Israel," followed by seven blessings spoken over a glass of wine.

At death, a corpse is washed, clothed, and buried according to rituals that differ slightly from denomination to denomination. After burial, there is usually a period of seven days of mourning, known as sitting **shiva**. Usually mourning is done for thirty days, except for parents. They are mourned for eleven months.

Symbols

On the entranceway to many Jewish homes, one may find a little case on the right side, based on the Biblical command in Deuteronomy: *And you shall write [the words that I command you today] on the doorposts of your house and on your gates. -Deuteronomy 6:9, 11:19*. The case is known as a **mezuzah** and contains a passage known as the **Shema** that basically testifies that God comes first. The Shema receives its name from the first two words of Deuteronomy 6: 4 "Shema Yisroel" (Hear, O Israel!), and is seen as encapsulating the monotheistic view of Judaism, as it continues, "the LORD our God, the LORD is one." Devout Jews often touch the mezuzah and kiss their fingers, expressing love for God. The protocol for an observant Jew is to remove the mezuzah if a Jewish family will no longer live in the household.

A MEZUZAH

The Star of David (Magen David)

Recently, the six-pointed star of David has become a popular symbol among many Jews. While there is no record to show that the Biblical David actually had such a symbol, the depiction has many interpretations, some of them mystical. The flag of the state of Israel has one such star of David upon it.

Judaism and Science

Judaism has never had any conflict with science and as such, we find that major contributions have been made by Jewish scientists and inventors. Israel is home to some of the world's most advanced research facilities.

Judaism and Other Religions

The relation of Judaism to Christianity has only recently seen a turn for the cordial, based on the centuries of teaching that Jews had rejected Jesus and were complicit in his crucifixion. After centuries of coexistence between Jews and Muslims in Muslim-majority lands, the establishment of the state of Israel has brought about a sometimes confrontational approach between adherents of Judaism and Islam. In America and many western countries, many conferences have been organized under the aegis of Pluralism to remove such animosity.

Judaism and Politics

The establishment of Israel has brought with it a strong support for Jews in many countries of the world. This means getting involved in politics to ensure, for example, in the United States, the American support for Israel remains strong. There are several ethical issues now that are under discussion in Israel, such as for example, the examination of how does Israel consider itself a Jewish state while acknowledging its Arab population.

Glossary

Abraham:	The Biblical patriarch, supposedly the first preacher of monotheism.
Abraham Geiger	German Rabbi and one of the founders of Reform Judaism
Antiochus IV	He was aSeleucid Ruler who desecrated the Temple in Jerusalem. He was defeated by the Maccabees.
Ark of the Covenant	The wooden chest in which the Ten Commandments were carried.
Beth Knesset	House of Assembly, the precursor of the synagogue.
Chumash	A name for the first five books of the Hebrew Bible
David	According to the Hebrew Bible, he was the second king of Israel
David Einhorn	American rabbi and one of the founders of Reform Judaism in the United States.
Decalogue	A term used to refer to the Ten Commandments.
Deuteronomist	According to the Documentary Hypothesis, this is one of the sources of the Hebrew Bible. It is also referred to as the "D" source.

Documentary Hypothesis   A theory put forth by Julius Wellhausen that the Hebrew Bible is composed of different books written by various authors in different periods.

Elohist   According to the Documentary Hypothesis, this in one of the sources of the Hebrew Bible. It is also referred to as the "E" document.

Essenes   One of the groups of Jews in the Second Temple era.

Ezra   One of the Torah scribes from Babylonia who returned to Jerusalem in 538 BCE.

Gemarah   Commentary on the Mishnah.

Halakah   Legal material of the Mishnah.

Ha Miqra   A term used to refer to the Hebrew Bible, meaning "The recitation."

Hanukkah   Commemoration of the victory of the Maccabees over the Seleucids, and a victory of monotheism over the desecration of the Temple and forced worship.

Hasidism   A form of Judaism that is based upon following a Zaddik, a holy teacher.

Herod's Temple   Between 20-18 BCE, Herod completed the reconstruction of the Second Temple and, until its destruction in 70 CE, it was known as Herod's Temple.

Israel   One of the names of Jacob, and also the name given to the Northern Kingdom or Samaria, when it broke away, after the death of Solomon, from the authority of Jerusalem.

Judea   The name given to the Southern Kingdom after the breakaway of states from the authority of Jerusalem after the death of Solomon

Judges	Those who were initially the rulers of Israel, administering by special authority endowed upon them by God. Also the name of one of the books of the Hebrew Bible.
Julius Wellhausen	The founder of the Documentary Hypothesis.
Kabbalah	A term used to refer to mystical Judaism.
Kashrut	Term referring to traditional Jewish dietary laws.
Kipa/Kippot	Skullcap worn by observant Jewish men.
Leopold Zunz	One of the founders of Reform Judaism
Levi (Tribe of)	One of the twelve tribes of Israel, named after one of the sons of Jacob
Magen David	The star of David.
Maimonides/Rambam	The most famous of the medieval Jewish thinkers.
Menorah	The candelabrum designed after the eight-branched light-holder that was used in the ancient temple. Today, there are nine branches. The ninth is traditionally for the candle used to light the other candles.
Messiah	An anointed king.
Mezuzah	A case containing the SHEMA, and often found on the right side of the doorway as one is entering a Jewish home.
Minyan	The quorum of 10 required for congregational daily worship.
Mishnah	The oral law, compiled in 63 tractates by Rabbi Judah Ha-Nasi
Modernism	The idea that reason triumphs over revelation.
Mitzvah/Mitzvot	Hebrew word meaning "a religious duty."

Mordecai Kaplan	The founder of Reconstructionist Judaism.
Moses de Leon	Author of the "Zohar."
Nehemiah	A governor who came back with the returning exiles to Jerusalem in 538 BCE.
Pentateuch	Another name for the five books of the Hebrew bible.
Pharisees	One of the groups in Israel during the Roman period.
Priestly (source)	According to the Documentary Hypothesis, this is one of the sources of the Hebrew Bible.
Purim	A joyous event in Judaism, celebrating the deliverance of the Jewish people from those who plotted to have them destroyed.
Rabbi	A traditional scholar in the Jewish tradition.
Rabbinic Judaism	As opposed to Biblical Judaism, this is that form of Judaism that is based upon rabbinic interpretation, after the fall of the Temple
Rosh Hashanah	The Jewish new year.
Saadia Gaon	One of the most famous medieval Jewish thinkers from Fayyum, Egypt.
Sabbath	The seventh day of the Jewish calendar, consecrated to the worship of God.
Sadducees	One of the groups of Jews in the Second Temple period.
Sanhedrin	The group of Jewish scholars who, in the Roman period, constituted the Supreme court and the legislative body.
Saul	According to the Hebrew Bible, the first King of Israel.

Second Temple   The rebuilt temple dedicated by the year 516 BCE. By 20-18 BCE, Herod completed the reconstruction and as such it was also known as Herod's Temple.

Sefirot   The term used to denote the ten emanations from the Divine Essence.

Semites   Descendants of Shem, son of Noah.

Shavuot   The commemoration of the Spring harvest and/or the giving of the Ten Commandments to Moses

Shekhinah   The Divine Presence.

Shema   The name given to a Biblical edict from Deuteronomy 6:4, beginning with "Hear, O Israel!"

Shem   According to the Hebrew Bible, one of the sons of Noah, from whom the Semites are descended.

Shiva   The seven days of mourning for the dead.

Solomon   Son of the Biblical David, third king of Israel, and the builder of the First Temple

Solomon Schecter   One of the founders of Conservative Judaism.

Synagogue   Worship center of Jews, established after the Temple was destroyed.

Tanakh   An acronym for the Hebrew Bible.

Theocracy   A state ruled by the law of God.

Theodicy   An explanation for the justification of evil in the presence of an omnipotent God.

Torah   The first five books of the Hebrew Bible.

Vespasian   Roman General who besieged Jerusalem and defeated the Zealots.

Yahwist   One of the sources of the Hebrew Bible, according to the Documentary Hypothesis. Also referred to as the "J" document.

Yitzhak   Hebrew for "Isaac," according to the Hebrew Bible, the son of Abraham from Sarah, and he through whom the inheritance of Abraham was passed on.

Yohanan ben Zakkai   The Rabbi who faked his death to escape Jerusalem and was promised by Vespasian to be allowed to set up an academy at Yavneh.

Yom Kippur   Day of Atonement, holiest day of the year in the Jewish tradition

Zadokim   The Hebrew name for the Sadducees.

Zakhor   "Remember," one of the most repeated commands in the Hebrew Bible.

Zealots   One of the groups of Jews in Jerusalem during the Roman Period.

Zionism   The idea of the establishment of a state for Jewish people in the homeland of the Hebrew patriarchs.

Zohar   The main text of the Kabbalah, supposedly authored by Moses de Leon.

CHRISTIANITY
Salvation through Christ

Angela Feres

A DEPICTION OF EARLY CHRISTIANS

- *Summarize social setting in which Christianity arose*
- *Discuss different sects in Jerusalem under Roman occupation*
- *Outline life and teachings of Jesus, according to Gospel accounts*
- *Explain Pauline influence*
- *Explain structure of Christian canon*
- *Analyze rejection and then acceptance of Christianity in Rome*
- *Discuss the early Churches and their structure*
- *Describe influence of Constantine on Christianity*
- *Analyze division of Eastern and Western Christianity*
- *Present very brief summary of Church Fathers*
- *Discuss movements such as monasticism, reform ideas in the Middle Ages*
- *Discuss Crusades*
- *Examine reasons for Martin Luther's Protest and other reform movements*
- *Discuss Christianity and rise of theology*
- *Examine rise of mysticism*
- *Discuss Christianity and modernity*

The Social Setting of the Emergence of Christianity

Christianity emerged from Judaism in the first century CE. The Jewish community had long been an unhappy member of the Roman world. In 63 BCE, the Roman General Pompey conquered the Jewish Kingdom of Judea. From that point forward, Rome occupied the region, subjecting the Jews to a Roman appointed governor, while the Jewish Council known as the Sanhedrin held juridical authority. The region later became a Roman administrative unit ruled by a **procurator**, of which Pontius Pilate (r. 26-36 CE) remains the best known. Many Jews resented Roman rule and efforts by the Jewish council to compromise with Roman authorities to preserve the community generated tensions and divisions.

STATUARY DEPICTION OF PONTIUS PILATE

Jews had traditionally attempted to create a theocratic community based on the Torah and other books of the Hebrew Bible. Religious life for Jews in Jerusalem consisted of sacrifices at the sacred Temple, and in Diaspora communities around synagogues. Despite a common adherence to the Mosaic laws of their ancestors, several religious and political movements divided the Jewish community. The **Sadducees**, an elite sector of Jewish society, were often the priests of the Temple, held great wealth, and wielded great political authority over the community. Dedicated to ritual purity and the letter of Jewish law, they faced criticism from some who viewed them as more interested in rituals than the social welfare of the community.

The **Pharisees**, not of the aristocratic rank of Jewish society, claimed to follow not just the written laws of Moses, but also an oral set of commandments passed on through from their ancestors. Rabbis, scribes, and lower level priests usually belonged to this political-religious group. The Pharisees, critical of the wealth and power of the Sadducees, embraced a less literal interpretation of the written Torah, ritual purity, and the belief in a coming messiah who would arrive before the end times when God would issue judgment on the people.

The **Zealots**, a militant activist group, embraced resolute worship of Yahweh and undertook violent attempts to overthrow Roman rule. Led by **Judah** of Galilee, they emerged ca. 6 CE. They believed that accepting Roman rule equated to forsaking God. Emphasizing the Jewish belief in a coming messiah, in the form of a heroic king, they actively sought a political savior and liberator who they hoped would destroy the Roman Empire and usher in a time of independence, peace, and prosperity for Jews.

DEPICTION OF JOHN THE BAPTIST[24]

One who actively prophesied the coming of the messiah was **John the Baptist**. John the Baptist may have been a member of a strict sect of Judaism, described in the Dead Sea Scrolls, called the **Essenes** who em-

---

[24] This attribution of this 1599 painting to Caravaggio is disputed.

braced a rigorous interpretation of Jewish law. The Essenes lived apart in pursuit of a renewed relationship to the Torah and revival of the covenant. They lived in Qumran, a community in the desert, embraced lives of frugality, participated in communal meals, avoided oath taking, and lived in anticipation of the coming Messiah and the end of days at which time they believed God would punish the wicked and restore the sovereignty of the Holy Land to the Jewish people.

Spiritual turmoil was also widespread throughout Roman world at this time. New mystery cults from the east, religions of salvation, gave a sense of purpose and promise of an afterlife to many in the Roman world. The Roman roads fostered religious expansion and syncretism. **Mithraism**, an Eastern religion, was popular with Roman soldiers. The **Cult of Isis** from Egypt was very popular, especially with women. The Roman State religion did not provide a great deal of spiritual comfort to people; a ritual and political religion, it failed to offer the promise of hope for personal salvation. Many of the older traditional rural cults of Rome regained popularity, but these nature cults did not provide the sense of salvation that came with the new mystery cults.

The Life and Teachings of Jesus

It was into this time of spiritual questing and tension that the foundational figure of Christianity emerged. Jesus of Nazareth was born to a Jewish family circa 4 BCEand helped give rise to a movement that has grown from humble roots to become, with its various denominations, the world's largest religion. While Christianity begins with Jesus, not much is known of his life; he produced no known writings of his own. His later followers wrote accounts of his life and purpose after his death ca. 30 CE. The earliest writings are a collection of letters by **Paul of Tarsus**, written ca. 50 CE. A collection of writings known as Gospels, literally "good news," were written down beginning in the 60s CE.

JOHN THE BAPTIST BAPTIZING JESUS[25]

The Canonical Gospels

Four of a multitude of **gospels**, "good news," eventually became part of the Christian canon. The Gospels of **Matthew, Mark, Luke,** and **John** provide Christians with accounts of Jesus' birth, life, teachings, and death. According to the writings, Jesus more than likely was born sometime around the year 4 BCE in **Galilee.** Until he accepted baptism at age thirty by John the Baptist, the canonical Gospels have little to say about his life.

Many scholars identify Mark as the earliest of the canonical Gospels. It is the oldest of the three synoptic Gospels, meaning of the same view, to be included in the New Testament. Scholars now argue that these three Gospels used the same source, called the Q source, which would have been a simple list of sayings attributed to Jesus. Though the Q source has not been found, it can be constructed from the similar sayings found in the three synoptic Gospels.

---

[25]John the Baptist baptizing Jesus. Trevisani. 1723.

The date for the composition of the gospel of Mark is ca. 60s CE. The Gospel of Mark focuses on the adult life and teachings of Jesus. Beginning with an encounter between John the Baptist and Jesus, Mark identifies Jesus as a charismatic Jewish teacher who taught devotion to God and love of humanity. According to Mark, Jesus attracted large crowds through his teaching and miracles. Jesus rejected the need to follow the letter of biblical law by emphasizing inward purity rather than rituals and sacrifices at the Jewish Temple. He instructed his followers that the "the kingdom of God" was at hand, emphasizing an imminent end time or an already inwardly manifested new kingdom. Emphasizing that God was a loving and forgiving father, Jesus welcomed marginalized groups such as the poor, sick, women, and tax collectors.

A FIFTH CENTURY MANUSCRIPT INCLUDING THE GOSPEL OF MARK[26]

The Gospel of Matthew, the next oldest of the three synoptic Gospels (ca. 70 CE) was written to persuade the Jewish community that Jesus was indeed the Messiah. Not all members of the Jewish community accepted claims that Jesus was the messiah or that he had any special knowledge of God. Only some Jews believed that Jesus was the Messiah about whom Jewish belief had spoken, a liberator who would free the Jews from captivity by foreign powers, because for many Jesus did not fit the predicted mold of the Messiah of the Hebrew Bible. Matthew attempted to sway Jews by providing a genealogy linking Jesus to the Davidic line and referencing the Hebrew book of Isaiah, where it was stated that a child would

---

[26]http://www.narrowgate-rmartin.com/theo10_classnotes/codex_washingtonias_mark.htm. Accessed March 4, 2014.

be born who would be called Emmanuel, which means "God is with us." Matthew shifts the original meaning of the Isaiah text to orient it towards his belief that Jesus was the product of a special birth and the Messiah.

The Gospel of Luke, written ca. 80 CE provides an account of Jesus' life from birth to annunciation. Luke's Gospel details visions and omens preceding the birth of Jesus that served to indicate to the reader that Jesus was indeed the heralded messianic figure of Jewish scripture. Luke lingers over the events related to the execution of Jesus, presenting him as an innocent victim of mob violence.

The final Gospel included in the official canon is John, which does not conform to the general constructs of the other three gospels. John was concerned with presenting Jesus as the messiah and the incarnation of the divine Logos, Word, of God, as understood in the Hellenistic world. John uses the word Christ to identify Jesus and express his understanding of the divine redemptive nature of his mission. In many ways the Gospel of John serves to indicate how far and entrenched the writings of Paul of Tarsus had become. The resemblance between the Christology of John to Paul is quite close.

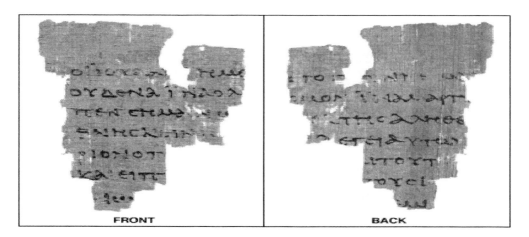

FRONT   BACK

FRAGMENT FROM THE EARLIEST MANUSCRIPT OF THE GOSPEL OF JOHN, DATING TO THE FIRST HALF OF THE SECOND CENTURY[27]

---

[27] http://www.nobeliefs.com/DarkBible/darkbible2.htm. Accessed March 4, 2014.

Though the canonical Christian Bible only contains four Gospels, hundreds of others were written. The 1945 discovery of the Nag Hammadi texts in Egypt has revealed a great deal about alternative forms of early Christian belief. Most of the text had been written in the second century. They are classified as gnostic texts. **Gnosticism** grew alongside other types of Christianity and competed with what would become termed as the orthodox position of the Roman Catholic Church, until it was suppressed. The texts that make up what is known as the Nag Hammadi Library were buried in terracotta jars and hidden, perhaps to protect them from destruction.

Christian Gnosticism embraced the belief that secret knowledge had been passed on by Jesus to some of his chosen followers. Those privileged few had **gnosis** (knowledge) of the hidden meaning of Christianity. Other forms of Gnosticism exist as well; there were Jewish Gnostics in the classical world. In general, Gnostics believe in a dualist universe. Goodness, light, and the spirit are in an eternal fight against the material, dark powers of evil. The material world, a trap for the spirit or soul, was a place of temptation and sins of the flesh that must be avoided in order to eventually liberate the soul from its prison in the body. For Christian Gnostics, Jesus was not a material flesh and blood man, but a spirit who was sent to wake people up and free them from their imprisonment, Orthodox Christian doctrine insisted that Jesus had been both fully human and fully divine; the Orthodox Church banned writings and suppressed Gnostic groups.

Resistance and Crucifixion
As earlier noted, the Jewish community did not uniformly accept the teachings of Jesus or his followers' claims to his special authority. The Pharisees considered Jesus' claims to be able to forgive sins blasphemous and the Sadducees were stung by his criticism. Jesus challenged the religious authorities in Judaism by teaching and healing in the Temple of Jerusalem. The Sadducees feared the crowds attracted to Jesus would provoke trouble as Jews from all over the Roman world entered Jerusalem to offer sacrifice at the temple during Passover.

A DEPICTION OF THE CRUCIFIXION, DATED TO 1622

Pontius Pilate, the Prefect of Judea and representative of Roman power, did not care about Jesus' teaching, but rather about keeping the peace. Jesus was attracting crowds and it was the time of Passover, always a highly emotional time, which alarmed Pilate. To avert riot and bloodshed, he arrested Jesus, who was later **crucified** under Roman law. Most accounts of the arrest and **crucifixion** were written after the First Jewish Revolt and may reflect anti-Jewish sentiment in the empire. To the Romans, the matter seemed settled, but after the **crucifixion** a rumor spread through Jerusalem that Jesus had been resurrected from the dead. Some accused the followers of Jesus of having stolen and hid the body, but belief in his resurrection became over time a central element of an emerging Christian faith.

The early followers of Jesus kept the movement alive by spreading Jesus' teachings through 30s-40s CE. They were called **Nazarenes**. Their message appealed especially to Hellenized Jews who were less committed to traditional Jewish doctrines. The first followers had no thought of breaking with Judaism, but because they adhered to Jewish laws, non-Jews were not eager to convert. Judaism of the first century required adherence to numerous rules regarding food, marriage, purity, and with whom one could interact. Circumcision was also mandated for converts, which may have added another barrier to wholesale conversion. These obstacles largely removed when Paul of Tarsus became an influential teacher and argued that one need not embrace the Jewish laws to become a Christian.

Paul of Tarsus

Paul of Tarsus (ca. 40 CE) is one of the most important figures in the spread of Christianity. He had been a Pharisee who persecuted the followers of Jesus; in 36 CE after a direct and personal encounter with the risen Jesus, converted. Paul taught that Jesus was the anointed one, the Son of God, who died to atone for humanity's sins and to bring salvation to all people, not just Jews. Paul stressed that adherence to Jewish ritual laws did not lead to salvation, but rather faith in Jesus as the messiah led to salvation. His missions to convert gentiles and Jewsled to the separation of a Christian community from Judaism.

DEPICTION OF PAUL

Thanks to Paul's efforts and those of his followers, Christianity experienced rapid growth. It strongly appealed to the lower classes, urban populations, and women. It also appealed to those who had already been attracted to the mystery cults. Paul and his companions established Christian communities throughout the Roman Empire. Though the Roman authority eventually executed Paul, the movement by then was firmly established and expanding in non-Jewish communities.

ARTIST HENRYK SIEMRADZKI'S (D. 1902) DEPICTION OF PERSECUTION OF CHRISTIANS

Persecution of Christians

Despite Christianity's rapid growth, many Romans initially perceived the movement as a subversive religion antithetical to Roman culture. The refusal of Christians to worship or offer sacrifice to the state cult on behalf of Emperor was a problem. Some Romans viewed them as a secret anti-social group. Also, many were pacifists who refused to serve in the army, denied legitimacy of other sects, and refused to associate with non-Christians. During the first two centuries persecution was sporadic and local, but in the late 3rd and 4th centuries, when the Empire was in danger of collapse, organized efforts were launched to suppress Christianity. The most systematic was launched in the fourth century by Emperor Diocletian, who imposed the death penalty on anyone who refused to sacrifice to the state cults of Rome.

Finally in 311 Emperor **Galerius** issued an edict of toleration making Christianity legal in the Eastern Roman Empire. He realized persecution had failed to eliminate faith and was counterproductive. In 313 Emperor Constantine granted Christians freedom of worship throughout east and west Empire by issuing the Edict of Milan. Emperor Theodosius I (r. 379-395 CE) made Christianity the official religion of the empire; in his zeal, he also persecuted pagans and attempted to force people to convert.

Organization of Early Christianity

Since early Christians had believed in the imminent second coming of Jesus, they had not constructed a hierarchical organization. When it became clear that the end was not as expected, they began to organize themselves based on Roman models. The earliest officials were **priests** who preached, taught, and conducted the **sacraments**, **deacons** who served the **priests**, and **bishops** who oversaw priests and deacons. By the 2nd century most Christian communities had organized in a hierarchical manner. Bishops came to be understood to be direct successors to the **apostles**. The term **Patriarch** is the title a bishop of an important city such as Rome or Constantinople. The **Patriarch** or **Bishop of Rome** rose to the position of preeminence in the west and was given title of Pope.

Women, who had acted as important patrons, teachers, and perhaps even priestesses in the earlier communities, were pushed to the margins when Christianity based its organization of the patriarchal values of the Roman world. Women who hoped to continue to serve the Christian community did so in subservient position to their male counterparts. Excluded from offering the sacraments, preaching, or teaching scripture, these women were only able to have a voice within the monastic communities that would later emerge.

The Role of Constantine and Authority in Christianity

Emperor Constantine, made Christianity a legal religion in the Empire and became an important supporter of and power within the Christian community. He did so after having a vision before an important battle. In this vision, he was shown the Christian cross in the sky and the words that by that sign he would conquer. Painting the inside of his soldiers' shields with the cross, Constantine rode to victory and the position of undisputed Emperor of Rome and champion of Christianity. Though Constantine made Christianity legal, he did not force conversion on anyone and tolerated the pagan faiths of the Empire. He refused to be baptized until on his deathbed partially because Christians of that time believed that baptism removed all sins from a person; Constantine was able to die in a state of sinless grace.

Constantine was interested in establishing religious as well as political order in the Empire. Religion could be a powerful stabilizing and unifying force. In order to achieve unity, he called the**Council of Nicaea** to establish orthodox doctrine and purge heretical teachings. Christianity went from being a religion with many voices and interpretations of Christ, to having one orthodox universal (catholic) view. Those who failed to hold true to orthodoxy were deemed heretical, followers of false belief, a crime that often became conflated with treason in the Middle Ages.

BUST OF CONSTANTINE

Constantine's active involvement in the formation of religious doctrine as well as secular laws is known as **caesaropapism**, a term used to describe Constantine's position as king (Caesar) and Pope. He claimed the power to intervene in theological matters and define orthodoxy and heresy, as well as to rule over secular matters. In the eastern Empire, Emperors would become absolute rulers over political, military, judicial, financial, and religious spheres, while in the West the Roman Catholic Church would emerge as an entity capable of making and breaking Kings and Emperors throughout the Middle Ages.

The Division of Eastern and Western Christianity
Over the years, Emperors in the east initiated and sat in councils to settle religious issues. Called in 325 CE, the **Council of Nicaea** highlights the role the state had in defining orthodox belief. The Council was called to decide the exact nature of Christ. A prominent Bishop named **Arius** (d. 336) taught that Jesus had been a **mortal** human being, created by God, rather than a divine being coeternal with God. Many theologians embraced the view of a rival bishop, **Athanasius** that Jesus was equally a human being and Divine, eternal, and begotten not made. The Emperor Constantine accepted this later view and used the **Council of Nicaea** to make sure Arius' views were declared heretical.

Other councils followed, during which divisions arose between the Bishop of Rome, Pope, and the Patriarch of Constantinople on questions of doctrine and conversion. By late 4th century, the Pope placed particular emphasis on the original primacy of Peter in a theory called **Petrine Prima-cy**.   Based on Matthew's gospel (16:16-18) the Pope claimed that Jesus had named Peter as the foundation upon which the church would be built. Since Peter had built the first church in Rome, the Bishops of Rome should lead the Church. The Eastern Patriarchs argued that all bishops should be equal.

To appease the eastern bishops, the Emperor encouraged the council to make the Patriarch of Constantinople second in power to the Pope, but Pope Leo I (d. 461) objected to the interference of the Emperor in religious matters, arguing that Emperors did not have the right to intervene in religion.   Subsequent Popes would argue that the power of the Church trumped that of any secular ruler because the Church focused on eternal souls and concerned with salvation, while secular leaders only rule bodies.

Another divisive issue emerged between Eastern and Western Catholics called iconoclasm.   Emperor Leo III (r 717- 741 CE.) declared that the veneration of religious images was sinful and banned the use of religious images in worship. The Pope of Rome condemned iconoclasm, supporting the religious use of icons as aids to spirituality, but emperors in the East continued the policy.

Although **iconoclasm** was abandoned in the East in the ninth century, other differences generated problems. The Eastern bishops objected to western priests shaving their beards and using unleavened bread in the mass. Arguments emerged about the precise relationship between Jesus, God, and the Holy Spirit.   Tensions grew, leading to the Great Schism of 1054 CE.   At this point, the Patriarch of Constantinople and the Pope in Rome excommunicated each other, splitting Christianity into **Roman Catholic** Christianity in the **west** and **Greek Orthodox** Christianity in the **east**.

DEPICTION OF PAUL, BY PETER RUBENS (D. 1640)

The Great Church Fathers
Several noted theologians helped craft the doctrines that would become a part of the institutional Roman Catholic position. St. Jerome, a monastic who lived in seclusion for part of his life in Palestine, was the first to complete a translation of the Bible into Latin. His definitive translation was not questioned until the Christian Humanists of the Renaissance revisited the Greek texts to compare them to the Latin Vulgate.

DEPICTION OF AUGUSTINE BY SANDRO BOTTICELLI (D. 1510)

One of the greatest was Bishop Augustine of Hippo (354-430). Augustine's remarkable account of his conversion to Christianity, *Confessions*, is a masterpiece of Christian literature. In it, he discusses his pagan roots, resistance to conversion and rather boisterous life, his intellectual development, and finally, the pivotal moment of his conversionary experience.

Augustine would go on after his conversion to tirelessly write about matters of theology, defining, for many, the essential elements of the faith. Augustine understood God as a real and present God who acted in the world. His own personal experience of God at his moment of conversion convinced him of that. He also firmly embraced the **Trinity** wherein God, Jesus, and the Holy Spirit were unified and equal, one and three, and the same. Eternal, ever-being, all powerful, and the source of all things, Augustine's God intervened in human history to punish the wicked, forgive the sinner, and reward the just.

Augustine developed a theology of original sin that viewed humans as creatures of weak and broken wills, as he himself had once been. Free will, endowed to man by God, allowed Adam a choice in the Garden of Eden, but Adam chose unwisely and through him all humans are born with original sin. The only way to remove the stain of original sin was through the grace and mercy of God, which God gives freely to all who ask.

To Augustine, the Church was a necessary entity. He argued that the Church was God's representative on Earth. There could be only one true Church, outside of which Augustine asserted one could not find salvation.

The Church delivered the sacraments and the words of God to the people that could not elsewhere be found. Augustine's thinking on the importance of the Church, its role as divine authority, and that only one true Christian community could exist would greatly influence the development of the Roman Catholic Church, as would his theories about original sin, grace, and free will. In the sixteenth century, Protestants would also find much to appreciate in Augustine regarding grace and God's mercy.

Origins of Monasticism

Asceticism developed first in the Eastern Empire. Some Christians believed that Christianity had strayed from its roots and become too urban. They sought to liberation from the contamination of politics and material wealth. Some left the cities to live in the desert, receiving the name Desert Fathers and Mothers. These men and women engaged in ascetic practices including extreme fasting, celibacy, self-inflicted beatings, or other acts of physical denial. It was out of these groups that the monasticism tradition emerged.

Leaders of the Church feared that ordinary people would be led into ascetic actions that they did not understand or be led into doctrinal error. The Patriarch of Constantinople demanded that rules be developed to regulate and enclose the growing number of ascetics. This led to the rule of Saint Basil, which focused on celibacy, fasting, and prayer. Monasticism would spread westward to become an important aspect of Roman Catholicism.

**ARTIST'S DEPICTION OF SAINT PAKHOM(C. 292-348),
CONSIDERED THE FOUNDER OF EASTERN MONASTICISM**

Western Europe in the Early Medieval Period

In Western Europe, the Roman Empire was replaced by Germanic fragmentary states. One of these, the Franks, helped to continue the impulse towards unity empire in the west and help lay the roots for the development of a Christian, Roman, Germanic cultural tradition. The Germanic chief Clovis led the Franks in defeating any lingering pockets of Roman authority in Gaul. He also conducted military campaigns against other Germanic peoples. Clovis' conversion to Roman Catholic Christianity facilitated his success in governing territories he conquered. Many Germanic people had converted to Arian Christianity, which had earlier been declared heretical at the Council of Nicaea. Clovis, however, supported the Roman Catholic Church thanks to the efforts of his Catholic wife Clotilda and active missionaries. His support of and subsequent conversion to Roman Catholicism gave Clovis the tools via which to govern what would be known as the Merovingian Dynasty.

The Merovingian Dynasty was located in modern day France, Germany, and the Rhineland. The Church supplied Clovis with scribes, accountants, and secretaries, which allowed him to build a literate administrative structure. He placed counts in charge of local areas within the kingdom to defend the borders and provide local justice. A mayor of the palace supervised legal and financial affairs and governed when the king was not present. The Roman Catholic Church gained numerous converts, but they gained the protection of an important and powerful King in the west. As the Pope grew more and more distant from the Emperor in the East, connections with powerful men in the west became increasingly important.

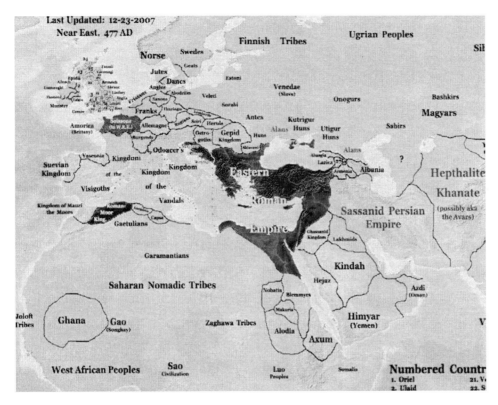

THE ROMAN EMPIRE IN 477 CE

The dynasty was short lived, but it left the renewed the desire for centralized rule in the west. The Carolingians capitalized on this impulse to centralization. The Carolingians were an aristocratic clan who asserted authority in the early eighth century Charles Martel (d. 741) of the Carolingian family was a mayor of palace in the Merovingian Dynasty. He made alliances with other families and demonstrating his prowess on the battlefield. In what was considered a major victory for Christianity, Martel defeated Muslim invaders in 732 C.E. at the Battle of Tours in central France. This victory solidified his position as the most powerful leader in the region, though he did not claim the title of Emperor.

Martel's grandson Charlemagne (r 768-814), Charles the Great, is the most important ruler of the Carolingian empire. Charlemagne ruled over

Gaul, parts of Northern Spain, Bavaria, and North Italy. Thanks to his alliance with and support of the Papacy, Pope Leo III proclaimed Charlemagne emperor on Christmas day 900 C.E. The title of Emperor allowed Charlemagne to claim a link to the power and prestige of the earlier Roman Empire while solidly linking himself to the Roman Church. The Pope gained the support of the imperial power, while symbolically indicated that he had the power to appoint secular rulers.

POPE ADRIAN MEETING WITH CHARLEMAGNE

Charlemagne helped facilitate a cultural revival that is known as the **Carolingian** Renaissance. During this period, monks wrote or copied books, produced illuminated manuscripts, and wrote law codes, letters, and sermons. Latin was the language used for all religious and state documents. Charlemagne's advisor on religion, Alcuin (735-804) established schools attached to monasteries and cathedrals, to educate priests in theology based on the Bible and the learned early Church Fathers, rhetoric, writing, geometry, and mathematics. Greek philosophy, Roman legal codes and speeches, and the writings of the Church Father were preserved by monks and formed the heart of the educational curriculum. Alcuin developed a theory that helped construct an understanding of the power and responsibilities of a Christian ruler, which allowed Charlemagne to assert that God had made him the legitimate ruler of Western Christendom, giving him spiritual and secular authority. This proclamation did not generate tensions while Charlemagne lived because he worked with the Pope, but later Popes and Emperors would fight over power and preeminence in the west.

THE VIKING EXPANSION

In the ninth century, Christianity suffered a major setback as non-Christians from the north, south, and east invaded Europe. The Vikings emerged from the northern lands of Europe. Expanding outward due to population pressure, the desire for wealth, and the need for resources, they used their seafaring skills to establish trade and raiding routes, and later colonies, throughout Eastern and Western Europe. As they expanded, they facilitated the formation of centralized rule in England as smaller territories joined forces with King Alfred (r. 871-899), which facilitated an intellectual revival in England, brought about political stability, and helped sponsor the development of a unified Christianity in England.

In the area now known as Germany witnessed Magyar invasions (modern day Hungary) from the east beginning in the late ninth century. The Magyars were not defeated until the mid-tenth century when King Otto I (r. 936-973) solidified the support of the Germanic local leaders and pushed the Magyars back. In return for his support of Christianity, the Church supported Otto I. He led armies to support the papacy in Italy and was anointed Emperor, as Charlemagne had earlier been. Otto I became the first Holy Roman Emperor and his relationship with the Church, though strong, set the stage for controversies between the Holy Roman Empire and the Roman Catholic Church.

Christian Europe in the Middle Ages
It took until the eleventh century for all of Western Europe to be converted to Roman Christianity. The conversion process experienced setbacks because of invasions.   When the Vikings, Magyars, and Muslims invaded, they attacked, pillaged, plundered, and destroyed monasteries and churches. Some religious communities disappeared, while others fell under the control of secular leaders who appointed themselves abbots or priests, but otherwise had no interest in religion. Some were greedy, dishonest, lecherous, and consumed with their own interests rather than being good leaders. People complained that the Church had become corrupt and worldly.

Western Monasticism and Reform Movements in the Middle Ages
The monastic communities experienced early success, but over time internal crisis. Devout Christians had embraced monasticism in the west just as they had earlier done in the east. Western monastics communities emerged by the fourth century. They developed rules by which the community would live. **St. Benedict** (480-547) developed a set of regulations, which stressed poverty, chastity, and obedience. Monasteries became an important component of the social life of Western Europe. Monasteries managed large tracts of land, producing goods, and employed laborers, which helped to support the infrastructure of communities. They also acted as inns, orphanages, hospitals, and schools. Monks established libraries, which preserved the knowledge of the classical world and supported the expansion of learning in Europe. Over time, however, some monastic communities became overly wealthy, lax in the observance of their rules, and corrupt.

Reform efforts began in the tenth century when new monastic communities were established. The **Abbey of Cluny** was formed in the tenth century as a result of reform impulses; it stressed strict observance of rules and high standards of behavior. **Celibacy** was strictly enforced at each of the more than 300 monasteries associated with the Order. They also did away with the common practice of **simony**, the selling of church offices. The monastery enjoyed the support of lay Catholics, who donated money and goods to the Order. As the wealth increased, however, lay influence began to have an influence, and the monks' lives became more luxurious.

Renewed calls for reform prompted the emergence of numerous Orders, each with its own set of rules and foci. **Robert of Molesmes** founder a new order called the **Cistercians**, members of which were known as the white monks because they did not dye their robes. The Cistercians sought to live in isolation from world, living lives of manual labor and prayer. They also became very popular and over time became wealthy. The most famous of the modern day Cistercians was **Thomas Merton**(d. 1968), who belonged to the Trappist Cistercians. His embrace of Zen Buddhism, meditation, and social activism made him a popular religious figure in the twentieth-century.

THOMAS MERTON[28]

At the highest levels of the Church, Popes also attempted to reform the institution. **Pope Leo IX** (r 1049-1054) issued decrees against violence, simony, and clerical marriage. **Celibacy** was the rule, but in tenth and eleventh centuries, many priests failed to live up to this ideal. Some were living with women, while others were married and had families. The Pope issued strict decrees regulating celibacy, sending Church officials out to visit parishes to ensure conformity. The Pope also attempted to limit the influence of elites from papal elections. The **Lateran Synod of 1059** asserted that cardinals were the only members of the Church with the power

---

[28]Downloaded fromhttp://www.merton.org/chrono.aspx Accessed, March 4, 2014.

to elect popes. Emperors could approve the choice made by the cardinals, but could not nominate Popes.

The Church in the High Middle Ages

After the period of invasions subsided, Europe began to revive. Regional states emerged in England, France, and the Italy, the economy revived nurtured by lines of trade established by Vikings and Muslim traders, and the Roman Catholic Church continued to expand its hold. Church efforts to reform and expand their hegemony generated tensions, as assertive secular leaders contended for more autonomy and power.

In the mid-eleventh century reformers appealed to the Pope to ensure the intellectual ability and moral behavior of the clergy. They asserted that secular rules had appointed men and women to positions in the church who were unfit. Holy Roman Emperors since Otto I had appointed important church officials, conferred office on them in the process known as **lay investiture.** The emperor provided the bishops with the symbols of office, which were comprised of a ring and pastoral staff. Conflict between the Papacy and the Holy Roman Emperor, called the **Investiture** contest, emerged because of demands by reformers that **lay investiture** stop. They not only believed that some of the choices were unfit for religious life, but also asserted that lay investiture implied that secular rulers had some authority over churchmen. Emperors were able to command the cooperation of important people by appointing them to high positions in the church.

MEDIEVAL KING INVESTING A BISHOP WITH SYMBOLS OF HIS OFFICE

Responding to the demands of reformers, Pope Gregory VII ordered an end to **lay investiture**. The Holy Roman Emperor, Henry IV, however, insisted upon his right to continue the practice. The Pope was forced to excommunicate him in 1076. Excommunication barred him and those in his realm from receiving the sacraments and left him without the protection of the Church. With the German nobility rising against him and the ordinary people fearing for their souls, in 1077 Henry IV sought the Pope's forgiveness, after which he reclaimed his position and refused to further challenge the Pope. Despite Henry's capitulation, the investiture controversy continued until 1122, as the Pope and Kings bickered about issues of authority and preeminence. It was not until the twelfth century that the **Concordat of Worms** effectively ended the dispute. It required that **bishopric election** would be conducted according to church law. Only after the church elected a bishop could a king invest him with the symbols and offices of secular authority.

Christianity and Scholastic Theology

In the High Middle Ages, the demand for educated leaders in the Church and in the secular world expanded. The growth of centralized states and expansion of cities helped create the need for highly educated workers to work as administers, accountant, lawyers, and to staff bureaucratic positions. Schools associated with cathedrals developed into universities. While some freedom to explore new topics existed within these Universities, the Roman Catholic Church still carefully monitored the curriculum.

Greek philosophy and Roman education models continued to have a hold over the educational establishment. Academics obtained the works of the great Greek philosopher Aristotle from Eastern Roman and Muslim philosophers. As a result, a system of theology known as scholasticism emerged. Scholastics attempted to use reason to inform their faith. The Scholastic theologian and **Archbishop Anselm** (ca. 1033-1109) used Aristotelian logic to argue for the existence of God. His ontological argument asserts that God is necessary and must exist as the greatest of all things that can be imagined.

Arguably one of the greatest scholastic theologians, St. Thomas Aquinas attempted to harmonize Aristotelian logic with Christianity. In the *Summa Theologica*, he used logic and reason to argue for the existence of God. Arguing from the observation of natural forces and human characteristics such as goodness, Aquinas sets forth to prove a possible, supremely good, primary, mover who sets things in motion according to a dine supremely good plan. His five proofs became the basis of Catholic doctrine and continues to influence Catholic theology as it is required reading in Seminary schools.

SAINT THOMAS AQUINAS[29]

Christian Mysticism in the Middle Ages
Many women and men claimed to have personal experiences of God through which they received special knowledge. This direct experience of the divine is part of **mysticism**. Unlike scholasticism, which used reason to support or inform faith, mystics claimed to experience the direct, real, presence of God during which they experienced a sense of unity that was without boundaries and hard to articulate in words. Mystics had to be careful lest Church officials misunderstand their words or intentions. Some mystics were condemned as heretics. Those who promoted loyalty to the Church, lived cloistered lives, or enjoyed elite support were able to more safely express their experiences.

Numerous male mystics were important during the Middle Ages. **St. Bernard of Clairvaux,** a noted Cistercian, wrote of his immensely visceral participation in unity with God through touching and consuming Christ's wounded flesh and blood. **Meister Eckhart**, a Dominican, wrote

---

[29]From a painting by Carlo Crivelli (1494). http://www.catholictradition.org/Tradition/faith4.htm. Accessed March 4, 2014

about the mystical experience as a removing of the veil that obscures the divine nature of humanity. Mysticism reveals the unity of self and God.

Though denied equality in the Church and prevented from administering the sacraments, women mystics not only experienced full mystical unity with God, but also could command great respect and authority within the religious establishment. **Abbess Hildegard Von Bingen** (1098-1179) began having visions when she was young and eventually wrote them down in a book called *Scivias*. Priests, nobles, and the Pope sought her advice on political, medical, and religious issues.

ARTIST'S DEPICTION OF ABBESS HILDEGARD VON BINGEN, LATER KNOWN AS SAINT HILDEGARD

The English mystic **Julian of Norwich** (c. 1342-1413) experienced visions over the course of two days. Her account of the visions, *Sixteen Revelations of Divine Love*, detailed her understanding of sin and God's love. Though she did not offer political advice, her discussion of the problems of free will, human sin, and the necessity of grace for salvation proved influential.

Many other mystics, men and women, wrote or had others write about their experiences. These mystics attracted a great deal of attention, some negative, from the Church. As long as they did not assertively challenge the institutional Church or its doctrine, some earned the support of the Church because mystics served as living reminders of God's presence and activity in the world.

Catholic Practice in the Middle Ages

The majority of people, however, had no access to the university, as the gap between the rich and poor was quite high. Elite theology was beyond the reach of most people. For most, the sacraments of baptism, marriage, communion, and last rights governed their Christianity. The most popular sacrament was the Eucharist. The Church taught that the bread and wine used in the mass were believed to transform into the body and blood of Jesus in a process known as **transubstantiation**.

During the Middle Ages, the Church promoted certain people to saint-hood. These people were viewed as saints thanks to their supposed ability to perform miracles. Saints were extremely popular as mediators to whom people could pray in times of need. Saints' relics, bones or objects associated with them, were believed to have the power to heal people or gain one release from purgatory, which encouraged many to undertake pilgrimages to holy sites where these items were stored.

Mary, the Mother of Jesus, held a special position among the saints. Though Mary was scarcely mentioned in the Bible, Christian theologians had developed a complex body of belief about her. Her **perpetual virginity** was asserted in the doctrine of virgin birth, while the **Doctrine of the Assumption** claimed her body was taken up to heaven where she reigns with her son and acts as an intermediary to whom Christians appeal for forgiveness. She was promoted as a suffering, self-sacrificing model for women, who could feel an affinity with her love and loss. Numerous cathedrals bear her name and the iconography associated with her cult was expansive. Mary remains an important figure in the Catholic Church in the modern world.

Every church contained a relic of some sort. In many cases, alter cloths had the bones of saints sewn into them. People traveled throughout Europe and into the Holy lands of the Middle East and Rome to visit holy sites. Relics stimulated cross-cultural interactions and trade, as well as helping to give people a tangible representation of their faith. Many traveled to see what were purported to be shards of the cross, vials of Jesus blood or the milk of Mary, or by the fourteenth century the purported burial shroud of Jesus, known as the Shroud of Turin.

Mendicant Orders and Reform

The twelfth century was a period of great urban poverty. Monastic orders, focused on their internal community, were ill equipped to deal with urban issues. Mendicant religious orders emerged that were able to confront the plight of the urban poor and address continuing reform needs in the Church. The Dominicans and Franciscans were urban-based mendicant orders that developed in the 12th century. They emerged to champion spiritual over materialist values and deter people from joining heterodox movements.

The **Franciscans** were a mendicant order founded by **Francis of Assisi** (d. 1226). Born to a merchant family, Francis led a life of luxury, although he showed an early leaning towards reading and care for the poor. After a serious illness, he changed his life, adopting a life of self-denial and meditation. He came to believe that spiritual liberation could only be achieved through embracing poverty.

Clara of Assisi founded an order for women based on the Franciscan Order. Though non-mendicant, the nuns of the order also took vows of poverty. Francis oversaw the order for a time, and then Clara took control and ruled the order, successfully resisting attempts to challenge the order's vows of poverty.

Francis called for the literal following of Gospel in which Jesus commanded his followers to preach in poverty. Francis gave away everything and became an itinerant preacher, attracting numerous followers. Known as the **begging brotherhood**, Francis' followers took vows of poverty. Francis was credited with numerous miracles and the stigmata, bleeding wounds on his body where Jesus had been injured. The Franciscans continue to be a popular and important mendicant group within the Catholic Church.

DEPICTION OF SAINT FRANCIS OF ASSISI

The mendicant Dominican Order was founded by Dominic de Guzman (d. 1221). After learning of the **Cathar** heresy spreading from Albi France, he requested permission to preach against heresy. Dominic was allowed to form an order based on the Rule of Saint Augustine. In order to reform the Church and combat heresy, his Order established schools throughout Europe. The Dominicans use money from donations to support the community and fund preaching tours and educational establishments. They became known as the **Black friars** because they wore black over their habits.

Challenges to the Orthodox Roman Catholic Doctrine

Two heresies became popular during the Middle Ages, the **Waldensian** and the **Cathar** movements (**Albigensian**). The Waldensian heresy began in 1173, when a wealthy merchant named Waldo decided to sell his property and give the proceeds to the poor. He then embraced a life of poverty and preaching, but did not join an order. Pope Alexander III (r 1159-1181) found his beliefs to be in conformity to the orthodox canon, but commanded that Waldo preach only when invited to do so by local bishops. Since Bishops resented his popularity, they did not invite Waldo to preach. Waldo did not stop preaching and as a result, in 1184 he and followers were declared heretics. Waldensians continue to exist, but their beliefs have moved farther from those of the Roman Catholic Church.

DEPICTION OF THE EXPULSION OF THE ALBIGENSIANS FROM CARCASSONE IN 1209

The Cathars posed the greatest threat to the Church due to sheer numbers, organization, and presence throughout Europe. Cathars thought the material body was an evil and degraded prison that enclosed the soul. The only way to liberate the soul within was to abstain from material life as much as possible. Most were vegetarians. The **Elect**, those at the highest levels, were celibate to avoid producing more trapped souls and to avoid bodily pleasure. The Cathar doctrine may have entered Western Europe through Bulgaria in 1140. Afterwards, it expanded partially because their attack against the Catholic Church for being greedy and corrupt resonated with city dwellers and the nobility. Women were attracted to the faith because Cathar groups allowed women to preach and teach.

The Roman Catholic Church tried converting the Cathars, but met with little success. The founder of the Dominican Order attempted to preach to Cathar groups. Finally, after a papal legate was murdered by a group of Cathars, a crusade was launched. Violence against Cathars continued throughout the 13th and 14th centuries, after which systematic oppression and the execution of unrepentant Cathars led to their demise as a group.

The Crusades
To the East, the movement of Muslim forces into the Holy Lands had begun in the seventh Century. Initially, Muslim leaders occupying Jerusalem and other shared holy sites had allowed Christians to come on pilgrimage and had not oppressed the native Christian population. Beginning in the Eleventh century, the newly converted Turkish Muslims, the Seljuq

Turks, conquered the region and began to expand. The Seljuq Turks were not tolerant and posed a threat to the neighboring Eastern Roman Empire.

The Emperor of the Eastern Roman Empire asked for help from the West. In response, Pope Urban II called upon Christian knights to liberate the Holy Lands. Not just knights, but people of all classes participated. Although the main impulse was religious, people participated for a variety of other reasons. Some men wanted to gain reputations, wealth, and power. Popes, weakened by the growth of centralized powers, hoped to regain power and perhaps even reunify the Eastern Orthodox and Roman Catholic Churches.

The first crusade began in 1096. It was disorganized and badly supplied, but despite this the Crusaders took Jerusalem in 1099. Between 1096-1270 eight crusades occurred, but none of them was very successful. During the 4th crusade (1202-1204), Christian armies from the west conquered Constantinople from the Muslim armies. They burned and sacked the city and stole the sacred relics. The Eastern Roman Empire was left weakened and divided, while the gulf between the Roman Catholic and Eastern Orthodox churches strengthened and still persists.

The legacy of the Crusades was to be heightened tensions between the majority Christian-countries and the majority Muslim bloc. Political relations between Islamic and Western Christian leaders worsened and religious persecution increased in both regions. Modern day strained relations can be partially traced back to the bloody battles of the crusades. This was a time of great tribulation for the Jewish communities in Europe as well, for the idea was that the Muslims were the enemy abroad, whereas the Jews—seen as Christ killers— were the enemy close at hand.

POPE URBAN AT THE COUNCIL OF CLERMONT, 1095

The Renaissance and the Church

The Middle Ages gave way to the Italian Renaissance in the fourteenth century. Urbanization, increased trade, and population growth nurtured new communities and change. The Roman Catholic Church, at many levels staffed by wealthy men with elite connections, engaged in the Renaissance spirit of conspicuous consumption and display. The Papacy acted as patron to artists, employed architects to beautify and restore cathedrals, and engaged in political machinations that provoked new calls for reform.

The availability of new texts and a spirit of investigation provoked many literate men to revisit the Bible, writings of the Church Fathers, and philosophical treatises from the classical world. Doing so raised questions about the sacraments, celibacy, the institutional Church, and the papacy. The Dutch scholar **Desiderius Erasmaus** (d. 1536)—more commonly known simply as **Erasmus**—was a leading Christian Humanist who called for a return to a simpler form of Christianity, stripped of the pomp and ceremony of the Roman Catholic hierarchy. Though Erasmus remained within the Church, others would launch critiques and calls for reform that would leave Christianity divided into numerous groups.

THE SISTINE CHAPEL

The Protestant Reformation

The Protestant reformation began as a call to reform the Roman Catholic Church, not to splinter Christendom. As literacy rates rose, vernacular languages gained strength at the expense of Latin, and some began to call for greater access to the Bible in their own languages. The Catholic Church had resisted publishing a full translation of the Bible into the common languages because it was feared that independent reading by those unskilled in theology might lead to doctrinal errors.

Into the spirit of literacy and calls for reform, an Augustinian Monk in Germany named **Martin Luther** (1483-1546) would emerge as the spokesperson for religious change. Luther had a vibrant personality, stubborn nature, and strong intellect. He began his reform efforts after the Church renewed and expanded the scope of the selling of **indulgences.** Indulgences were seen as the purchase of prayers that can earn early release from **Purgatory**

DEPICTION OF MARTIN LUTHER

Purgatory is a place where souls too good to go to hell, but still too stained from sin for heaven, are punished before ascending to heaven. The length of time a soul suffered in Purgatory depended on the gravity of one's sins. In 1517, Luther posted notice on the door of the church at **Wittenberg** calling of debate about the legitimacy of indulgences. This notice, which included 95 arguments critical of church practices, has come to be known as the **95 Theses**.

In 1521, Luther was called to the **Diet of Worms**[30] to recant his criticism. When he declared himself unable to recant, asserting that he had read scripture and convinced of its truth could not turn back. The Holy Roman Emperor Charles V censored Luther; The Pope excommunicated him. After his excommunication, Prince Frederick who supported Luther because he resented the power, wealth, and privileges of the Catholic Church protected Luther.

Once in hiding, Luther's critique of the Church expanded. Luther called for reform to call for a translation of the Bible into the vernacular language. He translated the Bible himself from Greek into German; His translation and other writings spread quickly thanks to the recent introduc-

---

[30] A "diet" is a formal deliberative assembly.

tion of the printing press with movable type (1456), which made the production of books less expensive and time consuming. Luther also called for the closure of all monasteries and convents because he asserted that no scriptural basis existed for clerical celibacy. Luther ended up marrying a former nun, with whom he had numerous children.

Luther also argued that **confession** to priests was unnecessary and did not assure one of salvation. Luther rejected the efficacy of confession and penance, key beliefs of the Catholic tradition, instead arguing that people were justified, saved from sin, **by faith alone**. He called upon all men to be priests within their own households, reading scripture, and directly addressing God not appealing to intercessors. To Luther, scripture provided all the laws and rituals one needed, not priests or the Pope. Luther's challenge moved from indulgences to radically call for a priesthood of believers without a hierarchy.

The progressive nature of Luther's call for spiritual equality did not, however, extend too far. Luther did not imagine a world with multiple forms of Christian belief. When he failed to reform the Catholic Church, Luther formed what he believed to be the one true church; The Catholic Church, he came to believe was a false church. Luther was also not a champion of social equality. When the peasants of Germany revolted against their oppressive landowners, inspired by his words, he denounced them. Many peasants left Luther's group to found a new Christian group, called the **Anabaptists**.

Luther continued to attract followers throughout Germany and Scandinavia. Lutheran communities continued to insist that scripture was the ultimate authority that helped lead one to God. Though they had split from Roman Catholicism, in many ways the structure of the Lutheran Church resembled that of the Catholics. Mass was still celebrated, though not in Latin, and the Eucharist was maintained, though Luther refrained from embracing transubstantiation, referring instead to the symbolic presence of Jesus rather than a literal material presence in the bread and wine. Priests conducted services and were overseen by bishops, but clerical celibacy was not required.

Anabaptists

Initially led by **Thomas Muntzer**, Anabaptists were also called **Separatists** because they held themselves apart from the civic institutions of their time. Believing that people should always make informed decisions based on their understanding of scripture, they did not believe in infant baptism; babies could not understand what was happening and could not knowingly accept Christianity. They believed that people should make a mature decision to embrace Christianity; Christianity should not be imposed.

Anabaptists rejected most forms of authority, outside of scripture. They did not attempt to construct institutions or a hierarchy, which meant that there was no centralizing force to unite Anabaptists over time and geography. They did not join political groups or the military. Their churches were home based and non-clerical, as they feared the institutionalization of faith and hierarchies led to abuse.

Increasingly oppressed by Catholic and other Protestant groups in the sixteenth century, many moved away from society to live apart. One group, led by **Menno Simons** formed **the Mennonites**. Many Mennonites fled to the Americas in the mid-1600s to escape persecution in Europe. In Pennsylvania, they became known as the **Pennsylvania Dutch**. One branch, known as the **Amish**, has rejected modern technology. Their clothing and technology remains at the level of the seventeenth century. Other Mennonites use modern technology, but prefer to live apart from urban centers.

John Calvin: Calvinism

Another challenge to Luther emerged in the form of the learned intellectual John Calvin (d. 1564). A lawyer and a classical scholar, Calvin became the intellectual leader of the reformation. Calvin's 1536 Institutes of the Christian Religion became the standard of Protestant thought throughout Europe. He argued that humans could only know peace through the knowledge of God. Seeking after knowledge is an act of faith that reveals God's creation and brings one closer to communion with God. Though attempts to impose a theocratic government based on his theology failed, Calvin's theology expanded and influenced the development of Protestant Christianity in Scotland, England, and the Americas.

PORTRAIT OF JOHN CALVIN, ATTRIBUTED TO HANS HOLBEIN, THE YOUNGER (D. 1543)

Calvin embraced a strict uncompromising view of God and salvation. Preserving all sovereignty for God, Calvin asserted a theory of **predestination.** He believed that God, all knowing and all-powerful, had determined the fate of all individuals even before creation. Humans, wretched and sinful due to their failed wills, could only achieve salvation through God's grace. Most were doomed to damnation; others were the select few predestined to salvation.

Calvin also attacked the Catholic doctrine of **transubstantiation**, labeling it akin to magic. Like Luther, Calvin believed that Christians should have access to the Bible in the vernacular. Calvin was also anti-monastic. Though he rejected the Catholic hierarchical priesthood, he did support a hierarchy of the Elect, those deemed of superior spiritual knowledge and behavior, other the non-elect in Calvinist communities.

As Calvinist thought expanded, some different groups within the faith emerged. In the Netherlands, **Jacobus Arminus** rejected predestination. His belief that free will and an all-powerful God were not in conflict was known as **Arminianism**. His views were condemned and his supporters were persecuted. In Scotland and England, Calvinists founded the Presbyterian churches, which like their continental counterparts did not have bishops. Instead, local communities sent representatives to an assembly that oversaw the governance of the community.

Sizable Presbyterian groups have emerged in Canada, the United States, Australia, and New Zealand, as well as remaining strong in Scotland and the Netherlands. Missionaries have also attempted to gain converts in Asia and the Middle East, with mixed results.

The English Reformation: Anglicans and Puritans

In England, the pace of reform was governed by political necessity. Henry VIII initially had championed the Catholic religion in England. When his wife failed to produce a male heir, Henry sought a divorce, which was not allowed by the Church. The Pope refused to budge despite Henry's pleas, which prompted Henry to split from the Catholic Church. Henry VIIIovernight became the Supreme Head of what would eventually become known as the Anglican Church. By doing so, he gained all the Church lands in England. After he closed the monasteries, he took that land and wealth as well. He became one of the wealthiest monarchs in Europe, as well as being the secular and religious leader in England.

Henry VIII was succeeded to the throne by his son Edward instituted more Calvinist inflected changes. His reign was short, however, and his sister Mary I took control, returning England to the Catholic Church. Mary also only ruled a short time. Her half-sister Elizabeth I (1558-1603) was longer lived. She returned England to the Protestant form of Christianity. As the Supreme Head, Elizabeth 1 ruled the Church and State just as Henry VIII had done.

Elizabeth 1 died in 1603 and James I (r. 1603-1625) became the head of the Stuart Dynasty of England. Under James I, the Anglican Church was divided between conservative Calvinist inflected Anglicans, known as **Puritans**, and the more ceremonial high Anglican Christians who in ceremonial rituals and hierarchy more resembled Catholics. Puritans wanted to reform the Anglican Church by stripping it of rituals and the hierarchy.

ELIZABETH 1 FROM A DARNLEY PORTRAIT, C. 1575

By the time of Charles I these religious divisions had become stronger. Charles supported the high Anglican Church, which prompted Puritans to leave England for the new American colony of Massachusetts Bay to escape oppression. Eventually, religious tensions erupted in the English Civil Wars (1642-1649), which ended when Charles I was beheaded, the monarchy was abolished, and the high Anglican Church was suppressed. A period of religious experimentation followed, with the end result being the eventual restoration of the monarchy and the Anglican Church in England.

The Anglican Church continues to be the State Church of England. It spread to the American colonies, where it became known as the Episcopalian Church. It is also strong in areas in which the British once had a colonial presence, such as Australia, New Zealand, and the Caribbean. The Anglican and Episcopalian communities tend to be progressive in matters sexuality and politics. This trend toward embracing progressive stances on issues of social justice has generated tensions in the church and many predict that the Anglican community may split into two churches.

The Catholic Reformation

The Roman Catholic Church had long been in a process of reform. The Protestant Reformation served to give added urgency to ongoing reform measures and stimulated new criticisms with which the Church would have to contend. The Holy Roman Emperor, beset with divisiveness and agitation over matters of religion, sought reform in order to restore stability and order to the continent. In response to requests from the Emperor and from within the church, Pope Paul III called the Council of Trent.

Council of Trent

Called in 1545, the Council of Trent was supposed to address reform and the redefinition of the Catholic faith. Protestant leaders were invited to the Council in the hope that unity in faith could be achieved. It soon became apparent that Catholic leaders had no desire to compromise with Protestants on Church practices or doctrine. The Council immediately reaffirmed Latin as the language of scripture, Catholic tradition as equal to scripture, the supreme and sole right of the Church to make decisions on matters of religion, all of the seven sacraments of the Catholic faith, and the position of works as an aid to faith in achieving salvation. The reaffirmation of these points made any discussion with the Protestant leaders moot, ending all hopes of a unified Christendom.

The Church did, however, undertake the daunting task of reforming the behavior of its members and increasing its outreach to the community. Clerical celibacy was reaffirmed and more closely regulated. Priests were required to be rigorously trained to ensure the quality of service. They were also instructed to provide sermons on the scripture to help educate the populace on the beliefs and practices necessary for salvation.

Jesuits

The Jesuit Order, founded in the sixteenth century by Ignatius Loyola, was central to the reform impulse. Loyola, a former Spanish nobleman and soldier, became the spearhead of a religious movement that emphasized missionary work, education, and obedience to the Church. The Jesuits emphasized a life of self-sacrifice in the service of Christ. Many agreed to staff missions in far-away places to convert lapsed Catholics or non-Christians.

Missions

DEPICTION OF IGNATIUS LOYOLA

The Jesuit missions in Europe and in newly discovered territories in the sixteenth century and beyond were highly successful. Jesuit missionaries masterfully adapted Catholic doctrine to new locations. They successfully converted many indigenous people in North and South America and Asia to Catholicism, while halting the spread of Protestantism in Europe. Skilled speakers, intelligent advisors, and well-trained theologians they served as advisors to Kings, helped staff government posts, and acted as intermediaries between the local people and colonial forces. Though over time their successes led to jealousy within the Catholic Church and attacks by Protestants from without, the Jesuits continue to be champions of reform, conversion, and the papacy into the modern day.

Christianity in the Seventeenth Century
The seventeenth century was a time of bloody wars of religion that expanded throughout Europe. The Holy Roman Emperor and the Pope sought to preserve their positions and the Catholic faith on the Continent, while Protestants sought religious liberty. The Thirty Years War (1618-1648) erupted when the Holy Roman Emperor attempted to use his position to compel Bohemia to remain in the Catholic Church. Underlying political issues exacerbated the tension and soon Europe was embroiled in a war that devastated the region. In 1648, the Peace of Westphalia granted Protestants freedom to worship in some areas, while retaining Catholic hegemony in others. England remained apart from the Thirty Years War, but did experience civil wars partially over religion as the Puritans resisted the ceremonial aspects of the Anglican Church.

Baptists
Many Puritans fled England for the Continent or the American colonies to escape oppression. One group that fled before the wars settled in Amsterdam where they were influenced by the Mennonites. Led by John Smyth, a group that came to be known as Baptists adopted the practice of adult baptism. Some Baptists returned to England to establish the First Baptist Church of England in 1612. They were noted for fully immersing people during baptism. In 1639, Baptists founded a church in Rhode Island from where they spread throughout the Americas, becoming particularly popular in the later southern states of the United States.

Congregationalist
Another group of English Puritan emigrants to the continent established the Congregationalist church. Congregationalists asserted that the Christian community is not composed of an imposed hierarchy, but rather one voluntarily chosen by the community and open to change. Each congregation was self-governing but responsible to provide support to all other Christians.

One group of Congregationalists returned to England in 1609 to organize a voyage to English held lands in America. Known as the Pilgrims, they sailed to North America on the Mayflower in 1620 and established the Plymouth colony in what would become Massachusetts. Joined by Puritans from England, Congregationalist groups established colonies throughout New England.

Quakers

New religious movements emerged in the seventeenth century. The Society of Friends, also known as the Quakers, emerged during the English Civil Wars. Founded by George Fox (1624-1691), the Quakers asserted that priests and other intermediaries were unnecessary to salvation. God, they believe, speaks directly to his worshippers and reveals his will to them individually. Quakers abstain from violence, oath taking, and sacraments. Quaker services begin with prayer, but mainly consist of silent mediation to allow God to speak to each person, male or female.

Quakers were persecuted in England due to their assertive practice of publically denouncing what they viewed as the empty ceremonies and rituals of other the state. Many Quakers left England for the English colony of Pennsylvania, founded in 1681 by William Penn as a haven for religious dissenters from the Church of England. Quakers continue to embrace their pacifist roots, are non-hierarchical, and believe in the personal revelation of God's will.

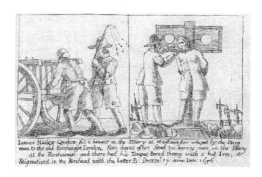

A QUAKER BEING PILLORIED

Eighteenth Century Christianity

Over the course of the eighteenth century, Protestantism continued to diversify, while the power of the Catholic Church continued to decline in many parts of Europe. It would not be until the nineteenth century that the papacy would witness a revival of power in some parts of Europe. The Enlightenment, a time of ongoing scientific, philosophical, and political investigation, saw not just Catholic but also protestant beliefs challenged.

Deism

New discoveries in science led many intellectuals to turn their analytical skills to politics, culture, and religion. In the area of Christianity, many religious leaders found themselves called upon to explain their beliefs about God that could be validated by scientific theories about the universe and the laws of gravity and the mechanical universe.

As a result, Deism emerged. Deists stripped the religion of the day of its supernatural elements. Viewing the universe in mechanical terms, they asserted that while God set the world in motion, He did not actively intervene or manifest Himself. While many still attended church services, they did not embrace the belief in the virginal birth, miracles, or mysticism. Instead, they viewed the universe as a rational and mathematical ordered place with laws that could be uncovered and understood.

Pietism

At the other end of the spectrum from the rational Deists, groups of Christians desiring a return to a more spiritual, less mathematical, view of the Christian experience emerged. Many of these more enthusiastic, heart-centered, Christians felt disaffected by the reasoned and measured faith of the Deists and sought to experience a sense of community and love within Christianity. Pietism, which refers to this more experiential and affective form of Christian worship, spread from Europe, to England, and into the Americas in the eighteen century.

Methodists

John Wesley established a reading group that would come to be known as known as the Methodists. Through his association with a group known as the Moravian Brethren, which stressed the personal experience of conversion to God, Wesley and friends preached throughout Britain. Displaying great emotion, lapsing into ecstatic states, and at times crying and passing out, Wesley and those who listened to his sermons claimed to directly experience God and to be changed, reborn, through their experiences into a new covenant with God. The movement spread to the American colonies via Methodist speakers whose charismatic preaching helped to spark a new religious awakening throughout the colonies.

DEPICTION OF JOHN WESLEY

The Great Awakenings: Revivalism in America

As pietism began to inflect Congregationalist communities throughout the Americas, a spirit of religious revival and renewal swept parts of the country. The eighteenth and the nineteenth century witnessed the first and second great awakenings were noted for tent meetings, charismatic preachers, and enthusiastic forms of Christian worship.

The Congregationalist John Edwards (1703-1758) was a leading figure of the first great awakening of the eighteenth century. His fiery preaching and creative interpretation of theology delighted and terrified his listeners. His sermon "Sinners at the Hands of an Angry God" warned people in graphic and theatric language of the hellfire that awaited the sinners who turned their backs on the life giving grace of God. Prayer meetings were held indoors and out, attracting large crowds of Christians hoping for direct experience of the saving grace of God. The revivalist impulse towards enthusiastic, person, and emotional sermons, conversions, and prayer meetings continued into nineteenth century.

New Religious Movements

New religious movements emerged in the nineteenth century, inspired by the revivalist movements. Joseph Smith (1805-1844) experienced revelations from God, through the angel Moroni, in which he was told that the true church would soon be restored. He founded a church called the Church of Jesus Christ in 1830, which would become known as the

Church of the Latter Day saints or Mormons. Smith claimed Moroni led him to find golden plates on which the Book of Mormon had been written. The Book of Mormon revealed that Jesus had visited the Americas, instructing the native people, before ascending to heaven.

Driven westward by those hostile to his teachings, Smith founded colonies in Missouri and Illinois. Initially he and his followers were polygamous, asserted that each member of the trinity was a separate being, and that humans can progress to become one with God. Smith's evolving views of the nature of God and humans caused division from within and without. He was eventually murdered by a hostile mob.

Smith's successor Brigham Young led a group of Mormons to Utah, those left behind in Missouri established the Reorganized Church of Jesus Christ of the Latter Day Saints. Young and his followers established the Utah with Young as their governor. Under pressure from the U.S. government, the church renounced polygamy though splinter groups not recognized by the Mormon church continue the practice.

The Mormon Church had thrived and thanks to an active mission it has expanded across to globe. Today, over thirteen million people identify themselves as Mormon. The modern church accepts all adult males as priests of an expansive community wide network. Mormons abstain from alcohol, tobacco. caffeine, and tithe yearly. All men must go on a two-year mission, which has helped to facilitate the spread of the faith. Women may go on mission, but are not required to do so; they are not allowed serve as priests, but women do serve in other important leadership roles particularly those related to charitable outreach.

Nineteenth Century Catholicism
The Roman Catholic Church developed new doctrines to refine their doctrine. Pope Pius IX issued the doctrine of the **Immaculate Conception**. Mary the Mother of Jesus had long been considered a virgin at the time of Jesus' birth, but the doctrine of original sin, which implied that original sin was transmitted through procreation, required that Mary be free of sin in order to not contaminate Jesus. That being the case, the doctrine of Immaculate Conception asserts that Mary was conceived immaculately and was never tainted by original sin.

In a move to protect the papacy from attack, the Syllabus of errors, issued by Pope Pius in 1864 denounced a multitude of modern developments including liberalism, modernism, communism, socialism, rationalism, as well as freedom of religion and of the press. In the First Vatican Council of 1870, to further prop up the eroded position of the papacy, the council of cardinals and leading bishops proclaimed that in matters of religion, the Pope was infallible. Despite these attempts to increase the religious authority of the Pope and to police the behavior and political ideologies of Catholics across the globe, the Italian government of Emperor Victor Emmanuel took some papal lands in Italy, reducing the size of the Papal States to their current size.

As the nineteenth century progressed some more liberal minded members of the Catholic community attempted to mediate a compromise between the conservative papacy and the modern world. The works of St. Thomas Aquinas, Thomism, were successfully revived in order to bridge the gap between reason and faith, allowing modern Catholics to enjoy a more harmonious relationship with science, technology, and discoveries in the social sciences.

Catholicism in the Twentieth Century: Vatican Council II

Pope John XXIII called for Vatican Council II to address any need for reform and to address issues specific to the modern age. Protestant and Catholic leaders, and members of the Orthodox communities were all invited to attend. After several meetings, the Church decided to support the use of the vernacular for mass, allow lay people active and authoritative roles as deacons, agreed that freedom of religion and conscience should be supported, and asserted that non-Catholics could achieve salvation. Anti-Semitism was explicitly condemned by the Catholic Church, partially in response to the devastation caused by the Holocaust.

As part of the reform measures called for by Vatican Council II, Pope Paul called the Synod of all Bishops to address doctrinal issues. Two divisive issues discussed at the Synod were birth control and clerical marriage. The Church continues to resist clerical marriage and any artificial forms of birth control, though liberal voices within the clerical and lay community have called for an end to clerical celibacy and an embrace of more birth control options. The ordination of women to the priesthood has also emerged in the modern age, as more women actively agitate for the right to offer the sacraments.

Christianity in the Modern World

The modern era has witnessed the growth of secular social and political philosophies. Some modern States have a separation of church and state, while others, such as some communist States, attempted to completely suppress religions. In some areas, atheism has become a growing force. Scientific theories and philosophies have emerged that prompted the need for a reanalysis of old belief systems.

Despite these changes and challenges, Christianity remains a potent force. Modernity has come with a series of problems. Economic dislocation, political instability, and the rapid pace of change have prompted many to return to religion in search of stability, order, and hope for a better future.

Evangelicals and Fundamentalism

The Evangelical movement has emerged within many Christian sects. Evangelicals, like Pietism and revivalist movements of the great awakenings in America, stress direct personal experiences of God and God's grace. Social issues associated with modernity have provoked the emergence of fundamentalist sects from within the evangelical Christian community. Christian fundamentalists resist any attempts to reconcile faith and the Bible with history or science. They assert that the Bible must be read literally and through the eyes of faith, not using critical or scientific methods.

Some fundamentalists, fearing that the inequality, poverty, and violence found in the modern world point to the end of the world, have embraced a black and white understanding of the world that accept little to no diversity of belief. This stance adopted by the minority of fundamentalists has led to oppression, intolerance, and at times violence. Some Christian fundamentalists governments have put in place oppressive laws. In some areas, Christian fundamentalists government officials have attempted to ban the teaching of evolution in schools, restrict or end the sale of contraceptives, and to make abortions in any circumstances illegal. Others have attempted to define marriage in such a way as to prevent same-sex marriages and to craft laws that would make homosexual acts illegal.

Some evangelical preachers, fundamentalist or not, have used their positions of authority within their communities as a launching pad for missions. Using modern technology, some have become noted televangelists who use television, radio, and the Internet to reach larger audiences. Many of these preachers are highly charismatic individuals who have become popular. The early pioneer Billy Graham commanded a huge audience of listeners who donated great amounts of money to help fund missions and activists. Graham now shares the stage with a multitude of preachers exhorting Christians to political activism and social conservatism.

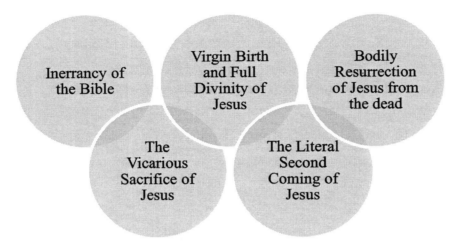

THE FIVE FUNDAMENTALS

Many Christian groups, however, have not embraced towards fundamentalism or evangelical style experiences. The Anglican and Episcopalian churches have embraced progressive stances on issues of contraception, homosexuality, and same-sex marriages. They have become inclusive of women and gay clergy. While the Roman Catholic Church has retained a conservative stance rooted in its traditions, it has under its current pope, Francis, embraced a more progressive attitude towards science, criticized inequality and unregulated capitalism, and taken steps towards the acceptance of homosexuals within the church. Nonetheless, a highly conservative strain of Catholicism continues to hold sway in many areas and the pace of reform has been slow.

Questions for Reflection

1. How did the Catholic Church emerge from the early Christian communities?
2. Discuss the differences the issues that split early Protestant reformers from the Catholic Church.
3. What issues have emerged in the modern era that has provoked challenges and changes within Christianity?

4. How has the position of women in Christian communities changed over time?
5. Discuss the differences between Lutherans, Anabaptists, and Calvinists.

Glossary

Anabaptists   A breakaway movement from Martin Luther's early Protestant movement, rejecting most forms of authority outside of Scripture.

Apostles   The Companions of Jesus.

Arius   A bishop who taught that Jesus was mortal, and not divine.

Begging brotherhood
Another name for the Franciscan order, started by St. Francis of Assisi.

Calvinism   One of the intellectual leaders of the Reformation, and famous for his concept of predestination within Christianity.

Christ   From Christos, meaning savior, and a Greek rendering of the Hebrew "Messiach." Specific title for Jesus whose death is seen as salvation for Christians.

Cistercians   Also known as the White Monks, because of the wearing of undyed robes.

Council of Nicea
A gathering held in 325 CE that defined orthodox belief regarding the nature of Jesus.

Clara of Assisi
Founder of a monastic order for women based upon the Franciscan order, although they did not adhere to the mendicant condition.

Constantine   Emperor who granted Christians freedom of worship throughout the Roman Empire.

Crucifixion   Jesus' death upon the cross.

Erasmus/Desiderius Erasmaus

A Christian humanist who called for a return to simple Christianity , without the pomp and ceremony of the Catholic hierarchy.

Franciscans Mendicant monastic order.

Galilee Likely birthplace of Jesus.

Gnosticism The idea that a secret knowledge had been passed from Jesus to some of his chosen followers, and the beliefs that are based upon this concept. Literally "hidden meaning" of Christianity.

Galerius Roman emperor who, in 311, issued the edict of toleration making Christianity legal in the Eastern Roman Empire.

Gospels Literally "good news." There were several gospels in early Christianity, but only four now form part of the Canon: Mark, Matthew, Luke, and John.

Iconoclasm The rejection of the use of icons in worship.

Indulgence The purchase of prayers that can earn early release from **Purgatory.**

Lay Investiture

The conferring of offices upon church officials by feudal non-Church lords and people of secular authority.

Martin Luther

Former Augustinian monk who protested against Papal indulgences and pioneered a movement of reform that started Protestantism.

Mithraism An eastern religion that was popular among Roman soldiers.

Monasticism An ascetic tradition governed by rules of celibacy, fasting and prayer.

Nazarenes Early followers of Jesus.

Patriarch Title of a bishop of one of the important cities in early Christianity.

Paul of Tarsus:

> One of the most influential figures in Christianity. Said to have converted by a unique spiritual experience and encounter with Jesus after the latter's crucifixion.

Petrine Primacy

> The concept of the primacy of Peter for leadership of the post-Jesus community.

Predestination

> (In Calvinist theory): The concept that God had determined the fate of all beings even before creation, and that only through God's grace would sinful humans achieve salvation. Without this, they were doomed for hell.

Purgatory A place where souls too good to go to hell, but still too stained from sin for heaven, are punished before ascending to heaven.

Sadducees Group in Jerusalem at time of Roman occupation; they had political power over the community.

Separatists Another name for Anabaptists.

Simony The selling of Church offices.

Theodosius 1 Emperor who made Christianity official religion of the Roman Empire and engaged in forced conversions.

Thomas Merton A famous Cistercian monk of the twentieth century.

Trinity A mystical concept in Christianity where God, Jesus and the Holy Spirit are unified and equal in a triune godhead.

ISLAM

Khaleel Mohammed

"There is no God but God"

**CALLIGRAPHIC REPRESENTATION OF THE SHAHADA: THE MUSLIM DEC-
LARATION THAT TRANSLATES AS "THERE IS NO GOD BUT GOD, AND MU-
HAMMAD IS THE MESSENGER OF GOD."**

- *Explain Social Setting to which Muhammad came*
- *Discuss the Birth and Life of Muhammad*
- *Discuss etymology of Islam, Muslim*
- *Explain Sources*
- *Discuss early development, beliefs*
- *Discuss Compilation of Quran*
- *Discuss Caliphate*
- *Explain Qur'an, Islamic law.*
- *Crusades, Spread of Islam*
- *Explain Islam in America.*
- *Political Islam/Extremism*

Sitz im Leben

The Hijaz region –located in present day Saudi Arabia—was the meeting place of many religions in the seventh century. Entire tribes identified themselves as Christian or Jewish, or being devoted to gods or goddesses that were specific to Arabia. In the city of Mecca, there was the **Ka'aba**, a worship site said to contain 360 idols, representative of the various tribes and their deities. Each year there was a pilgrimage during specific months, at which time there was a general truce. This **Ka'aba** was said to be the worship site built by Abraham and his son Ishmael, and the presences of idols only came about when later generations strayed from monotheism.

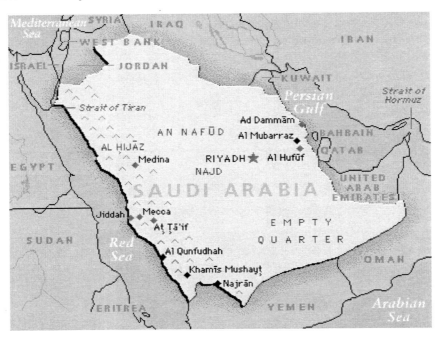

MAP OF SAUDI ARABIA, SHOWING MECCA AND MEDINA

Mecca was known for its trade with Syria and Yemen. The influence of the Byzantine and Persian empires was felt even in the desert. We are not sure of the exact types of Judaisms or Christianities that may have been present, but the writings of historians indicate that there were many sectarian movements, and Arabia was even referred to as *haeresium fera*— 'the mother of all heresies."

Flavius Josephus, the first century historian wrote of the biblical practices that were among the Arabs, among them circumcision. In 135 CE, when the Jews were exiled from Israel, many of them made their way into the Arab desert and, over the centuries, established their own communities, adhering to their ancestral religion. These people were known as the Banu

Isra'il. Rome had representatives in Arabia as well, and it would seem that many of the traditions of the region were shared. The story of Abraham is one of these traditions: the Jews saw themselves as his descendants by way of Isaac and Sarah, while the Arabs saw themselves as his descendants by way of Hagar and Ishmael.

Birth and Life of Muhammad

Muhammad, later to be the prophet of Islam, was born in the city of Mecca. He is said to have been born in 570 CE, but this date seems to be more in keeping with tradition rather than with any provable historical accuracy. Records seem to suggest he started preaching in the year 610 CE. The maturity required for acknowledged leadership and scholarship was deemed to be forty in the Judeo-Christian lore, and so, with some retroactive calculations, if Muhammad's spiritual maturity were assumed to have come when he was forty years old, it followed that he would have been born in the year 570.

Muslim chroniclers tell us that Muhammad was born to the **Quraysh** tribe. His father had predeceased his birth, and he also lost his mother while still a child. He became a ward of his grandfather, **Abdul Muttalib**, and upon the latter's death, was placed in the care of his uncle **Abu Talib**.

We know little that can be deemed as reliable about the young years of Muhammad. Many stories—as is a trait in prophetology—are panegyrical and mythical in nature, ascribing to him numerous miracles and wondrous deeds, although it must be noted that the **Qur'an**, Islam's scripture, does not make these claims for Muhammad.

Muslim historians tell us Muhammad was seen to be a person of great integrity and honesty. He was employed by a rich widow, **Khadijah**, to take care of her trading caravans. When he was about twenty five years old, he married his employer who, according to the traditional reports was fifteen years his senior. Four daughters were born of that marriage, although there are some claims that only one child was the result of that union.

It was during this time that Muhammad received his spiritual experience that was to forever change his life. He was meditating in the cave of Hira, in the mountains around Mecca, when he received his first revelation. Many Muslim traditions report that he was visited by the angel Gabriel. Some chroniclers point out that the story is seemingly structured upon the experience of Jacob in the Hebrew Bible, and that the Qur'an instead refers to revelation that he received "upon his heart."

FOURTEENTH CENTURY DEPICTION OF GABRIEL VISITING MUHAMMAD

Muhammad then began preaching his message which, in summary, was a call to return to the monotheism of the Abrahamic religion, to respect and honor the prophets and books of the antecedent Judaism and Christianity. The monotheism to which Muhammad called was an uncompromising belief and worship of one God. In doing so, he was going against the culture of the Meccans with their many gods.

While many members of his own tribe, the Quraysh did not pay attention to his message, there were some early converts, and their numbers kept rising. Among the early converts were **Khadijah, Ali,** Muhammad's cousin, and **Abu Bakr**, a close friend. The poor and downtrodden were quickly drawn to the message of equality, charity and ethics. Those who opposed the new faith were adamant, however, that it not spread, and devised all sorts of means to oppress the followers of Muhammad.

It was decided to completely boycott Muhammad's tribe, and the little group suffered terribly. In 619, during the time of this boycott, Muhammad lost his wife Khadijah. Later some of the Muslims, as the followers of the new faith were called, went to Abyssinia (modern day Ethiopia) to escape persecution. The Quraysh tribe tried to get the Negus, the Christian leader of Abyssinia, to return the band of Muslims. Tradition reports that the Negus summoned the Muslims and questioned them about the founder of their new religion as well as its tenets. They told him that Muhammad was a man of ethics who had not been known to aspire to any position of power, and then they recited for him one of the revelations about Jesus and Mary. The Negus supposedly said that these teachings were in accord with what he knew, and that he would not return the Muslims. As such, Muslim tradition recognizes Ethiopia as the first place where they found refuge.

In 620, a delegation from Yathrib visited Mecca and after being impressed by Muhammad's teachings, invited him to come to their city. The delegation converted to Islam, as the new religion was called, and returned to Yathrib to pave the way for his going to them. In the meanwhile, with Muhammad's influence growing, and the members of his new faith increasing, several Meccan clans decided to assassinate him. If, however, one man did the deed, then revenge would be sought against his tribe by Muhammad's clan members. It was therefore decided that forty men would do the deed; in this manner, no single person would bear blame, and that Muhammad's tribe would not dare wage war against all the tribes.

QUBA MOSQUE, SITE OF THE OLDEST MOSQUE IN THE WORLD. THIS WAS THE FIRST MOSQUE BUILT BY MUHAMMAD WHEN HE ARRIVED IN MEDINA FROM MECCA

Muhammad was staying at Abu Bakr's house, surrounded by the people who were plotting his death. Under the cover of night, Ali, Muhammad's cousin took his place in his bed, and Muhammad and Abu Bakr fled the city. This was in the year **622. The occasion was so significant that the Muslim calendar starts from this year.** This flight was known as the

HIJRAH (Arabic word for emigration), and as such, today when we refer to the Muslim calendar, we put the letters A.H. after the date thus: 1423 A.H.—the abbreviation for **Anno Hegirae**: the Latin expression for "the year of the Hijra."

The city of **Yathrib** was later renamed *"Medinat al-Nabi"*—city of the Prophet, and has retained that name ever since, in its shortened format of *"Medina."* Upon arrival, Muhammad became the leader of a polity, thus becoming prophet and state leader. He enacted what is known as the Constitution of Medina, probably the world's first agreement on anything resembling an interfaith alliance. It was decided that Muslim, Christian and Jew would defend their new state, and that a wrong committed against one was as a wrong committed against the entire state.

Many fled from Mecca to Medina leaving behind their wealth and belongings. These people were known as the *MUHAJIRUN*: the emigrants. When they arrived in Medina, they were assisted by the new Muslims there, known as the *ANSAR* (the Helpers). There are several stories in the Muslim tradition about the selfless devotion with which the **Ansar** treated their coreligionists.

THE DISTANCE BETWEEN MECCA AND MEDINA IS APPROXIMATELY 210 MILES

Muhammad continued to receive revelations, and his followers grew in number. The **Quraysh** in Mecca were not happy with these developments, especially with Muhammad gaining allies from surrounding tribes. It was the norm in those days for warring parties to raid each other's caravans, and Muhammad's forces attacked a Meccan caravan. The Meccans decided to strike back and in 624 (2 A.H.) led a force of 900 troops against Medina, which only had 313 defenders. The Muslims, despite the smaller numbers, soundly repulsed their enemy in what came to be known as the battle of Badr. The Muslims lost only fourteen men while the attackers lost seventy.

The following year, the Meccans marched upon Medina with 3000 men, including two hundred cavalry, while the Muslims could only muster 700 defenders. Ali, Muhammad's cousin, distinguished himself on this day, as he had in the Battle of Badr. Initially, it looked like the Quraysh and their allies would be defeated, but some Muslim warriors left their positions, and the Muslims suffered a crushing defeat, with Muhammad being injured in the fighting. The Quraysh, however, had their own casualties, and withdrew from the battle.

In 627, the Meccans again sought to overrun Muhammad and his band of Muslims, and attacked Mecca with 10000 fighting men. Muhammad heeded the advice of one of his followers, and dug a huge ditch around his position. As such, this event is known as the **Battle of the Trench**. It is significant for other reasons, and also called the battle of the Confederates, for in this confrontation, the Quraysh persuaded some Jewish tribes that had professed their allegiance with Muhammad to renege on their promise. The harsh weather and spirited defence worked in favor of the Muslims and the Quraysh were forced to withdraw.

The following year, taking advantage of the truce that governed the months of pilgrimage, Muhammad set out for Mecca with about fourteen hundred men. Some of the Quraysh were prepared to violate the terms of truce that had been the custom for so long, and sought to stop Muhammad and his band from taking the normal route to Mecca. The Prophet took a different road, and arrived at Hudaibiyya, a few miles outside of Mecca. The opposing parties agreed to certain terms at the Truce of Hudaibiyya. Muhammad would not make the pilgrimage that year but would be allowed to do so the following year. A general truce for ten years was also declared, and in this time, any Meccan going to Medina to join Muhammad would be returned. The tribes would be free to make alliances with either Muhammad or the Quraysh.

Muhammad returned to Medina, and continued to seek converts to his new religion. It was during this time too that he fought wars with several Jewish tribes, and emerged successfully. In 630, the Quraysh attacked a tribe that was allied with Muhammad, and the Prophet had no choice but to retaliate. With a force of 10000, he marched against Mecca. There was not much opposition to this army, and Muhammad entered the city in victory. He entered the Ka'aba and destroyed the idols that were there, thus purifying the place, said to have been built by Abraham, from polytheism. Some traditions report that Muhammad only allowed a statue of Mary, mother of Jesus and her infant child to remain.

THE KA'ABA

He had thus completed his mission, restoring monotheism to the most important shrine. In 632 he made pilgrimage and then returned to Medina where he died. In returning to his birthplace in triumph, to establish a state in his birthplace, he did something that had not been accomplished by the leaders of the two antecedent Abrahamic traditions. Moses had not been allowed to enter Israel, and Jesus had never set up a polity.

Sacred Teachings and Scripture
In the twenty-three years of his ministry, Muhammad completely transformed the Hijaz, setting the foundations of a religion that was later to become the majority faith of the Middle East. He called his religion "*Islam*"—explained by many as meaning "submission to God." While Islam does inculcate the concept of submission to the will of God, the actual meaning is ***to seek to become whole and perfect***, as much as it is possible for a human being to do so. The word comes from the Arabic root of *SaLiMa*, and is a cognate of the Hebrew term "*shalom*," which encompasses the same meaning.

CALLIGRAPHIC DEPICTION OF AL FATIHA, THE FIRST CHAPTER OF THE QUR'AN

Islam has many concepts that are common with the older religions of Judaism and Christianity. This is so because Muhammad did not see himself as founding a new religion and thus superseding the older faiths. He saw himself instead as continuing the message of the previous prophets who preached the Abrahamic belief in one God. As such, the scripture that Muhammad brought, the Qur'an, has many shared narratives with the Bible, and mentions many of the biblical personalities.

Perhaps what is most notable about Islam is its rigid monotheism, known as **TAWHID**. This means that God has no partners, no humans share in divinity. God's uniqueness means that the Divine does not have children, and cannot be described.

The scripture of Islam is known as the **Qur'an**. This word comes from the Arabic term *QaRa'a* which means "to recite." Incidentally, at the time of Muhammad, the Hebrew Bible was known as *"Miqra"*—the recitation. The Qur'an contains 114 chapters—known as *Suras.* To this day, many Muslims memorize the entire document, chanting it in measured tones, following specific rules of recitation. A person who memorizes the Qur'an is known as a **Hafiz**.

While translations of the Qur'an are available in many languages, the normal practice is to refer to the Arabic original. Muslims point out that there are several reasons for this. The idea is that the Qur'an was revealed directly to Muhammad and is therefore the word of God. This concept of the word of God being manifested in book form is called **INLIBRA-TION**—as opposed to **INCARNATION**: the Christian concept of the word of God becoming manifested in the person of Jesus.

There is a specific euphonic way of reciting the Qur'an that is known as *TAJWID*. This is defined as recitation of the Qur'an in measured tones, with the pronunciation of each letter of the Qur'an being maintained in a specific manner so that its intrinsic and acquired properties are not lost.

The Five Pillars of Islam
The sacred teachings of the faith may best be summarized under what is known as the **FIVE PILLARS OF ISLAM**. As shown in the above image, the reason for this nomenclature is that Islam is seen almost in architectural terms, with the religion, ISLAM, supported by five pillars. These five pillars are, to use their Arabic terms, known as:

1. **Shahada**
2. **Salat**
3. **Zakat**
4. **Sawm**
5. **Hajj**

**THE FIVE PILLARS OF ISLAM--SHOWING ISLAM AS A STRUCTURE SUP-
PORTED BY FIVE PILLARS**

Shahada

The **shahada** is a testimony of creed, normally recited in Arabic, which means "There is no god but God, and Muhammad is His messenger." It is the statement by which one becomes a Muslim, and is all that is required for converts to accept Islam. It is often represented in calligraphy.

Salat

Salat is the Arabic word for "prayer"—and observant Muslims perform five prayers per day. There are specific rituals involved in these prayers, involved standing, bending, and prostrating. Verses from the Qur'an are recited in certain aspects of the standing phase. To prepare for prayer, there is a ritual ablution done, known in Arabic as **WUDU**. This involves, among other things, washing the hands and face. Sometimes, conditions do not allow for the prayers to be done in their normal ritual performance, and in such cases, there are rules and regulations to be followed for an alternative action.

DIFFERENT STAGES IN THE MUSLIM RITUAL PRAYER

On Friday, the early afternoon prayer, called the ***DHUHR***, is usually replaced by the FRIDAY PRAYER, **Salat al-Jumu'a**—where Muslims congregate at the place of worship known as the ***MASJID***, or mosque. The nomenclature for prayer places is a very important one in Muslim majority countries. Sometimes, people in a big company may congregate for prayer in an area that is not designated as a mosque. Such a place is known in Arabic as a ***Musalla***. The designated mosques where members of the community congregate for daily prayer, summoned by the ***adhan*** or prayer call is called a ***masjid*** or mosque. The Friday prayer is of such importance that the delivery of the sermon is usually done by a senior preacher. In some areas, mosques may be closed for this prayer so that their congregations may assemble in a larger mosque to listen to a senior imam. A mosque wherein the Friday prayer is held (in addition to the regularly mandated prayers) is known as a ***Jaa'mi'***.

In prayer, Muslims turn towards the Ka'aba, located in Mecca, the place of worship said to have been built by Abraham and his son Ishmael. This idea of a specific direction is expressed as "**facing the *QIBLA*.**" In the early days of Islam, Muslims turned towards Jerusalem, but in 624 C.E, by Qur'anic revelation the Prophet was directed to turn towards Mecca.

Zakat

The zakat is a form of obligatory charity paid by those whose savings, in the course of a year, are over and above normal needs. In traditional Muslim majority countries, there are often government institutions to supervise this collection. In North America, however, while many mosques may have committees to facilitate this duty, many Muslims go about it on an individual basis—either by giving money to those they identify as needy, or in some cases, sending it to charitable organizations.

Sawm

The religious calendar of Islam is a lunar one, and the ninth month is known as RAMADAN. During this month, observant Muslims perform *SAWM*, or *SIYAM*, fasting from food and drink from just before sunrise to dusk. The Qur'an states that this practice was enjoined upon older religious communities as well, and that the purpose is to teach people **TA-QWA,** or God-consciousness. The month comes to an end with the commemoration **of Eid al-Fitr**, an event in which there is a communal prayer, often followed by celebrations.

Hajj

The Qur'an states that at least once during their lifetime, if they can afford it and do so in a safe manner, Muslims should make a pilgrimage to Mecca, during a specific time. This is known as the *Hajj*. Throughout the year, many Muslims do make a pilgrimage to Mecca, but do not observe all the rituals of the formal *hajj*. This is known as *'umra*.

SOURCES OF MUSLIM PRACTICE

Muslims see the *Qur'an* and *Sunnah* as the sources of Muslim belief and Practice. **The Qur'an is defined as the words of God, revealed unto Muhammad, and is said to be protected by God from corruption.** The *Sunna* is the practice of the Prophet and the early community, the mimetic form by which Muslims know how to practice Islam. The idea of **mimesis**—action by imitation—engendered a sort of hierarchy in Islam regarding authority. As such, Muhammad was seen as the prime exemplar. His contemporaries who accepted Islam and learned directly from him remained Muslims for the remainder of their lives are referred to as the **COMPANIONS (As'haab, singular Sahabi).** The generation after theirs is known as that of the **SUCCESSORS** or **Taabi'un (singular Taabi'i).**

The **Sunna** is often reported in the form of traditions known as the **HAD-ITH**, defined as '**that which is attributed to the prophet in terms of word, deed, or tacit approval.**" This is also called the Oral Tradition of Islam. Muslims say that the proper practice of the Qur'anic teachings and the Sunna allow for the observance of the Shariah. This term is explained by Professor Fazlur Rahman 'the highway of good life', i.e. religious values, expressed functionally and in concrete terms, to direct man's life.

TRANSLATION OF SAHIH MUSLIM, ONE OF THE AUTHORITATIVE COLLECTIONS OF HADITH

The most important and comprehensive concept for describing Islam as a function is the concept of the **Shari'a** or **'Shar'** This word originally means 'the path or the road leading to the water', i.e. a way to the very source of life. The verb **shara'a** means literally 'to chalk out or mark out a clear road to water'. In its religious usage, from the earliest period, it has meant 'the highway of good life', i.e. religious values, expressed functionally and in concrete terms, to direct man's life. It differs from the term 'Sunna' in that the subject of the Sunna 'leads the way' by actual example and, therefore, his action as such is of the same kind as those who follow him in accepting the example, whereas the subject of **Shar'** shows or ordains the way and is, therefore, an abstract concept. The human attempt to understand this abstract, based on the reading of the Qur'an and the study of the Prophet's example, or the application of the intellect to understand what Islam requires of its adherents is known as *FIQH*, often translated as "Islamic Law," but more literally rendered as "understanding."

The Qur'an, however, does not outline the proper manner of doing every action, nor does it provide the solution to every issue that the Muslims might face. The solution to such issues is done by the reflections of the learned jurist, through the process of 'FIQH'. This **FIQH**—coming from the word "understanding," as earlier noted—connotes that interpretation and solution to any matter is built upon the reflection of the fallible human mind. As such, there may be different views put forth by different scholars. The process of such reasoning is done through the process of **IJTI-HAD**—learned intellectual reasoning, by analysis of the sources of Islamic law.

The Caliphate and Sectarian Developments

The Prophet's death in 632 was a surprise for the Muslim community, for he was only in his sixties. It is at this point that, for historians, a particular truism becomes obvious: that the past is what it is, and that reports are simply perspectives that reflect the bias of chroniclers. For some Muslims, the Prophet left no clear instructions as to who should lead the community after his demise. For others, he did leave instructions that his son-in-law Ali should be the leader. The word used in Islamic vocabulary for this leader is "*caliph*"-from the Arabic meaning successor or deputy.

This argument was to expand in later years into a full-blown sectarian war between two groups: the **Sunnis** and the **Shias**. The *Sunni* claim is that the prophet died without leaving a clear successor, but that he had in various ways indicated that his father-in-law, Abu Bakr was to lead in his absence. The other group avers that on more than one occasion, the Prophet had noted Ali's closeness to him and even said that whoever has taken him as their leader, has also acknowledged Ali as such.

The political divide in these two groups were to grow into theological differences, with the Shias branching out into subsects, although their common belief was in the caliphate of Ali. There seems to be agreement on one crucial aspect however: that whether or not Ali was indeed the rightful ruler, he did not challenge the leadership of the first three leaders. In the common Shi'ite view, it was political intrigue that kept him out of his rightful position, and he held his peace so as to not foster dissent within the Muslim community.

The first leader after Muhammad's death was Abu Bakr who looked after the affairs of the post-Muhammadan community for two years. On his death bed, he ordered that another Companion, **Umar b. al-Khattab** be the caliph. Umar held this office for ten years, and it was under his caliphate that the Muslim polity extended its borders. During his time, Iraq, Egypt, and the lands that we now know as Jordan, Syria, and Israel were captured by the Muslim armies.

In 644, Umar was mortally injured by the knife of an assassin. He asked that a committee of elders appoint a successor, and he left strict instructions regarding the procedure for such choice. After some time, ***Uthman b. Affan***, also a Companion, and one of Muhammad's sons-in-law was appointed. His caliphate, however, was marred by reports of nepotism, and in a revolt in 656, he was killed. It was then that Ali b. Abi Talib became the caliph. His rule, however, from the very beginning met with dissent from certain quarters. Some of Uthman's clansmen felt that the caliph should make the bringing to justice of him murderers the matter of prime concern. Ali noted that there were other matters of state that needed to be dealt with. This led to a civil war, the rebel party led by Muawiya b. Abi Sufyan, one of Uthman's kinsmen. It ended in 661 when Ali was assassinated. At this time Muawiya became caliph.

The partisans of Ali, in this war were known as "*shi'at Ali*" (partisans of Ali). After his death, they were persecuted terribly. They developed the idea that the caliphate was not by election, but rather by succession through the line of Ali and Fatima. Anyone belonging to this ancestry is known as a ***sayyid***, and is not unlike the status given to Aaron's children according to Exodus in the Tanakh.

The leadership of Islam was never to see peaceful resolution after this war, and the Umayyads, as the dynasty of Muawiya was known (from belonging to the Umayya clan) were overthrown in 750 by the Abbasids. In 1258, with the invasion of the Mongols, the last Abbasid caliph was killed, and a new series of rulerships occurred. In 1517, a new group of Turkic peoples founded the Ottoman caliphate and it was under this leadership that Islam entered modernity.

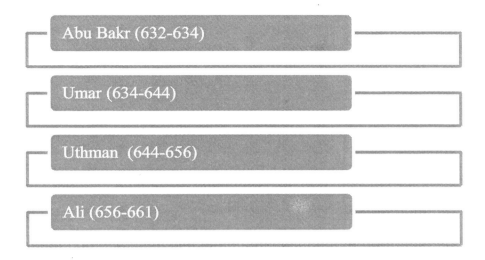

List of the first four caliphs.

The caliphate floundered in modernity, with modern armament and technology being the tools through which Europe gained ascendancy over the majority Muslim countries. In 1797, Napoleon defeated the Muslim armies in Egypt and the Muslim countries were to enter an era where they were, for the most part, colonized by European powers. In 1919, Kemal Ataturk revolted against the Turkish government and by 1921 assumed leadership. In 1923, he abolished the caliphate, and established a secular government.

For many Muslims, the Islamic path is one that takes the Middle Way between Judaism and Christianity, the former with a focus upon law, and the latter with its concept of salvation through grace. For Muslims, Islam is a religion that has certain laws, tempered by the concept of God's grace. Yet, in normative Islam, there is a heavy focus on the interpretation of the law. This varies from one **MADHHAB** to another, with the word **MADHHAB** often being translated as "School." There are several such **MADHHABS** in place. The most famous are the following:

Maliki—named after Malik b. Anas (d. 795)

Hanafi—named after Abu Hanifa (d. 767)

Shafi—named after Muhammad al-Shafi'I (d. 820)

Hanbali—named after Ahmad Ibn Hanbal (d. 855)

Ja'fari—named after Imam Ja'far as Sadiq (d. 765)

Zaidi—named after the fourth imam, Zayd Ibn Ali (d. 740)

Zahiri—supposedly made famous by Ibn Hazm (d. 1064)

Ibadi—named after Abdullah Ibn Ibad (circa late seventh century).

The Imams

In the Shi'ite view, after Ali's death, his oldest son Hasan was the rightful successor. Hasan renounced his right in order to prevent further war, but was still poisoned. Hasan's younger brother also fought against the Umayyads but was killed in 680 at an ambush near to the city of *Karbala*. To this date, the commemoration of this battle is a significant event among the Shias. Researchers believe that this was the foundation of the Shia movement as we know it today. As noted earlier, succession in the Shi'ite view is based on heredity. There is a divine grace from God granted that makes the imams infallible in matters of religion, as exemplars to the community. The most famous sub-sect of the Shi'as is the *Twelver* or *Ithna Ashari* group, so called because there are twelve imams. This group is also known as the *Ja'fari* Shias. There are other groups of Shias, among them the *Zaydis*, also known as the Fivers, and the *Ismailis*, known as the Seveners.

 In the Twelver belief, the last imam, *Muhammad al-Mahdi* was kept from public view after his father, al-Askari died in 873 CE. From that time until 941 CE, he remained in contact with his followers via intermediaries. This period is known as *"al ghaybat al-sughra"*—the minor occultation.

In 941, the last intermediary announced that, based upon the knowledge and orders of the hidden imam, the intermediary would soon die, and that the imam would go into *major occultation*, reappearing at some time in the future.   This belief is of importance to us because from that time until 1979, the Twelver Shias were deemed a quietist movement, awaiting the appearance of the imam before they could have any effective leadership under his direct guidance.

AYATOLLAH KHOMEINI, WHO OVERTHREW THE SHAH IN 1979

In 1979, Ayatollah Ruhollah Khomeini led a revolution in Iran which deposed the Shah and instituted a religious government. Ayatollah Khomeini instituted the doctrine of "*wilayat al-faqih*"—the guardianship of the jurist—**meaning that a qualified jurist from the family of sayyids, in the absence of the imam, can lead the community.**

DEPICTION OF IMAM HUSAYN, ON A PENDANT. ALTHOUGH AN ARTIST'S RENDERING, THIS DEPICTION IS QUITE POPULAR.[31]

---

[31]http://www.zazzle.com/imam_hussein_necklace-177143634567877210. Accessed April 2, 2014.

The Crusades

The Muslim polity was threatened by a series of wars from the 1095 until the thirteenth century, initiated by Pope Urban II whose stated reason was to rescue the Holy Land from the Muslims. During this time too, the Crusaders targeted the Jews as "the closer enemy" and as such, the European Jews in particular suffered terribly. Even though the Muslims eventually triumphed, the cost of these wars sapped the economic strength and political stability of the Muslim polity. The continuing weakness led to the beginning of European colonization in 1797. The establishment of the state of Israel in 1948 was cause for another period of unrest that has continued up to the present time, along with several wars among the Muslim nations in the Middle East region. The invasion of Iraq after 9/11, and several revolutions have led changes of government.

Islam and Calligraphy

Many early Muslims, based on the argument of Islam against graven images, felt that statuary and other concrete depictions of living things were problematic, in that God is the only true Creator. Their artistic impulse was fulfilled by calligraphy, which is still one of the most amazing artforms among Muslims.

THE SCRIPT READS, "IN THE NAME OF GOD, THE BENEFICENT, THE MERCIFUL."

AN EXAMPLE OF CALLIGRAPHY: THE SCRIPT READS, "I TESTIFY THAT THERE IS NO GOD BUT GOD AND THAT MUHAMMAD IS THE MESSENGER OF GOD."

Islam and the Veil

One of the modern controversies in Islam is regarding the woman's head covering. In medieval Mediterranean society, it would appear that women who were not slaves covered their head. This seems to have been especially so among Jews and Christians, based on scriptural edicts.

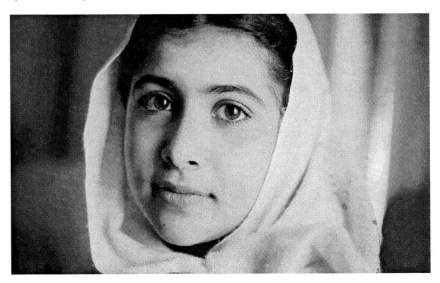

THE HEAD COVERING IS WORN IN DIFFERENT WAYS. HERE IS MALALA YOUSUFZAI, THE FAMOUS PAKISTANI ACTIVIST WEARING HERS IN CUSTOMARY MANNER THAT SHOWS THE HAIR, BUT STILL COVERS THE HEAD.

The Qur'an, addressing the people of that time, had an edict for the Muslim women to draw their head-coverings over their breasts (Q24:31).The interpretation of these verses is the source of the difference of opinion among Muslims on the issue. For some, the Qur'an's rules are permanent, and therefore cannot be changed. For others, the verse is to be contextualized by its having provided a reason for such covering, and if such reason no longer exists, then the result of that reason therefore no longer exists. Others say that in an age of modernity, where there is no demarcation between free-persons and slaves, and where a woman's dress ought not to define who she is, there is no need for such head-covering. And yet others say that the freedom of religion gives them the choice to do as they wish, and that if they prefer to wear a head covering—or even a full face-veil— then they are simply exercising their rights.

A common name for the veil is "**hijab**"—a misnomer that comes from a word that indicates seclusion. The actual word used in the Qur'an to indicate the woman's head cover is *khimar*.

Sufi Islam

Early Islam saw the rise of a tendency towards mysticism, wherein the Qur'an was often seen as a document with esoteric interpretations decipherable only to the enlightened, as opposed to the exoteric understanding which was left for those who did not truly grasp its deeper meaning. That difference of opinions exists to this day, with those who follow they more esoteric mystic path, being referred to as "*Sufis*." There are many different groups of Sufis, among them the Naqshabandi, Alevi, Bektashi, Chisti, Rifa'i, Qadiriyyah, and Suhrawardiyya orders.

There are often different practices for the various orders. There is focus on *DHIKR*, chanting the name of God. The word *Dhikr* is derived from the root that means "to remember," and it generally refers to reciting the various names of God as expressed in the Qur'an. Over the years, Sufis have developed ways of chanting this, or focusing upon a single such name with a specific mode of utterance. This may be done by actual chanting only, or by incorporation this with other forms. One such is the dance of the dervishes of the *Mawlawi /Mevlevi* order. The Mawlawi believe in performing their *dhikr* in the form of a "dance" and musical ceremony known as the *Sama* which involves whirling from which the order acquired its nickname. The *Sama* represents a mystical journey of man's spiritual ascent through mind and love to the "Perfect."Turning towards the truth, the follower grows through love, deserts his ego, finds the truth, and arrives at the "Perfect". He then returns from this spiritual journey as a man who has reached maturity and a greater perfection, able to love and to be of service to the whole of creation.

WHIRLING DERVISHES

Islam and Modernity

Before colonization, the majority of Muslims lived in the Middle East, parts of Africa and Eastern Europe. As the majority, they had their own laws and norms. After colonization and the mass immigration to the West, Muslims began arriving in large numbers, removed from their majority status in their home countries, to live as minorities in places that did not know, or were hostile to Islamic concepts. In 1966, when the United States started allowing non-European immigrants to settle in its lands, large numbers of Muslims started coming. At this time, the majority of Muslims can trace their ancestry to a foreign land, and many still have practices that some Americans see as foreign.

The colonial era, the political upheavals, and the American involvement in the Middle East, as well as the fallout from 9/11 have made many Muslims see themselves as a beleagueredcommunity in Europe and North America. The term "Islamophobia" has been coined to describe this situation. While lexical purists point out that the term refers to "morbid fear of Muslims," others note that regardless of the origin of the term, the record shows more than just fear, but rather discrimination and outright hate.

Many hate groups function on campus, their express focus on demonizing Muslims. Among the foremost hatemongers are Pam Geller, Robert Spencer, Ann Coulter and Walid Shoebat. In the case of Walid Shoebat, who claims to have been a former terrorist, his assertions have been debunked. Yet, he continues to draw a lot of supporters.

To combat this, many governments and private enterprises have started interfaith movements that seek to educate about and interact with Muslims. The numbers of Muslims in the United States continues to grow and is estimated at between 6-9 million.

After 1966, the numbers of Muslims have grown tremendously in the United States, this increase coming from the number of immigrants from primarily Asia, Africa and the Caribbean.

Islam and Science

In the medieval period, the time that was known as "The Dark Ages" was in fact an era of great scientific advancement in the Muslim world. It was Muslim scientists, or those working under the aegis of the Muslim state, that introduced algebraic concepts to the world, the science of optics and even approaches to philosophy. It is said that the maps that Columbus used to travel to the New World were from Moorish cartographers.

With the Renaissance and the Industrial revolution in Europe, however, the Western nations went on a spur of discovery and activity that were to surpass the Muslim world. In 1797, Napoleon invaded Egypt, using modern armament, including cannons that decimated the Mamluk defenders. That was the beginning of the decline in the technological strength of the Muslim world, since many of the Muslim majority countries were under the yoke of colonization, their resources exploited, and their educational institutions controlled by outsiders who did not want them to advance and gain scientific advancement. When Turkey sided with the Axis bloc in the two world wars, the rift between the Muslim majority countries and Europe only grew stronger. With the establishment of the state of Israel in 1948, the Muslim majority nations were seen as enemies and there has been a constant adversarial approach to them from the G-8 countries, wherein embargoes have been placed on the sharing of technological equipment and knowledge.

Relationship to Other Religions

Islam sees itself not as a religion of supersession, but of continuation. As such, the Qur'an recognizes and grants rights to other faiths in a manner that was seen in the Muslim heyday as exemplary. The Crusades, colonization and modern international relations have changed much of what was once harmonious. The fact that Muslim rule supplanted Christian rule in the Middle East is still a factor that rankles some.

Like Christianity, Islam is a proselytizing religion, and has been the only major faith to challenge Christendom for supremacy in numbers and influence over the world. The legacy of the Crusades still exists in subtle, if not overt, ways, and Muslims often complain about their faith being misrepresented in western academic institutions. Among such misrepresentations, for example, is the idea of Jihad, presented in many texts, as "Holy War" and an element of Islam. Muslim scholars point out that Holy War actually is a concept in both Judaism and Christianity, and that while Muslims are exhorted to take up arms to defend their state (assuming that such a state exists), their battle is only to repel an invader, not to aggress.

Especially after 9/11, there has been a terrible backlash. Afghanistan and Iraq were invaded with several hundreds of thousands of people killed, displaced or imprisoned. The continuing revelations of CIA torture of detainees, the imprisonment of Muslims without trial, the employment of trainers who present Islamophobic material as academic information are all issues that concern many Muslim legal rights associations. One such organization is CAIR (Council for American Islamic Relations), that monitors cases where the rights of Muslim citizens and residents of the United States are violated. Many mosque burnings, acts of vandalism, assault, and in some case, even murder have been reported. Despite this animus towards Islam and its followers, Muslims are making their presence felt in many ways in North America, occupying positions of prestige in both the public and private spheres.

Today, Muslims number in excess of two billion people and they are located in almost every nation in the world, and as such one may find mosques in places that are far removed from the origins of Muhammad's preaching.

MOSQUE IN CORRIVERTON, GUYANA, SOUTH AMERICA.

Glossary

Abdul Muttalib   Grandfather of the Prophet Muhammad.

Abu Talib   Uncle of the Prophet Muhammad.

Alevi   Name of one of the Sufi groups.

Ali (ibn Abi Talib)   Cousin and son-in-law of the Prophet, and fourth caliph of Islam.

Ansar   "The Helpers:"collective name given to the inhabitants of Medina who aided the early Muslim refugees from Mecca.

Bektashi   Name of one of the Sufi groups.

Chisti   Name of one of the Sufi groups.

Dhikr   Derived from the root that means "to remember," and it generally refers to reciting the various names of God as expressed in the Qur'an.

Hafiz   Title used for one who has memorized the Qur'an.

Hajj	Pilgrimage to Mecca: the last of the five pillars of Islam. It differs from the other four in that it is only to be done if there is safety and economic ability.
haeresium fera	Latin term "mother of all heresies" used to refer to Arabia in the second century of the common era.
Hijab	Literally meaning curtain or seclusion, it is the misnomer often applied to the head covering worn by some Muslim women in deference to their interpretation of Islamic sartorial regulations.
Hijra	Arabic term for "emigration." It refers to the flight of the Prophet from Mecca to Medina in the year 622, from which the Muslim calendar starts.
Incarnation	The Christian concept of the word of God manifesting itself in human form (Jesus).
Inlibration	Concept of the word of God being manifested in the form of a book (the Qur'an).
Islam	Often wrongly defined as "submission to God," the term more accurately refers to the seeking of wholeness by turning to God.
Ka'aba	The most revered site in Islam, this is the mosque located in Mecca and said to have been originally built by Abraham and Ishmael.
Khadijah	The first wife of Muhammad.
Khimar	The proper name of the head covering worn by some Muslim women. The term comes from the Qur'an.
Mecca	The city in which the Kaaba is located.
Medina	"The City:" abbreviated form of Medinat al-Nabi (city of the Prophet) given to Yathrib after the Prophet Muhammad settled there.
Miqra	"The recitation."Medieval Hebrew term used for the Tanakh.

Muhajirun	"The Emigrants"—a name used to refer to the early Muslim refugees who fled persecution in Mecca to settle in Yathrib.
Naqshbandi	Name of one of the Sufi groups.
Qadiriyyah	Name of one of the Sufi groups.
Qur'an	The Muslim Scripture, generally defined as that which has been revealed by God unto Muhammad, starting from the sura known as "al-Fatiha" and ending at "al-Nas." It consists of 114 chapters.
Quraysh	The tribe of the Prophet Muhammad.
Ramadan	The ninth lunar month of Islam; also the month of fasting (sawm/siyam)for observant Muslims.
Rifa'i	Name of one of the Sufi groups.
Sahabi/Ashaab/Sahaba:	
	One of the contemporaries of the Prophet Muhammad who accepted Islam during the Prophet's lifetime. Generally translated as "Companion."
Salat	The Muslim ritual prayer, one of the pillars of Islam.
Sama	Part of a Sufi ceremony performed as ***dhikr***.
Sawm/Siyam	Fasting:One of the pillars of Islam
Sayyid	A term used to refer to one who can trace ancestry through the Prophet Muhammad. In Shi'ite Islam, only such a person may be the Imam of the Muslim community, insofar as it refers to the entire Shi'ite community.
Shahada	The declaration that there is no God but God. This is the first of the five pillars of Islam.
Siyam	See Sawm.
Sufi	A name used to refer to one who generally follows a more esoteric, or mystical interpretation of Islam

Suhrawardiyya	Name of one of the Sufi groups.
Tabi'i/Tabi'un	The generation that comes after the *Ashaab/Sahabas*.
Tajwid	Recitation of the Qur'an in measured tones, with the pronunciation of each letter of the Qur'an being maintained in a specific manner so that its intrinsic and acquired properties are not lost.
Tawhid	The rigid monotheistic concept meaning that God has no partners, and that no humans share in divinity.
Umar	*Umar b. al-Khattab.* Father-in-law of the Prophet Muhammad and second Caliph of Islam.
'Umra	Often referred to by the misnomer "lesser hajj," this does involve a visit to the Kaaba, but may be done at any time of the year, and does not include all the rituals of the time-specific *Hajj.*
Uthman	Son-in-law of the Prophet Muhammad, and third caliph of Islam.
wilayat al-faqih	The guardianship of the jurist—A modern Shia concept *meaning that a qualified jurist from the family of sayyids, in the absence of the imam, can lead the community.*
Wudu	Ritual ablution involving, among other things, washing the hands and face.
Yathrib	Name of the city to which Muhammad fled from Mecca; later renamed Medina.
Zakat	Stipulated charity;Fourth of the five pillars of Islam.

BAHÁ'Í FAITH

Progressive Revelation

Dr. Arashmidos Monjazeb and Duane L. Herrmann

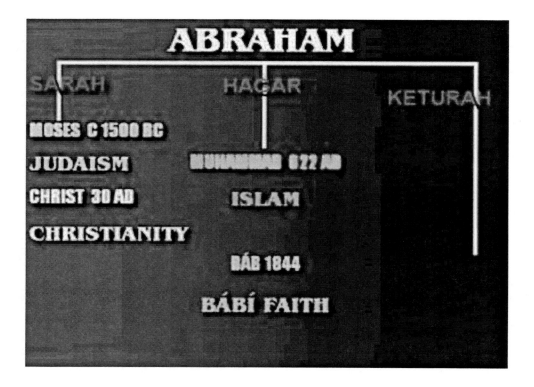

- *Discuss social setting of Iran at time of the Bab*
- *Discuss persecution of the Bab*
- *Explain the coming of Baha'ullah and his doctrines and teachings*
- *Summarize teachings of the Baha'i faith*
- *Refer to different scriptural writings of the faith*
- *Discuss Houses of Worship/Community Life and the Baha'i calendar*
- *Analyze relationship to other religions*

Many faiths have the concept of a sort of redeemer who will come towards the end of time. The Abrahamic faiths, with their shared concepts, also have the idea: some Jews speak of the Messiah, Christians expect a returning Jesus, and many Muslims speak of the Mahdi or the Imam. In the mid-nineteenth century, the situation in the Middle East was such that many looked forward to the appearance of such a figure. And in 1844, Sayyid Ali Muhammad Shirazi, later to be known as the Bāb ("The Gate"), declared himself to be that awaited personality. He was 25 years old when he declared his mission in Shiraz, Persia. As his name suggests, he was of noble parentage, for "sayyid" in Islamic terminology, is a title denoting that he was from the family of the prophet Muhammad.

The Bāb's first disciple was Mulla Husayn Bushrú'í, and to him he said: O Thou who are the first to believe in Me! Verily I say, I am the Bāb, the Gate of God and thou art the Bābu'l-Bāb, the gate of that Gate. Eighteen souls must, in the beginning, spontaneously and of their own accord, accept me and recognize the truth of my Revelation."[1.]

ROOM OF THE BĀB'S HOME IN SHIRAZ, IRAN WHERE HE DECLARED HIS MISSION IN MAY 1844

After eighteen religious scholars, having made their own research, recognized him, he made his declaration public. Some of his teachings shocked the country as they seemed to clash with the Islamic worldview. His claim to be a Messenger of God, succeeding Muhammad, was deemed to be heretical. His proclamation that women were equal to men was seen as undermining the social order with saw the male gender as being superior.

For six years, the Bāb was subject to different types of torment and torture. He was arrested and held in one prison after another. One prison, Mah-ku, was located in the mountains, was snow-covered for most of the year. He stayed there for nine months. From there he was transferred to Chihriq, on another mountain, and kept there for a little more than two years. During this time, he was kept in darkness, not even allowed a candle for light or warmth.

Finally the religious leaders and government decided to end this religious movement. The number of his followers had grown rapidly, more and more people had become aware of his message and declared their adherence to it. In attempts to put it down an estimated 20,000 of his followers were martyred. This repression was not enough to stop people from recognizing and accepting the Bāb as a new Messenger from God.

The Bāb was eventually brought to Tabriz for trial. When asked; 'Who are you and what is your claim?' He answered: "I am, I am, I am the Promised One! I am the One Whose name you have for a thousand years invoked, at Whose mention you have risen, Whose advent you have longed to witness, and the hour of Whose Revelation you have prayed God to hasten. Verily, I say, it is incumbent upon the peoples of both the

East and the West to obey My word, and to pledge allegiance to My person."[2.]

The Barrack-square in Tabriz where the Bab suffered Martyrdom. Pillar on the right marked X is the place where He was suspended and shot

From there He was taken to a military prison. The religious leaders issued a ruling condemning Him to death. The Bāb and one young follower were brought to the courtyard of the barracks and tied to be executed. After the smoke from the rifles cleared, the multitude who were watching the event noticed that the companion of the Bāb was standing and unhurt while the Bāb was absent. After a short search by the military they found the Bāb back in the cell.

There he was finishing a conversation with His secretary which had been interrupted earlier. This escape so excited the watching crowd that it was reported to foreigners who reported it to their governments. The Bāb was taken back to the courtyard, and the Bāb and His young disciple were tied again for execution in the courtyard.

The Bāb's addressed the crowd which had assembled to watch the execution: "'O wayward generation!' were the last words of the Bāb to the gazing multitude, as the regiment prepared to fire its volley, 'Had you believed in Me every one of you would have followed the example of this youth, who stood in rank above most of you, and would have willingly sacrificed himself in My path. The day will come when you will have recognized Me; that day I shall have ceased to be with you.'"[3.]

The second firing squad, also composed of 750 men, was successful. Afterwards the mangled bodies were thrown into a dry moat outside the city.

It was expected that animals would eat them. Some followers of the Bāb guarded the bodies until night when they could be rescued and kept safe.

For fifty years the bodies were hid in one place or other so officials would not find them. They were eventually transferred to their resting place today, on the slopes of Mt Carmel in Haifa, Israel at the Bahá'í World Center.

During the six years of His ministry, the Bāb prepared His followers for the appearance of another Divine Teacher whom He referred to as, 'One Whom God will make manifest.' After the Bāb's death His followers were expectant. The coming of two Divine Teachers, in quick succession, had been prophesied in past scriptures.

Bahá'u'lláh "The Glory of God" (1817-1892)

After the death of the Bāb, His followers searched for the next Divine Educator. One of his followers was Bahá'u'lláh, which means the Glory of God. This title had been given to him by the Bāb. Bahá'u'lláh's father had been a minister in the Court of the Shah, the Ruler of Persia. On his father's death, Bahá'u'lláh had been offered his father's position but he declined since his interests lay elsewhere. His family was well respected because of their integrity and fair behavior.

In 1852 Bahá'u'lláhwas arrested, led through the streets of the capital, and imprisoned. His properties and belongings were confiscated. His family had to escape from their home and seek refuge in a relative's house. The prison Bahá'u'lláh was taken to was so horrible it was called the Black Pit. It had been built as a cistern for storing water. He described the experience later: "Upon Our arrival We were first conducted along a pitch-black corridor, from whence We descended three steep flights of stairs to the place of confinement assigned to Us. The dungeon was wrapped in thick darkness, and Our fellow prisoners numbered nearly a hundred and fifty souls: thieves, assassins and highwaymen. Though crowded, it had no other outlet than the passage by which We entered. No pen can depict that place, nor any tongue describe its loathsome smell. Most of these men had neither clothes nor bedding to lie on. God alone knoweth what befell Us in that most foul-smelling and gloomy place"[4.]

The Black Pit Prison in Tehran

A chain weighing about a hundred pounds was placed around His neck. The weight was so great that a piece of wood had to be placed under His chin to keep His head up. Because of his noble status, the government did not dare kill Him. His companions, however, were martyred one by one.

"Every day Our jailers, entering Our cell, would call the name of one of Our companions, bidding him arise and follow them to the foot of the gallows. With what eagerness would the owner of that name respond to that solemn call! Relieved of his chains, he would spring to his feet and, in a state of uncontrollable delight, would approach and embrace Us. We would seek to comfort him with the assurance of an everlasting life in the world beyond, and, filling his heart with hope and joy, would send him forth to win the crown of glory. He would embrace, in turn, the rest of his fellow-prisoners and then proceed to die as dauntlessly as he had lived. Soon after the martyrdom of each of these companions, We would be informed by the executioner, who had grown to be friendly to Us, of the circumstances of the death of his victim, and of the joy with which he had endured his sufferings to the very end."[5.]

While in this prison Bahá'u'lláh received the Revelation which would change His life. He described it later: "O King! I was but a man like others, asleep upon my couch, when lo, the breezes of the All-Glorious were wafted over me, and taught Me the knowledge of all that hath been. This thing is not from me, but from One Who is Almighty and All-Knowing. And He bade me lift up My voice between earth and heaven…"[6.]

After four months in this prison Bahá'u'lláh was released and exiled from the country. He was sent to Baghdad, in the Ottoman Empire. He, His family and a few fellow believers had to leave Tehran ill-prepared, in mid-

winter and travel over 500 miles on foot and horseback through mountains. For water they had to melt ice. The trip took four months.

For ten years they were in Baghdad. It was a difficult time. Other followers of the Bāb traveled from Persia to Baghdad to see Bahá'u'lláh. This
traffic caused religious leaders in Persia great concern and they pressured
Ottoman officials to send Bahá'u'lláh even further from the Persian border. In this they succeeded.

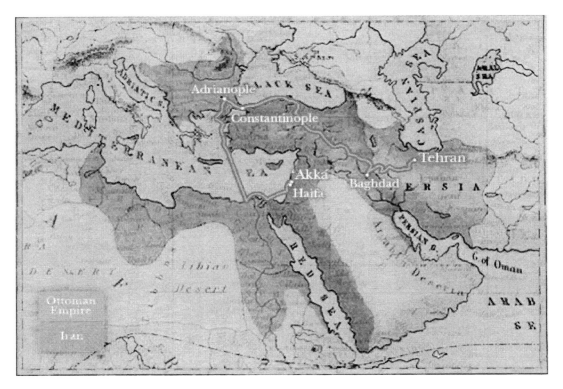

MAP SHOWING BAHA'ULLAH'S EXILE LOCATIONS

On His departure from Baghdad, in April 1863, Bahá'u'lláh proclaimed
that He was the 'One Whom God shall make manifest.' He revealed hundreds of tablets (letters), books and prayers. From Baghdad He was sent
to Constantinople (now, Istanbul) and then Adrianople (now, Edir-
ne).From Adrianople, Bahá'u'lláh sent His first letters to kings and other
rulers of the world, including religious leaders, calling them to establish
peace on the planet. Some of the statements in these letters include:

"O Czar of Russia! Incline thine ear unto the voice of God, the King, the
Holy, and turn thou unto Paradise... "[7.]

"O Queen in London! Incline thine ear unto the voice of thy Lord, the Lord of all mankind."[8.]

"Say: O King of Berlin! Give ear unto the Voice calling from this manifest Temple..."[9.]

"O Emperor of Austria! He Who is the Dayspring of God's Light dwelt in the prison of 'Akká..."[10.]

Eventually Ottoman authorities decided to send Bahá'u'lláh and His companions to a prison reserved for the worst criminals and from which few left alive. This was Akka (present-day Acre, Israel) where, according to tradition, birds flying over the city would die from the filth and stench of it. Bahá'u'lláh and His companions were sent by ship. "Notorious throughout the empire for the foulness of its climate and the prevalence of many diseases, Akká was a penal colony used by the Ottoman State for the incarceration of dangerous criminals who could be expected not to survive too long their imprisonment there"[11.]

Still a prisoner of the Ottoman Empire, Bahá'u'lláh died near the prison city of Akka in 1892. His words, recorded in thousands of documents, address issues of contemporary society such as international collective security, atmospheric contamination, globalization, the rights and responsibilities of individuals, the limits of government and other concerns of an increasingly interdependent planet. These documents are preserved, studied, translated and published at the Bahá'í World Center in present-day Haifa, Israel, near Akka.

In Bahá'u'lláh's will and testament, he appointed his oldest son Abbas ('Abdu'l-Bahá) to be head of the Bahá'í Faith. He was designated the 'Center of the Covenant.' All Bahá'ís were to turn to Him as they had turned to Bahá'u'lláh. No previous religion has had such a covenant. This Covenant would preserve the new faith from schism.

Abdu'l-Bahá (1844-1921)

'ABDU'L-BAHÁ

'Abdu'l-Bahá was born in Persia in 1844. In 1853 He accompanied his father, Bahá'u'lláh, on his exile from Tehran to Baghdad. Given the name Abbas, he preferred the title "'Abdu'l-Bahá" to indicate his station of servitude to his Father. He was a prisoner of the Ottoman Empire until 1908. Of this he said: "Forty years I endured in a Turkish prison. Then in 1908 the Young Turks 'Committee of Union and Progress' shook the gates of despotism and set all prisoners free, myself among them. I pray that blessing may be upon all who work for Union and Progress."[12.]

'Abdu'l-Bahá built a modest building on Mt Carmel in which to place the remains of the Bāb. This would become the first level of the Shrine of the Bāb as later completed. With his encouragement, the Bahá'ís in Ishqabad (now Ashgabat), Russia, built the first Bahá'í House of Worship.

In 1911-1913 'Abdu'l-Bahá traveled to America and Europe, visiting such countries as: Egypt, England, France, Germany, Hungary, the United States and Canada. He spent more than eighteen months traveling to proclaim his father's teachings. Although he had no schooling, he was able to converse with engineers, professors and others with specialized knowledge.

SHRINE OF THE BAB AT MOUNT CARMEL

When he was in America he laid the cornerstone for a second Bahá'í House of Worship, in Wilmette, IL, just north of Chicago. 'Abdu'l-Bahá died in 1921. In His Will and Testament He designated his grandson, Shoghi Rabbani (1897-1957), later more popularly known as Shoghi Effendi, as the Guardian of the Faith.

Bahá'u'lláh forbade the creation of a priesthood or clergy, and directed that each Bahá'í community would be guided by elected councils, one in every locality. Nine Bahá'ís from the local community are elected to serve on these councils. He also ordained an international council. Though the first local council had been formed in the 1880s, few had been created after that. Shoghi Effendi guided the Bahá'í community in creating these councils, and the intermediate, national level, in preparation for the international council. Bahá'í elections are carried out by secret ballot with no nominating or campaigning.

Upon his death in 1957, a group of twenty-seven individuals, designated by the Guardian as "Hands of the Cause of God," finished his plans to prepare the world community to elect the first Universal House of Justice. This was achieved in 1963. These elections are held every five years.

Some Teachings of the Bahá'í Faith
The Bahá'í teachings are based upon what is known as Progressive Revelation. This is the concept that religious truth is revealed by God progressively and cyclically over time through a series of divinely sent messen-

gers, and that the teachings are tailored to suit the needs of the time and place of their appearance. As such, the Bahá'í teachings recognize the divine origin of world religions as different stages in the history of one religion, while believing that the revelation of Bahá'u'lláh is the most recent (though not the last), and therefore the most relevant to modern society.

Among the teachings too are that we can never adequately describe God. In the same way that a painting cannot describe the painter who created it, we are like that painting in our inability to understand or describe God. Certainly some attributes of God are known to us, but we also have free will and responsibilities, and ought not to blame God for our own mistakes. We should accept the consequences of our actions. We use our intellect and God-given perception to learn about God. Indeed the very purpose of our existence is to know and to love God.

Among some of the teachings that are particularly relevant in modern society are the need for unity among humankind, abandonment of the concept of holy war, eschewal of prejudice, the need to associate in harmony with members of other religions, the pursuit of science and knowledge, and the equality of the sexes. Worship includes work, for each person should engage in some form of occupation, such as crafts, trades and the like. One teaching states, "The most despised of men in the sight of God are those who sit idly and beg . . . When anyone occupieth himself in a craft or trade, such occupation itself is regarding by God as worship."13.

Bahá'í teachings promote the idea of a universal language. In addition to the different languages around the world, if one other was adopted by everyone, then people would only need two languages to be able to communicate with anyone on earth. This would lead to the whole earth being regarded as a single country.

Prayer is what assists in the development of a spiritual nature. Bahá'u'lláh instructed his followers to pray and read scriptures in the morning and night. Daily prayers are essential and he revealed three specific prayers for such use, all affirming the relationship of the individual soul to God. Meditation is another activity that is encouraged, and seen as a key for opening the doors of mysteries, promoting withdrawal from the mundane, and focus upon the divine.

World peace is a major emphasis of the Bahá'í teachings. Bahá'u'lláh called the rulers and leaders of the world to reduce their armaments and consult together to solve their differences by consultation not conflict. In the century and some since then progress towards peace has been made.

Bahá'ís are confident that world peace will be achieved, though the process will not be easy or smooth.

Scripture

The teachings of Bahá'u'lláh were written or dictated by the Messenger of God himself. He used his own seal to verify that the words came from him and not from someone else. Some of His writings, individually or collectively, include the following:

The Kitab-i-Aqdas (The Most Holy Book)
Epistle to the Son of the Wolf
Gleanings from the Writings of Baha'u'llah
The Hidden Words of Baha'u'llah
The Kitab-i-Iqan (The Book of Certitude)
Prayers and Meditations
Proclamation of Bahá'u'lláh
The Seven Valleys and the Four Valleys
Tablets of Bahá'u'lláh Revealed after the Kitab-i-Aqdas

Houses of Worship

Bahá'u'lláh specified that each Bahá'í House of Worship is to have nine sides and gave their formal designation of, 'Dawning Place of the Mention of God.' In Persian it is Mashriqu'l-Adhkár. They are also known as Temples. 'Abdu'l-Bahá specified that the nine sides form a circle, or nonagon. The Guardian determined that each should have a central dome. The architecture of each is different and many closely reflect the culture in which they are built. In Panama Meso-American designs are used and the one in India is in the shape of a lotus blossom. It is even called the Lotus Temple. These buildings are to be as perfect as possible, adorned with that which is befitting, not with images and effigies. They are supposed to be places where, with radiance and joy, the praises of God are celebrated. In them preaching or sermons are forbidden. At first they were built on a continental level, national and local ones will follow.

The number nine is significant in that nine is the highest single digit and therefore represents unity. Also in the Abjad system of numbering, where letters of the alphabet are given numbers, the number value of the word, 'baha,' is nine. The number nine, therefore, is a reference to the name of Bahá'u'lláh.

The institution of the Mashriqu'l-Adhkár is to consist of not only the central House of Worship, but also of institutions of social service such as a hospital, an orphanage, a university, etc. It incorporates the concept of service to others as worship. People of all religions, races, colors, and nationalities are welcome to these Temples.

BAHA'I HOUSE OF WORSHIP, WILMETTE, ILLINOIS

Community Life
Bahá'ís often pray in their own homes with other Bahá'ís or friends and family. Anyone may attend these gatherings. Another way is by study circles where scripture and beliefs are studied and discussed. There are also observances of holy days to commemorate significant events in Bahá'í history. In addition there is a regular community gathering for worship and community business on the first day of each month of the Bahá'í calendar. These are called Nineteen-day Feasts.

The Bahá'í Calendar
The Bahá'í calendar, ordained by the Bāb and verified by Bahá'u'lláh, is a solar calendar of nineteen months of nineteen days each. These 361 days almost equal the days it takes the earth the make one orbit around the sun. To make it even, intercalary days are added, four in normal years, five in leap years. These days do not form part of any month. Instead they are special days for hospitality, gifts and philanthropy. The new year begins on March 21, the first day of spring (in the Northern Hemisphere).

Relationship to Other Religions

The teachings of the Bahá'í Faith foster harmonious interaction with other religions since it recognizes all religions in its concept of progressive revelation. Bahá'ís are encouraged to: "Consort with the followers of all religions in a spirit of friendliness and fellowship"[14.]

This does not mean that Baha'is are treated well. They are terribly persecuted in Iran, where their faith is still viewed as a heretical offshoot of Islam. They are forbidden to have their own schools, places of worship, and even from attending higher study at educational institutions.

What is a Bahá'í?

Once 'Abdu'l-Bahá was asked, 'What is a Bahá'í?' He gave a general answer. "To be a Bahá'í simply means to love all the world; to love humanity and try to serve it; to work for universal peace and universal brotherhood.". On another occasion He said a Bahá'í was: "...one endowed with all the perfections of man in activity."[15.] Essentially, he is saying that one who is following the teachings of Bahá'u'lláh is a Bahá'í.

To formally become a member of the Bahá'í community one expresses to a local or national Spiritual Assembly that one has accepted Bahá'u'lláh as the Messenger from God for this age and wishes to be part of the Bahá'í community. By becoming a member of the Bahá'í community one's efforts are joined with the efforts of others around the world to improve their community and world. It is an adventure whose goal is to spiritualize your life and the world. An informative website is www.bahai.org

The following is a prayer by 'Abdu'l-Bahá expressing a summary of the teachings of Bahá'u'lláh:

"O Thou kind Lord! Unite all. Let the religions agree and make the nations one, so that they may see each other as one family and the whole earth as one home. May they all live together in perfect harmony.

O God! Raise aloft the banner of the oneness of mankind.

O God! Establish the Most Great Peace.

Cement Thou, O God, the hearts together.

O Thou kind Father, God! Gladden our hearts through the fragrance of Thy love. Brighten our eyes through the Light of Thy Guidance. Delight our ears with the melody of Thy Word, and shelter us all in the Stronghold of Thy Providence.

Thou art the Mighty and Powerful, Thou art the Forgiving and Thou art the One Who overlooketh the shortcomings of all mankind." 16.

SHRINE OF BAHÁ'U'LLÁH NEAR AKKA

Notes

1. Shoghi Effendi (trans), *The Dawn-Breakers* (Bahá'í Publishing Trust: Wilmette, 1996) p.63.
2. Shoghi Effendi, *God Passes By* (Bahá'í Publishing Trust: Wilmette, 1974) p.21.

3. ibid. p.53
4. Bahá'u'lláh, *Epistle to the Son of the Wolf* (Bahá'í Publishing Trust: Wilmette, 1988) pp.20-21.

5. Shoghi Effendi, *Dawn-Breakers*, pp.632-33.

6. Bahá'u'lláh, *Epistle*, p.11.

7. ibid, p.57.

8. ibid, p.59.

9. Bahá'u'lláh, *The Kitáb-i-Aqdas, Most Holy Book* (Bahá'í World Center: Haifa, 1992) p.51.

10. Bahá'u'lláh, *Kitáb-i-Aqdas*, p.50.

11. *Bahá'u'lláh* (Baha'i International Community Office of Public Information: New York, 1992 May 29) p.21.

12. 'Abdu'l-Bahá, *'Abdu'l-Bahá in London* (Bahá'í Publishing Society: Chicago, 1921) p.39.

13. Bahá'u'lláh, *Tablets of Baha'u'llah Revealed after the Kitáb-i-Aqdas,* (Bahá'í World Center: Haifa, 1988) p.26.
14. ibid, pp.22, 35 & 87.
15. J.E. Esslemont, *Bahá'u'lláh and the New Era* (Bahá'í Publishing Trust: Wilmette, 1980) p.71.

16. 'Abdu'l-Bahá, *The Promulgation of Universal Peace* (Bahá'í Publishing Trust: Wilmette, 1982)p.100.

Photos courtesy of the National Spiritual Assembly of the Bahá'ís of the United States, Inc.

Glossary

Kitab-i-Aqdas "The Most Holy Book:--one of the Baha'i scriptures.

Kitab-i-Iqan "The Book of Certitude"—one of the Baha'i scriptures.

Mashriqu'l-Adhkár The Persian term for the Baha'i place of worship.

Progressive Revelation
The concept that religious truth is revealed by God progressively and cyclically over time, through a process of divinely sent messengers, with their teachings tailored to suit the needs of the time and place of their appearance.

INDEX